MAN OF THE WORLD
THE ODYSSEY EXPEDITION: BOOK 1

Graham Hughes

Man Of The World
The Odyssey Expedition: Book 1

Graham Hughes

Cover Design, Maps and Text
Copyright © 2017 by Graham Hughes

ISBN – 9781626130814
Library of Congress Control Number - 2017932935

Published by ATBOSH Media ltd.
Cleveland, Ohio, USA

www.atbosh.com

2nd Printing

For Mum

Contents

Prologue

The Odyssey Expedition, Book 1

As far back as I can remember, I always wanted to be an adventurer. The road at my feet, a song in my heart and five hundred miles to the horizon.

On January 1st 2009, I boarded a ferryboat in Argentina and crossed over the River Plate into Uruguay and thus began one of the most daring, epic, and dare I say hilarious, solo travel adventures of all time.

My goal? To become the first person to visit every country in the world without flying.

The scale of the challenge laid out before me was simply gargantuan: 192 members of the United Nations plus Vatican City, Taiwan, Palestine, Kosovo and Western Sahara.

Nobody had ever attempted it before, I had bugger-all money and I would have no professional support along the way.

Getting into (and out of) Somalia, Afghanistan and North Korea would be one thing. But getting to far-flung island nations such as Nauru, Kiribati and Comoros without flying would be another matter entirely.

No planes, no helicopters, no hitchhiking, no driving. Only public transport — buses, coaches, shared taxis — and a variety of maritime transportation — yachts, cruise ships, cargo ships and the like.

More than 200,000 kilometres over land and sea. Crossing over 200 borders requiring more than 100 visas in the process of over 1,000 individual journeys.

Over and over again I was told it couldn't be done, it was impossible, a fool's errand.

But what they didn't know is that I eat impossible for breakfast.

One book alone simply cannot do justice to the incredible people, history, and culture of all the places I visited, and so *Man of the World* covers the first 12 months and 133 countries of the expedition. I don't want to give away too much *yet* — suffice it to say, it was one hell of a year.

My hope is that *Man of the World* (and its two sequels) provide not just a unique snapshot of this crazy little planet, but also inspire you to go and see the world for yourself.

If this adventure taught me one thing, it's that the world isn't such a bad place — it isn't going to hell in a handcart (although it might sometimes seem that way if you only listen to our increasingly hysterical news media).

At every twist and turn of the journey, I met kind, generous and supportive people. It just goes to show — you can't judge people by the actions of their government.

Yes, at times it was difficult, but then so is life. Most of the time *The Odyssey Expedition* was, quite simply, a bloody good laugh.

Here's to my family, my friends and the good eggs all over the world who helped make *The Odyssey Expedition* the incredible story I'm about to tell. And hey, if you're ever in Panama...!

Graham David Hughes

Jinja Island
Bocas Del Toro
Panama

Christmas 2016

Chapter 1
This Is My Quest

It was the summer of 1985.[1] I was six years old and wearing a Ghostbusters T-shirt. We had just been to visit the European micronation of Andorra, high up in the Pyrenees. As our old campervan wound down the mountainside, my dad cheerfully (and truthfully) announced that the brakes had failed.

Hilariously enough, Harry Chapin's *30,000 Pounds of Bananas* was actually playing on the radio.

Dad was a full-time mechanic and a part-time racing driver, so he kept his cool and used the gears and handbrake to bring us to a stop. Maybe I was too young to comprehend the gravity of the situation — only an Armco barrier stood between us and certain death. All I remember thinking is 'wow this is fun.'

And thus began my life-long love-affair with travel. Maps, camping, weird food, exotic languages, living out of a backpack, waking up each day somewhere new. Brilliant.

In 1988 my family went on another road-trip, this time around to, what was then, West Germany. Since my brother Alex and I would fight in the back of the car, my parents would be forced to split us up and one of us would get to sit up front. The front seat meant you got to unfold the Michelin map and be navigator — and I loved being navigator. Game theory, as understood by kids.

At one point we drove to the border crossing of the GDR, also known as East Germany, behind the Iron Curtain. My dad attempted to talk his way in without a visa, but the border guards were having none of it.

---

[1] Editor's Note: Since Graham Hughes is a well-travelled *British* national and the publisher/editor of this book is an *American,* the editor has, on occasion, interjected footnotes to translate Graham's English into, well, English. This was done only with Graham's begrudging consent. He implores that I emphasize that the Editor's Notes are not meant to insult the British audience, but rather the Americans for whom they are intended ☺

However, they did allow us to turn around at the checkpoint. For a few glorious seconds we were inside the "Sphere of Soviet Influence". As far as I was concerned, it totally counted.

We returned to Germany in 1990, just six months after the fall of the Berlin Wall. I didn't understand the political implications at the time, but looking back it was a thrilling time to be an (albeit young) gentleman of the road. The forbidden lands of Hungary, Czechoslovakia and Poland were suddenly and wonderfully accessible. That summer, I chipped a chunk of concrete off of the Berlin Wall. To this day it sits in a place of pride on my mantelpiece.

In 1999 I booked my first overland adventure as a grown-up — Cairo to Istanbul on a backpacker bus with my friends Dino and Dan. It was on the Egyptian section of that journey, between pyramids and temples, when I met the irrepressible Mandy. It wasn't exactly love at first sight (I annoyed the crap out of her), and considering she was from Australia and I'm a Brit and these were the dark days before Skype came along, I assumed we'd remain just good friends.

Three years later however, I purchased a round-the-world ticket. I planned to backpack on my own to the Indian Subcontinent, South East Asia, Australia, New Zealand and South America.

On the Australian leg of the journey, Mandy met me at the airport and we — rather unexpectedly — started kissing. From that moment on we were as thick as thieves, travelling through the red centre and down the east coast of Oz together in a beat-up Holden panel van we called Monty. She bought me my first Akubra hat in the desert town of Alice Springs.

A few months later I found myself sitting on top of a train in Ecuador scribbling down a list of all the countries I had visited in my life thus far — Andorra, Argentina, Australia... To my great satisfaction, I had clocked over 50 — and I entered most of them overland. Here, at the tender age of 23, I'd already been to over a quarter of the countries of the world. I found myself wondering how difficult would it be to go to *all* of them?

I thought back to Michael Palin's wonderful TV series *Around the World in 80 Days*. In it, he retraced the footsteps of Phileas Fogg and circumnavigated the globe without flying. I remember asking my mum if this meant he would be visiting every country in the world along the way — something that made sense to my 9-year-old brain. I admit to being a little disappointed to learn that — no, it didn't work that way.

I soon discovered that there were plenty of people who had travelled around the world without flying and that there were dozens of people who had visited every country in the world, but, as far as I was aware, nobody had done both at the same time.

How many countries are there anyway? Back in the summer of 2002 there were 189 members of the United Nations, plus Vatican City which had special observer status. By the end of that year, Switzerland and East Timor had joined, making 191.

Then there were also states of limited recognition: Taiwan, Kosovo and Palestine. Strangely, Western Sahara is a member of the African Union although Morocco is not. The Scottish and Welsh get rather upset when they aren't counted as separate countries, therefore it would be unfair not to count the four home nations of the United Kingdom as separate entities.

Yes, there are weird little places like Abkhazia, South Ossetia, Nagorno-Karabakh and Transnistria. There are places with separatist move-ments like Catalonia, West Papua, Somaliland, Mindanao and Tibet. There are places that have some degree of autonomy but are still tech-nically part of another country — like French Guiana, Greenland and Niue. And there are places like Bermuda, Tokelau and Guam that are self-governing but not sovereign.

But I didn't want to be travelling forever.

When I returned to my hometown of Liverpool, I jumped the bus to the Central Library and looted every copy of Lonely Planet I could get my grubby mitts on. I started connecting the dots from The Americas to New Zealand via Europe, Africa, Asia and Australia. I made copious notes on border posts, visa regulations, bus routes, train lines and ferry times, whilst also assessing which areas were (or seemed) safe to travel through and which were not.

After one long and extremely productive night, I emerged blinking into the crisp morning sunlight, clutching a definitive itinerary detailing how to get in and out of every single country in the world over land and sea. And what's more, according to my calculations, it could — if everything went swimmingly — be done in a year. Little did I really know.

In hopes of funding, I took my plan to *The Guardian* newspaper in London. In return for funding I would write a weekly column about my adventures on the road. The meeting with the travel editor went well — until he asked about safety.

My own personal safety was and is something I take very seriously. In the first few years of the 21st century, pretty much all of the civil wars that had torn through Africa had fizzled out, but some of the countries I intended to visit were still unstable and prone to sudden and unpredictable outbursts of violence. I had workarounds in place (such as visiting the peaceful Somaliland region of Somalia, and the Autonomous Kurdish Region of Iraq) but the possibility of a kidnapped or dead backpacker on *The Guardian's* payroll gave them cause for concern.

Until the world became a bit more settled, my dream of visiting every

country in the world without flying would have to remain exactly that —
a dream.

In the meantime, Mandy flew to the UK and I set up an independent
video production company, making short films, filming live events and
rocking Liverpool's burgeoning music scene. Mandy and I travelled
whenever we could, and with the advent of YouTube in 2005, I now had
a way of sharing my backpacker vids with the entire world.

By 2008 the number of UN members had risen to 192 but the "complete
no-go" countries (according to the UK's Foreign and Commonwealth
Office) had dwindled down to just one — Somalia. But even that was
possible to enter safely, so long as I visited the aforementioned region
of Somaliland in the north.

In February, I received an email from Lonely Planet in Australia — they
liked one of my YouTube videos and wanted to buy it. This gave me an
"in" with the biggest travel book company in the world. What's more,
the BBC had just bought a 75% stake in the company *and* that summer
I'd be travelling to Melbourne for Mandy's sister's wedding.

It felt as if the stars were aligning. Maybe Lonely Planet would dare do
what *The Guardian* would not. So instead of writing a column, what if
I could film a weekly video series for Lonely Planet's YouTube channel?
It would be incredible — and well within my abilities.

All I needed was a meeting.

So together with my friends Matt, Laura, Stuart, and Jewles, I put
together a punchy pitch video, laying out my plan to visit every country
in the world without flying. I used footage I had accumulated from
previous backpacking adventures — shots of me at the Pyramids, the
Taj Mahal, Machu Picchu. I also included footage of an insane bungee
jump I did in New Zealand, skydiving over Magnetic Island in Australia,
and swinging on vines through the Amazon jungle.

I planned to call the expedition "*The Odyssey*".

After arriving in Australia, I sent the video to my contact at Lonely
Planet. I told them I was in Melbourne and would love a meeting.

The response was a polite but dispiriting 'It is always nice to hear from
our contributors.'

'Oh well', I thought. 'Back to the drawing board...'

But then, a few hours later, I received another message.

David Collins, the Head of Development at Lonely Planet TV, had
watched the pitch video. And he liked it! Not as a YouTube series — but
as a bona fide *TV* series. A meeting at Lonely Planet HQ was set up for
the next day.

Weirdly enough, Mandy and I happened to be staying with a friend of hers for that one night and her house was walking distance from Lonely Planet HQ, a converted warehouse down by Footscray Docks.

David met me at reception and we made our way through the cavernous building to the staff canteen.

After getting the usual pleasantries out of the way, he had just one question:

'Is it possible?'

I pulled out a copy of my itinerary and placed it on the table.

'Yes. Yes it's possible.'

'Says who?'

I was ready for this. 'Says Lonely Planet!'

For such a complex undertaking, the plan was relatively simple. I would fly to Argentina and begin my expedition by crossing into Uruguay (country #1), and then head north to the east coast of Canada via every country in The Americas. From there I'd take a cargo ship across the Atlantic to Iceland and then on to Europe.

Europe, with its open borders and excellent public transport, would be a walk in the park. Next, I would head down the west coast of Africa, wiggle my way in and out of the landlocked countries of the continent, before shooting up the east coast and into the Middle East, Central Asia, the Indian Subcontinent, The Far East and South East Asia.

Finally, it was down to Australasia and into the endless blue of the Pacific. A journey through 200 countries, a great big sine wave from one side of the map to the other.

There were, of course, several outliers along the way. Unfortunately for me, countries are not all arranged in a nice neat line. I knew that Cape Verde and São Tomé off the west coast of Africa and Comoros, Mauritius, Madagascar, Seychelles and Maldives in the Indian Ocean would present a few headaches. As for how I was going to reach the 12 sovereign states of Oceania, *I simply didn't have a clue.*

My plan petered out once I hit Papua New Guinea.

Of course, I didn't tell David that.

The upshot of all this was that the Head of Development for Lonely Planet TV loved the idea. The stage was set for me to unleash *The Odyssey Expedition* on an unsuspecting world, beginning January 1st 2009.

With the expedition finally in the offing, I contacted the folks at

Guinness World Records™ (GWR) to agree on the rules of the challenge. They were as follows:

I.   I cannot fly *as part of the journey.*

II.   I cannot drive my own vehicle *as part of the journey.*

III.   I cannot hitchhike on public roads *as part of the journey.*

IV.   I must step foot on dry land — sailing into territorial waters does not count.

V.   A visit to a far-flung territory does not count as a visit to "the motherland".

Rules II and III were added at the behest of GWR, as they cannot sanction or condone a race on public roads (too many jokers contacting them to say they've driven from Liverpool to London in an hour). I'd have to rely on buses, trains and shared taxis from start to finish.

Okay, if I was going to visit every country in the world without flying I'd have to learn how to sail. Or at least how not to make a nuisance of myself on the high seas. Upon returning to the UK, I travelled over to Holyhead in Wales with my friend Hugh Sheridan and went out for a day on his family's yacht.

I can't claim to have learnt much. Although I did discover that sailors never call anything by its most obvious name and that sailboats move slowly compared to pretty much every other form of transport, short of riding on the back of a giant tortoise.

A yacht, in a good wind, can truck along at 7 knots. That's 8 miles an hour. I think I can run faster than that. It's probably why Hugh just laughed and shook his head when I asked how long it would take to sail to Iceland.

Back in Liverpool I had other things to attend to: wrapping up my video production business, giving notice on my flat and city centre office, getting all the necessary vaccinations (because I'm not a total moron), buying everything I would need: a mini laptop, GPS tracker, battery charger, spare mobile phone, and all that jazz. Happily, being Lonely Planet's newest bezzie-mate meant that I could have all the guidebooks I could eat, for free!

There wasn't much point in getting visas. At this stage as they would almost certainly expire before I could use them. Instead, I bought a second UK passport to leave with my parents so that they could get any visas I couldn't pick up on the road and then Fed-Ex it over to me.

I wanted to travel to these places for the same reason Mallory wanted to climb Everest: *because they're there.* I do not see myself as some kind of great white saviour. Nevertheless, I do believe all humans have a basic right to clean, safe drinking water.

So I travelled down to London to meet with Mel Tompkins, the media officer for the charity WaterAid, to find out how I could go about raising money and awareness for them whilst on the road. As well as encouraging people to donate, I roped my dad into making a special "WaterAid" toilet seat to hang off the back of my backpack.

It seemed appropriate, as my level of humour hovers somewhere around "toilet".

Meanwhile, over in Australia, David Collins was busy targeting specific broadcasters he thought might be interested in an excitable British chap bumming his way around the world. At the beginning of December 2008 we got a bite.

National Geographic Adventure offered 75% of the projected budget. They wanted eight episodes, and they would be shown in 50 countries across Africa, Asia and Australia.

The Odyssey Expedition was a GO.

There was no turning back now.

If you want to travel fast, you have to travel light. That being the case, here is a list of *everything* I took with me:

(1) Timex digital compass watch

(1) small Lowe Alpine Pax 25 backpack

(1) canvas courier bag

(1) small canvas shoulder bag

(1) pair of jeans (Levis)

(1) pair of shorts

(1) pair of shoes (Vans)

(7) underwear

(7) t-shirts/shirts

(7) pairs of socks (thin)

(1) jumper (which doubled as a towel)

(1) leather jacket

(1) tiny sleeping bag

(1) simple first aid kit (Band-Aids, Imodium, Vaseline, antiseptic cream, painkillers, electrolyte packets, etc.)

(100) anti-malaria tablets

(1) copy of Lonely Planet's *South America on a Shoestring*

(1) small laptop (Dell Latitude X1)

(1) video camera (Sony HVR-A1E)

(10) MiniDV tapes

(1) iPod nano

(1) pocket camera (Sony Cybershot)

(1) lighter socket power inverter (12v DC to 19v DC for my laptop)

(1) mobile phone (Nokia 7360)

(1) satellite phone (Iridium)

(1) packet of wet-wipes

(1) toilet seat

(2) glasses

(20) disposable contact lenses

(1) Swiss army knife

(1) GPS logger

(1) USB powered AA battery charger

(1) toothbrush & toothpaste

(1) hand sanitizer

(1) awesome hat (kangaroo hide Akubra)

- - - -

Christmas 2008 was a whirlwind of action and emotion. Mandy and I had to come to terms with the fact that we would not see each other for an entire year. When I flew to South America, she would fly home to Australia.

The plan was to reunite in Australia at the end of the year.

Or should I say, our "wildly optimistic" plan was to reunite in Australia at the end of the year.

Even though National Geographic had agreed to stump up 75% of the budget of the TV show, nobody had offered to make up the other 25%. I'd have to start the journey without any backup. I would be on my own.

It isn't that I thought I'd be followed around by a couple of Land Rovers and a make-up artist; but it would have been nice to have somebody whose job it was to make phone calls to shipping companies on my behalf.

Just to make things interesting, on Boxing Day[2] I broke a tooth. Then my video camera, the camera I planned to take around the world with me, stopped working.

So instead of taking the train to London to make our flights, Mandy and I ended up driving through the night to Tottenham Court Road in order to buy a new video camera (thank goodness for credit cards).

We dumped the car in South London for my friend Danny to drive back to Liverpool. *Sod the tooth, I could live with it broken.* As for the TV show, I was doing this with or without them.

For Mandy and I, that night would be our last together until God knew when. As a treat, we booked ourselves into a gorgeous hotel that we found on lastminute.com, bought a bottle of wine and a got ourselves a delicious take away. Heroically, I fell asleep at 9pm, probably out of nervous exhaustion.

The next morning Mandy and I travelled to Heathrow airport. We said goodbye twice. Once for the camera, held at arm's length, and a second time "for real".

By the time we went our separate ways we were both big blubbering messes.

What the blithering heck was I doing?

Twenty hours later I arrived in Rio de Janeiro, Brazil.

I know what you are thinking. If Uruguay is country #1 — and I'm crossing into it from Argentina, then why am I flying into Brazil? Because doing it this way worked out £200 cheaper. With the TV show not set in stone, this still needed to be a shoestring effort.

I had saved £10,000. It was time to see just how far around the world £10,000 would get me.

I headed straight to the bus station. The bus to Buenos Aires (1,500 miles away) left at 4pm. Since it was still early in the morning, I bought a ticket for the bus, put my backpack in a locker, and jumped a taxi to Copacabana beach.

The last time I was on Copacabana beach, Brazil had just won the FIFA World Cup for the fifth time. It was good to be back. It was even better to leave behind the cold wet winter of the UK for the summer skies, hot

---

[2] Editor's Note: Boxing Day is December 26th (a holiday in the UK and countries that were part of the British Empire).

sand and cool fresh coconut water of Brazil.

What was less good was that when I arrived in Brazil I accidentally set my watch back one hour too many. This meant that when I returned to the bus station at what I thought was 3:30pm, it was actually 4:30pm. The bus to Buenos Aires left 30 minutes earlier and there wasn't another until the next day. It wouldn't arrive until the afternoon of January 1st. This would throw my entire evil scheme out of kip — who'd be interested in an expedition that began on January 2nd?

Nobody, that's who.

Plus I'd miss all the New Year's Eve parties and that was totally unacceptable.

Desperate times call for desperate measures — I grabbed my bags and flagged down a taxi.

'Rio domestic airport *por favor.*'

As you will learn, languages are not my strong suit. The bus I missed stopped in São Paulo at 8pm that night. If I took a plane to São Paulo and the traffic wasn't too insane when I got there, I could *just* make it.

Yes, I wasn't supposed to fly, but it was still 2008 – the challenge hadn't started yet!

And so I tentatively boarded an "Oceanic Air" flight, even though I was a big fan of the TV show *Lost*. Thankfully I didn't end up on a tropical island with a polar bear, I ended up in São Paulo. The taxi ride from the airport to the bus station left me with little in the way of fingernails left to bite, but as the taxi pulled in, so did the bus to Buenos Aires.

I clambered aboard and took my rightful seat. When I say seat, I mean "armchair". Latin America really knows how to *bus*.

Back on track! The only downside being that after factoring in the cost of the bus ticket, flight and taxis, the direct flight from the UK to Argentina would have worked out cheaper.

I arrived in Buenos Aires on the morning of December 31st. It was raining so I headed straight for the backpacker hostel. I rang Mandy — now back in Melbourne and a good 16 hours ahead of me — to wish her a Happy New Year. I still hadn't got my head around the fact that we wouldn't see each other for a whole 12 months. To be honest, I still hadn't got my head around the fact that any of this utter madness was actually happening.

Although the funding was not yet secured, Lonely Planet didn't want to miss the start of the adventure. They hired Carlos Pauluk, a local camera op, to document the first 48 hours of *The Odyssey Expedition.*

I assumed that Argentines saw in the New Year like the rest of us — they go to a party, hug complete strangers, and crash into the gutter around 6am after a frantic but ultimately fruitless hunt for a taxi home.

But Maia, my only friend in Buenos Aires, told me that *Porteños* like herself don't do that. They see in the New Year with a family meal. This really didn't come as much of a surprise to me. I knew from past experience that Argies don't usually go out partying until well after midnight — no matter what night of the year it is.

That in mind, I headed over to the Milhouse Backpackers New Year's Eve disco. I saw in the great year of 2009 with travellers from all over the world, covered in foam and dancing to *Human* by The Killers.

Wave goodbye, wish me well. You gotta let me go...

Around 2am, drunk and fairly disorderly, Carlos and I left to meet with Maia. She invited me to an authentic Argentine house party — which is a lot like a British house party only with everyone speaking Spanish. I wasn't at the party long before a weird herbal concoction was thrust into my hand: an apparently "classic" Argentinean beverage which tasted like tree bark and which signalled the end of my ability to string together a coherent sentence in English (never mind Spanish).

I didn't remember it at the time, but Carlos filmed my drunken trek back to my hostel. The boat to Uruguay left in just under four hours. Stumbling, slurring and starry-eyed I directly addressed the camera with what became the de facto motto of *The Odyssey Expedition*.

'I'm a little bit drunk, but that's not going to stop me.'

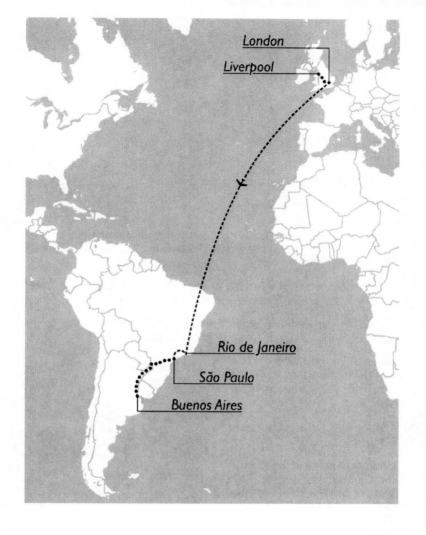

London
Liverpool

Rio de Janeiro
São Paulo
Buenos Aires

Chapter 2
Hey Ho Let's Go

Three hours later I awoke, fully clothed and in desperate need of water and Aspirin. I looked at my watch. It was 8am. The ferry to Uruguay departed at 8:30.

I jumped out of bed, grabbed my bags, checked out of the hostel, hailed a taxi and tore across Buenos Aires to the ferry terminal.

Carlos the Cameraman, bedraggled and bewildered, met me at the entrance to the terminal. 'Go go go go!', I hollered.

We made the boat by the skin of our teeth. The last to board, hungover as hell, we crossed the River Plate.

A fitting start to the craziest year of my life.

Uruguay[3] is one of those countries that many people have heard of, but few know anything about. This is probably because it's: (a) tiny and (b) harmless. It keeps to itself and does little to upset or destabilise the world — something I feel should be commended in this day and age.

I disembarked in the picture-postcard port town of Colonia and ambled over to the nearby bus station. Unfortunately, my plan to hit the ground running tripped

URUGUAY 001/200

🏛 MONTEVIDEO

👥 3.36m

❓ Spanish

💵 Uruguayan Peso

💰 $9,064.71

Uruguay has won the FIFA World Cup twice as many times as England.

---

[3] Author's Note: With each new country, I have included an information card which includes the location of the country, the capital, its language, currency, population and GDP per capita (correct for 2009 — the year of the expedition).

at the first hurdle. Uruguay was, for all intents and purposes, closed. January 1st is a public holiday. All long distance buses had the day off.

Very little on my expedition was pre-booked — bus tickets, hostel rooms etc. It was mostly a case of turning up and hoping for the best. This was not laziness, it was just impractical to reserve and/or pay for things in advance when any one of a number of things could prevent me from arriving on time. Having said that, it would have taken me 10 seconds on Google to discover that the buses in Uruguay weren't running. This was just piss poor preparation!

With no other options for travelling across Uruguay, the first modification to *The Odyssey Expedition* route was required — instead of crossing the border into Brazil, I would have to return to **Argentina**, back the way I came.

Thank goodness that, unlike in Uruguay, the Buenos Aires bus station was open. In fact, half the city seemed to be there. I downed a can of Coke and threw myself into the throng.

Bus stations in Latin America are like bustling markets — hundreds of stalls and a bewildering number of logos and timetables. Finding a company that serves your destination can be a mission in itself.

Luckily, I had Carlos on hand to help out. Within a few hours we were on a bus hurtling towards the Argentinian town of Posadas, 500 miles to the north.

ARGENTINA 002/200

🏛 **BUENOS AIRES**

👥 40.02m

❓ Spanish

💵 **Argentine Peso**

💰 $9,456.82

The name 'Argentina' comes from the Latin 'argentum' meaning 'silver'.

PARAGUAY 003/200

🏛 **ASUNCIÓN**

👥 6.347m

❓ Spanish

💵 **Paraguayan Guaraní**

💰 $2,509.68

Paraguay boasts the only national flag that has different designs on either side.

It was the small hours of the morning before we arrived at our destination. I hopped over the border into **Paraguay**, got my entry/exit stamp, and then hopped back into Argentina.

I had been to Paraguay before, several years earlier and I hadn't had a particularly good experience: I had arrived in the capital Asunción as it was getting dark only to discover that none of the ATMs would accept my bank cards. I therefore had to find somewhere that would exchange my travellers cheques (remember them?).

However, all the places listed in my guidebook had either closed down or moved. After three hours of lugging around my backpack, I finally found a hotel that would accept them. It was only when I crashed out exhausted on my bed and the sounds of what would politely be called "romance" began to echo down the corridor did it dawn on me that the hotel in question doubled as a knocking shop. I should have noted the hourly rates on the wall.

From that previous trip, I knew that the fastest way to get to Bolivia was not to brave the dirt track through north-west Paraguay, but instead to hurtle west across Argentina's Chaco region and then head north at the wonderfully named San Salvador de Jujuy[4]. And so for the second time that day I crossed back over into Argentina.

The bus to the town of Resistencia would have been uneventful had I not stupidly left my GPS tracker on the damn thing.

Thank heavens then for Carlos and the friendly guys in the Resistencia ticket office — a couple of phone calls and it was returned to me on the next bus — smiles and hi-fives all around.

In San Salvador de Jujuy I had to say *adios* to Carlos — his allotted time was up. For the next 35 countries of *The Odyssey Expedition* I'd have to film everything myself, holding my camcorder at arms-length and talking to it like a demented hobo conversing with his homemade sock puppet.

I ventured northwards to country number four, **Bolivia**, and arrived at the border early the next day. There were a few hundred people standing in line to see the one guy with the rubber entry stamp. Oh Bolivia, how I've missed you...

Bolivia is not just my favourite

BOLIVIA 004/200

🏛 **LA PAZ**

👥 **9.993m**

💬 **Spanish**

💵 **Bolivian Boliviano**

💰 **$1735.14**

The lithium in your mobile phone battery probably came from Bolivia's vast salt flats.

---

[4] Author's Note: Pronounced "who-who-ee".

country in South America, it's one of my favourite countries *in the world.*

It's the only place on Earth a person can walk in the reflected sky of the Salar de Uyuni salt flats, go for an excursion down a notoriously dangerous silver mine, buy dynamite in a shop like you're Wile E. Coyote, enjoy a guided tour around the capital's main prison (given, *of course,* by one of the inmates), go for a bike ride down a "Road of Death" and swim with the anacondas, piranhas and crocodiles of the Amazon basin.

I like to refer to Bolivia as "The Land That Health and Safety Forgot". To say that Bolivia was a bit nuts would be an understatement — I love it.

Having said that, there is one thing I most certainly *don't* love about Bolivia: the buses. In contrast to Brazil and Argentina, Bolivian buses are generally filthy, uncomfortable and seemingly held together with duct tape. The roads range from pretty awful to the official "most dangerous road in the world", and the drivers have a tendency to drive like they're playing Mario Kart.

In short, I'd much rather have taken the train, but by the time I got over the border all of the day's tickets were sold out. So I reluctantly clambered aboard a bus to the mountain town of Oruro. As nightmare coach journeys go, this one was a corker; windows that didn't shut properly; an unsealed road up through The Andes littered with switchbacks and sheer drop-offs; and to top it all, the journey was a shut-your-eyes-and-hope-for-the-best overnighter. Bolivia isn't big on streetlights, cats-eyes or, for that matter, crash barriers.

I have a total of six superpowers that would be utterly useless for fighting evil, but are super handy when travelling.

Firstly I can hold in a poo for up to a week. Go me!

Secondly, I hardly ever get ill when I'm travelling. Both of these abilities may stem from my misspent youth eating dodgy kebabs at muddy European music festivals.

Thirdly, given the choice, mosquitoes will bite somebody else rather than me. That might have something to do with my blood-type being A Positive, I dunno.

Fourthly, I always seem to make it back to where I'm staying no matter how drunk I get. My beer-scooter has one hell of a GPS installed.

Fifthly, I can wake up when I want to without the aid of an alarm clock, even after a relatively short period of time.

And finally (I saved the best till last) I can *always* sleep. Anytime, anyplace, anywhere.

Uncomfortable seat? No head rest? Bus driver gunning it around twisting mountain roads? Freezing cold air blasting through the window? No matter. I simply place my head on the seatback in front of me and sleep through the night, no Temazepam required.

However, the next day was not so hunky dory. Not only did I foolishly leave my copy of Lonely Planet's *South America on a Shoestring* in a cyber café in Oruro, but the pass over the Andes into Chile reached as high as 4,000 metres above sea level. Of course you're not supposed to go that high so quickly. Before long my head felt like Joe Pesci had put it in a vice.

All I wanted to do was curl up in my sleeping bag at the back of the bus, but once we reached the mountaintop border-crossing I was made to stand in a queue for over two hours in the freezing cold in order to get stamped out of Bolivia. A thousand invisible elephants were dancing the flamenco on my head while the arid Andean air whipped my face like a giant sandblasting machine.

After being stamped into **Chile**, I returned to the coach, did my best to ignore the stench of the nearby baby getting its nappy changed, the frigid air streaming through the inexplicably open windows and the overwhelming urge to chuck my guts up all over the chemical toilet, and I fell fast asleep.

CHILE 005/200

🏛 **SANTIAGO**

👥 **16.99m**

❓ **Spanish**

💵 **Chilean Peso**

💰 **$10,141.60**

Parts of Chile's Atacama Desert have not experienced a drop of rain since records began, yet quite remarkably, over a million people eke out an existence there.

We reached the dusty Atacaman surf town of Arica around midnight. Having descended to sea level in less than half a day. Joe Pesci decided to let my head out of the vice.

The bus station was all but closed, so I had to change my Bolivian bolivianos into Chilean pesos with some shifty looking guy who kept asking me if I wanted "anything more". I asked him for "more pesos", but I don't think the joke translated well. A ruddy-faced Chilean lady asked in English if I needed somewhere to stay. Wracked and weary from my journey I said yes.

Throwing caution to the wind, I followed her down some terrifyingly dark alleyways. Happily, I wasn't mugged. The lady's homestay was cosy enough for one night. After I had checked-in she offered me a "Christmas drink". I didn't want to be rude and it's not like me to turn down a glass of anything that is (a) wet and (b) alcoholic. It tasted like a mixture of cold coffee, vodka and rotten eggs. It was all I could do not to vomit it back up all over the table.

The next morning I took a shared taxi to the border with country number six, **Peru** — the cradle of the Inca Empire.

After being stamped into the country I hopped on the bus for the 18-hour journey to Lima. The Pan-American Highway stretched north all the way to the horizon. To the left were the crashing waves of the Pacific Ocean, to the right was the inhospitable desert that reaches the foothills of the Andes.

By the afternoon the bus was hot, cramped and uncomfortable. I had pins and needles in my right foot.

But we were making good time and I was in high spirits.

Around 7pm we stopped to get some food and to change

PERU   006/200

🏛 **LIMA**

👥 **28.93m**

💬 **Spanish**

💵 **Peruvian Sol**

💰 **$4,188.81**

Conquistador Francisco Pizarro captured Incan emperor Atahualpa and ransomed him for a "room of gold". Pizarro got his room of gold but killed Atahualpa anyway.

drivers, our new driver being the unholy offspring of Evel Knievel and Donald Campbell.[5] Even when winding our way along narrow mountain roads there was nothing he wouldn't overtake, often whilst going around blind corners in the dark with a sheer drop just inches away. Lewis Hamilton[6] could be blasting his way out of hell, dressed as Batman, in a rocket-powered Bugatti Veyron and this guy would be right behind him flashing his lights and beeping his horn. It was by some damn miracle that we survived.

Upon my arrival in Lima I took a stroll in the morning sun around the picturesque central square with its colonial-era buildings, decked out in yellow and white. People were milling about, getting ready for the *Fiesta des Tres Reios*, the Spanish celebration of the Epiphany. I had been to a couple of these before in Spain — there is a big colourful parade and they throw sweets to the kids. Taking candy from babies sounded like a lark, but I had another 194 countries to visit, so I reluctantly pressed on towards Ecuador.

When there isn't allocated seating, there's a moment when you get on a long-distance coach and you have to quickly decide where you'll be sitting for the next several hours, or maybe even have to sleep through

---

[5] Editor's Note: Donald Campbell CBE was a British speed record breaker who broke eight absolute world speed records on water and on land in the 1950s and 1960s.

[6] Editor's Note: Lewis Hamilton MBE is a British Formula One racing driver.

the night. I always try to get a window seat on the side that the sun isn't and preferably behind the driver — in order to piggyback on his instinctive sense of self-preservation in an emergency.

But sometimes you don't get a choice. Sometimes, the bus is sold out, there is just one seat available, and it's next to a sketchy looking weirdo. The only thing that would make it worse is if said weirdo smiled when you sat down next to him and placed his hand on your knee. And left it there. Shudder.

It was 16 hours to the border.

The next day I entered my 7th country, **Ecuador**, from the town of Tumbes. I couldn't find a direct bus to Quito so instead I took the bus to the city of Guayaquil thinking "near enough". When I arrived, I realized that it was a good 80 miles out of my way. That's what happens when you lose your guidebook.

I arrived in Quito at midnight and *just* missed the weekly bus that would have whizzed me directly through country number 8, Colombia, into country number 9, Venezuela.

ECUADOR	007/200

🏛️ **QUITO**

👥 **14.76m**

❓ **Spanish**

💵 **US Dollar**

💰 **$4,236.78**

A common street food in Ecuador is "cuy" — spit-roasted guinea pig on a stick.

I wandered around for a good hour looking for somewhere to rest my weary bones. Even though Quito is just a couple of miles south of the Equator, it doesn't feel particularly equatorial — possibly something to do with the fact it has an elevation of 2,850 metres above sea level. At night it can be positively freezing. Eventually I found a little guest house for $10 and crashed. I was knackered.

The following morning I made the executive decision to take the day off. I had been travelling pretty much non-stop for more than a week and my batteries needed recharging — literally and metaphorically. While my laptop, phone and video camera got back up to 100%, I spent the best part of the day strolling around Quito's beautiful old town, some of it remains unchanged since the great French Geodesic Expedition of the 1730s, which spent five years here meticulously measuring one arc of the meridian at the equator, paving the way for what we now call the "metre", as well as the independent nation of Ecuador itself.

The next day I caught the bus to the town of Ipiales on the border with **Colombia**. It's less than 90 miles as the crow flies, but I wasn't allowed to fly, and the Andes don't facilitate straight roads. By the time I got to the frontier it was getting dark.

Like with Bolivia, hundreds of people queued to see one guy with the entry stamp. I had two choices: stand like a chump in the queue, miss the last bus out of the border town, and spend the night in a dingy overpriced "hostel" (which may or may not also be a brothel), or I could pick a random backpacker in the queue closer to the front, pretend he's my mate, bribe him with a cold can of Coke to keep quiet, and save myself a lot of time and bother.

COLOMBIA 008/200

🏛 **BOGOTÁ**

👥 45.8m

Spanish

💵 Colombian Peso

💰 $5,104.99

At the height of his infamy, Colombian drug lord Pablo Escobar was the richest and most powerful criminal in human history.

Being a terrible person, I chose the latter.

Once in, I changed money, bought a new SIM card and took a taxi to the bus station. Next stop: Bogotá.

Make no bones about it, Colombia is *beautiful*. As I travelled along the spine of the northern Andes, the view out of the window was a feast for the eyes — lush green tropical mountains — a world away from the concrete monotony of the British Motorway Network.

The Colombians themselves are disarmingly friendly, happy to share their snacks and natter away nineteen to the dozen[7].

There is a perception that Colombia is an outrageously dangerous place. It may have been 25 years ago, but it has made great strides since those dark, dark days. Still, when police/army types with big guns and no smiles interrupted our journey every 30 minutes, I figured it was a sad necessity. Better safe than sorry.

Once in Bogotá, there was barely time to dig my undies out my arse before I was on another overnight bus, this time heading to the border with Venezuela.

For some reason, Colombian buses are kept at a constant temperature of what felt like minus 25°C. Forced to wear pretty much all the clothing I was carrying with me, I crawled into my sleeping bag and hoped not to die of hypothermia in the night.

We were roused from our collective slumbers at about 7am for breakfast on top of a mountain, shrouded in early morning mist. And I thought

---

[7] Editor's Note: British slang for something happening very fast, in this case people talking very quickly.

the bus was cold! The driver kept us all locked out of the coach for half an hour so we all got to experience the full bollock-shattering chill of an Andean mountain pass on an early Sunday morning.

But at least there was coffee. Milk and plenty of sugar please.

I arrived at the border with **Venezuela** around noon. In the queue I chatted with a Venezuelan teenager called Mario who had been visiting his relatives in Colombia with his mum. Like many people his age, Mario was less than impressed with the antics of the then-president Hugo Chavez, and correctly predicted the economic collapse that ensued a few years later.

My first taste of Venezuela involved a rip-off. The taxi guy who drove me from the border to Ureña bus station wanted $30 — for a journey of less than a mile. It would be outrageous in London, but it's taking the absolute piss when you consider

VENEZUELA 009/200

🏛 **CARACAS**

👥 **28.58m**

💬 **Spanish**

💵 **Venezuelan Bolívar**

💰 **$11,524.99**

The first Europeans to reach this part of the world saw that the indigenous people built stilt homes on the water. That's why "Venezuela" means "Little Venice".

that at the time, petrol in Venezuela cost less than a *penny* a litre. That is not a typo.

Matters didn't improve when I arrived at the sprawl of concrete and pollution they called a bus station. Up to this point, *The Odyssey Expedition* had pretty much been a no-brainer. I turned up, bought a ticket to my next destination and hopped aboard — easy! However, Venezuela did things... erm... *differently.*

I can only assume there was a meeting of the government's public transport department that went something like this: 'Let's not put enough buses on! Let's have no express services! Let's make it impossible to pay by credit card! Let's employ thoroughly unpleasant and unhelpful staff! And, just to kick a guy when he's down, let's make sure the only ATM in the bus terminal is out of action!'

To further complicate matters, the following day was a public holiday, so the world and his mate was trying to cross the country by bus. I was told there would be no availability for *any* bus going *anywhere* for at least three days.

By some outrageous fortune I ran into Mario and his mum again. What's more, they were heading the same way as me. I don't know how they did it, but they managed to wangle me a ticket on the bus for Cuidad Guyana, a city on the way to the actual country of Guyana. They

28

also persuaded the coach company to let me pay in US dollars. I got a crappy exchange rate, but I didn't care — Ureña was not a town in which I wished to spend the next three days. Thank goodness for lovely people, eh?

I woke up the next morning to the sound of *Death Race* starring Jason Statham being played at a volume that would make a jet engine quiver. This continued for about three minutes until, rather inexplicably, the televisions turned themselves off. I guess that's what passes for an alarm clock on a Venezuelan bus.

Rudely awoken, I realised we were passing through Caracas, the capital of Venezuela. Maybe I didn't see the best of it from the bus window, but I was more than happy to be just passing through. The bus then headed east along the coast and I saw the glorious azure blue of the Caribbean Sea for the first time in my life.

We pulled into Cuidad Guyana's bus terminal at 10pm, after 36 hours of travel, just in time to see my connecting bus leave the terminal *at that exact moment*. Goddamnit. This meant I had nowhere to go *and* nowhere to stay.

Once again my guardian angels came to my aid. Mario and his mum said I could kip at their place and take the next bus in the morning. How could I say no?

That night I got to tuck into a delicious traditional soup made by Mario's Colombian-born father, have a hot shower and stay up late with Mario talking shit and playing *Guitar Hero* like a goddamn normal person. It was heavenly.

In the morning, the family and I ate breakfast together and Mario's brother dropped me off at the bus station. Their generosity was humbling. I can't stress how much this journey re-affirmed my faith in humanity.

Now even though they're next-door neighbours, you can't enter Guyana from Venezuela. This is because the Venezuelan government believes 80% of Guyana belongs to Venezuela. It is even marked on official maps as *'Zona en Reclamación'*. Unsurprisingly, this somewhat irks the Guyanese.

Consequently, the border between the two countries is well and truly closed. To get to Guyana from Venezuela overland I'd have to dip in and out of Brazil via the north-western city of Boa Vista. But that was all right — I had to visit Brazil again anyway (this time as part of the challenge).

The bus to the border travelled down through the Grand Savannah — an area of Venezuela filled with vast table-top mountains called *tepuis* — home of the Angel Falls, the highest waterfall in the world — 16 times higher than Niagara. The only way to see it for yourself is to fly or hike for several days, so it wasn't on my itinerary — this time around.

I found myself sitting next to a guy named Francisco. He was 81 years old, his parents were from Trinidad, he was born in Venezuela, his wife was from Grenada and he now lives in Washington DC, where he would be selling flags for President Obama's inauguration which would be taking place the following week.

Until that day I had successfully avoided being stuck in a border town for the night. It is invariably a grim undertaking, and the grotty little town of Pacaraima did not disappoint. As I arrived 15 minutes after the border closed, I was forced to check into a grubby little guesthouse. The shower was cold, my room smelt of turnip and the mattress was damp.

BRAZIL 010/200

I really, really missed Mario's gaff.

In the morning, I popped over to Pacaraima's solitary ATM only to find that it did not accept my filthy foreign cards. But once again it was wonderful people to the rescue as a taxi driver offered to take me the full two-hour journey to Boa Vista, **Brazil** on a promise that I'd pay him upon arrival. That was if I could find an ATM that worked.

BRASÍLIA

193.5m

Portuguese

Brazilian Real

$8,373.46

South America was split between Portuguese and Spanish lands by the Treaty of Tordesillas (1494) which specified the line of demarcation in leagues from the Cape Verde Islands.

Thankfully for the sake of Anglo-Brazilian relations, I did.

After paying the driver (and leaving a decent tip), I transferred to a minibus that ran up to the town of Lethem on the border with Guyana.

Guyana — a country endearingly called "Conradian" *in its own tourist material*. As in Joseph Conrad. As in *Heart of Darkness*. To add to my concerns, the unsealed jungle track from Lethem to the capital Georgetown was, according to my (now-lost) copy of Lonely Planet, "prone to robbery and hijacking".

At the border, a toothless old guy rowed me across the Takutu river. The finishing touches were being added to the shiny new concrete bridge. 'Won't have this job much longer', he mused.

I stepped off the boat and I found myself transported, as if by magic, to the Caribbean proper. Goodbye gauchos and *jamón y queso* sandwiches — hello spicy food, reggae beats and good old-fashioned cricket.

Although geographically part of the South American mainland, culturally, socially and historically, Guyana very much identifies itself with its northern, more islandy neighbours. It is part of Caricom (the Caribbean Community) and they even drive on the left, like normal people.

The only building on the Guyanese side of the Takutu river was a café-bar called T&M. A large lady sitting behind a desk welcomed me in. She stamped my passport, changed my money into Guyanese dollars, and sold me a ticket for the next minibus to Georgetown. Not only that, she passed me an ice-cold beer and fed me dinner. Now THAT, ladies and gentleman, is how you welcome a stranger into your country!

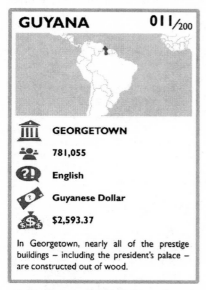

GUYANA   011/200

🏛 **GEORGETOWN**

👥 **781,055**

💬 **English**

💵 **Guyanese Dollar**

💰 **$2,593.37**

In Georgetown, nearly all of the prestige buildings – including the president's palace – are constructed out of wood.

The bus left at dusk. We bumped and grinded our way through the rainforest for a few hours before the minibus stopped at a clearing. I thought we were stopping for food, but no — we were handed a hammock each, told to hang it up in the nearby gazebo and get some sleep. Thank heavens mosquitoes don't fancy me much.

The journey through the jungle recommenced at the crack of dawn, and was made more interesting (and perhaps a little safer) by the fact it was no longer pitch black. The road wasn't as bad as the guidebook made out — okay, so there were a few river crossings on fixed pulley rafts made of rusty metal and wooden planks, but if that was the limit of the Conradianness of Guyana, I wasn't complaining — it was actually rather fun.

It stopped being fun around midday when the minibus stopped, the driver pointed at the road ahead and said 'roll over, roll over', before hopping out of the vehicle. My fellow passengers and I followed him down the track until we stood on a small bridge that spanned a rocky stream, around twenty metres below.

In the stream was a smashed minibus, exactly the same colour and make as the one we were travelling in. It lay on its side, half-submerged in water.

Our driver scurried down the bank, climbed on top of the wreck, wiped the mud off the side window and looked inside. He shouted something in the local lingo. The guy next to me translated. 'He says there are five dead bodies inside. He thinks they're Brazilians'.

Jesus Christ.

'Should we get them out?', I asked.

The guy shrugged. 'Nah. The police will do it.'

As the minibus guys quietly looted some bits and bobs from the wreck, I mused on the fact that for the next 12 months, maybe longer, I'd be putting my life in other people's hands. The majority of my journey would be in places where Health and Safety, seatbelts, speed limits and decent roads are an undiscovered country. Suddenly my merry little jaunt around the planet became a lot more real, and a lot more dangerous.

It was late afternoon before we arrived in Georgetown. I wouldn't make it to my final country of South America — **Suriname** — before dark, so I thought it best to leave it until morning.

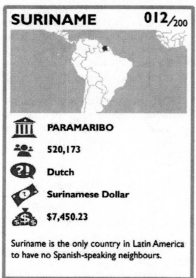

SURINAME 012/200

🏛 **PARAMARIBO**

👥 520,173

❓ Dutch

💵 Surinamese Dollar

💰 $7,450.23

Suriname is the only country in Latin America to have no Spanish-speaking neighbours.

That night I chatted to Mandy on Skype. It had only been a couple of weeks since I last saw her, but it felt a lot longer. The fact that it would be at least another 50 weeks before we'd be together again didn't bear thinking about. It was all going well, I told her — just a day behind schedule.

The best thing about travelling around the Americas with a British passport back in 2009 was that you didn't need to ask prior permission to visit pretty much any of the 35 nation states of North America, Latin America, or the Caribbean. You could just turn up.

But there is always an exception that proves the rule. In this case it's Suriname. Old Dutch Guiana requires you to apply for a visa in advance. This takes time and money. Since I was short on both and didn't have to travel through Suriname (French Guiana being, well, French) I didn't see the point of getting a visa. Like Paraguay, Suriname would just be a border hop.

So I took a bus to the Guyanese town of Corriverton and from there a large panga boat took me and a bunch of other passengers over Molston Creek to Nieuw Nickerie in Suriname. I may not have got a passport stamp, but my GPS tracker and video footage proved I crossed the border.

Stepping off the boat onto Surinamese soil was an exhilarating experience. I'll admit allowing myself a "woo" even though I'm British and we tend not to go in for that sort of thing.

I had made it to my 12th and final country of South America in two weeks using just buses and boats.

But that was the easy bit. I still had 188 countries to visit; 48 of which were islands, and a quarter of them were in The Caribbean — a place where scheduled ferry services are few and far between.

The real challenge was about to begin.

Chapter 3
The Hitchhiker's Guide
To The Caribbean

The lack of ferry services in The Caribbean meant that in order for me to hop from one nation to the next, I could no longer expect to get by on my own. I needed help. It was time for "Team Odyssey" to step into the limelight.

Team Odyssey consisted of my Liverpool friends Lorna Brookes and Dino Deasha, my girlfriend Mandy, my cousins Leo Skelly and Christian Olsen, my family lawyer John Howell, and my mum and dad. Others helped out along the way, but they were the core group. This was a strict tea-and-biscuits affair, everyone helped out when they could while juggling full time jobs, children, and in Lorna's case, working on her PhD.

Their job? To get me onto cargo boats, sailing boats, fishing boats, banana boats — anything so long as it was going my way and appeared to float.

With the notable exceptions of Barbados, Jamaica and The Bahamas, the island nations of The Caribbean are laid out in a convenient arc running from Trinidad to Cuba, each rarely more than 100 miles from its nearest neighbour. That's a few hours on a fast ferry, about 7 hours on a large cargo ship, or 15 hours on a yacht.

But first I had to get to Trinidad! Apparently, there was some sort of ferry that left from north-east Venezuela, but information on it was sketchy and getting back to Venezuela would entail braving the jungle death road again. Sod that for a game of soldiers.

If I wanted to get to Trinidad directly from Guyana I would have to hitchhike my way onto a container ship. Technically, catching a ride on a container ship isn't considered hitchhiking, but you get what I mean. For several days, Team Odyssey had been emailing Gulf Shipping, a Guyanese company that might be able to help.

I returned to Georgetown around 3pm to find an email waiting for me from Lorna. It said that Gulf Shipping had been in touch and that there was a boat leaving for Trinidad in two hours' time and I had myself a berth!

I emailed Lorna informing her that she was a goddamn legend and when I'm Prime Minister she can have free Haribo Starmix for life.

Bevaun, the shipping agent, picked me up from the guesthouse and drove me across town to the shipping office where I was handed over to his colleague, Cedric. Cedric sorted out my exit stamp and took me to the port — grabbing some damn tasty Guyanese tucker, pepper pot, Cajun beef and jerk chicken, along the way.

We arrived at the boat within the hour. There she was — the *MV Miriam*. What a magnificent beastie. Although I come from a city famed for its maritime history, I had never actually *been* on a cargo ship before. It was all rather exciting. I was introduced to the captain and the crew. Everyone on board was from the Philippines, perhaps the last great seafaring nation. It wasn't long before we were chasing the setting sun towards Trinidad.

The first thing I learned about modern cargo ships is that they are utterly mind-bogglingly big. The amount of stuff that is transported around the world on any given day is astronomical. I thought sussing out the logistics of *The Odyssey Expedition* was tricky, I had no idea.

Consider this: the big ships, the "Post-Panamax" ships (too big to fit through the old Panama canal) transport up to 13,000 containers. If those containers were placed end-to-end (say, on a train), the train would be *fifty miles* long. That's a train stretching from Oxford to Central London. Manhattan to Trenton. Melbourne to Ballarat. That's *one* ship, ladies and gents. Maersk has over 500 ships in their fleet. Admittedly, they aren't all Post-Panamax sized but still, if all of Maersk's containers were stacked on top of each other they'd be 8,850 times the height of the Eiffel Tower.

And Maersk is just one of many big shipping companies.

Thinking about it makes my brain ache.

Now on most ships there are two cabins that are rarely used, one for the owner and another for the pilot. The pilot is a local who comes aboard and helps the captain guide the ship in and out of their port. It's rare that the pilot stays overnight, so it was his cabin I had purloined for the duration.

These ships have around 20 people living on them full time: the captain, the chief officers, the chief engineer, the supercargo (in charge of cargo), the bosun (in charge of, er, stuff), the cook, the thief, his wife and her lover. Something like that.

The guys who know their ropes are called "line handlers" and the cargo movers are called "stevedores", although I never found out whom exactly Steve adores[8]. I was down on the crew manifest as a "supernumerary" which sounds like a caped crusader that helps you with your maths homework, but really it's just a fancy way of saying "passenger".

The crew went out of their way to make me feel incredibly welcome, and were happy to ply me with more alcohol than my guts could handle, something of a baptism of fire for a wee ginger man still trying to find his sea legs.

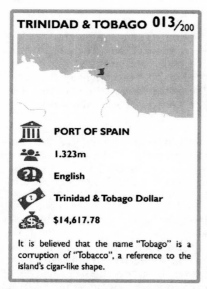

TRINIDAD & TOBAGO 013/200

🏛 **PORT OF SPAIN**

👥 1.323m

❓ English

💵 Trinidad & Tobago Dollar

💰 $14,617.78

It is believed that the name "Tobago" is a corruption of "Tobacco", a reference to the island's cigar-like shape.

Point Lisas on the west coast of **Trinidad** was supposed to be a quick stopover on the way to Port of Spain further up the coast. However, once in port, our electric generator failed, which meant that cargo operations could not take place. It also meant there was no power for the galley. The cook, not one to be bested by a little thing like non-working ovens, found a pallet of wood, smashed it apart with a fire axe, dug out an old barbecue set and began cooking a hog-roast on deck, laughing as he worked.

I could have split for the capital, as it was only 24 miles away, but it was a Sunday. Nothing happens on a Sunday. The weather was perfect, the crew were in good spirits and damn that was a fine looking roast. Needless to say, I held off going to Port of Spain for a few hours.

That evening I said goodbye the fabulous crew of the *MV Miriam* and took the bus over to the capital. Port of Spain has a somewhat lousy reputation, but I had a fine old time, making new friends and tucking into some of Trinidad's legendary fried chicken.

Early Monday morning I set off for the Caricom dock, situated to the left of the Port of Port of Spain. One might say I was *port of the Port of Port of Spain.*[9]

While the main port handled the big container ships, the Caricom dock was for small independent cargo boats transporting bits and bobs around The Caribbean.

---

[8] Editor's Note: Groan
[9] Editor's Note: Double Groan

I asked around if anybody was heading to Grenada. 'Not until Wednesday', came the reply.

The cargo ship I was hoping to take across the Atlantic was leaving in less than three weeks. If I was to make that (admittedly tight) connection I couldn't waste even a couple of days.

A bit of a pickle, to be sure, but there was little I could do about it. I headed back into town to pick up a couple of things from DHL: a copy of Lonely Planet's *Caribbean Islands* and, more importantly, a free international mobile internet USB dongle from the lovely people at Vodafone UK. It was time to upload some of my videos from the road.

After I got setup over a hot coffee, Lorna called me on Skype. She had set up a meeting with Annette Callender, the manager of a yacht hire company at the nearby marina.

Annette was a total legend. She got on the marina's VHF radio and found me a space on a private sailboat heading to Grenada. Go Annette! It wouldn't be leaving until the evening of the next day, but it would get me there a day earlier than any ship from the Caricom dock. It also meant we could watch President Obama's inauguration on the telly before I left. Annette cried with joy to see the US's first black president be sworn into office. Great days.

The sailboat to Grenada was called the *September Song* and was helmed by Ted, John and Linda from the UK. Not having learnt a thing from my experience on board the *MV Miriam*, I ate pizza and drank beer before getting on board. As a fairly direct consequence I spent most of the journey to Grenada chucking my guts up. Good thing there were only 46 more island nations for me to get to on a boat after this one.

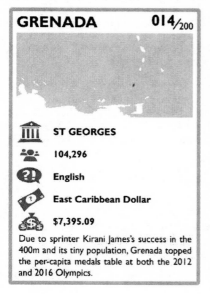

GRENADA 014/200

🏛 ST GEORGES

👥 104,296

💬 English

💰 East Caribbean Dollar

💵 $7,395.09

Due to sprinter Kirani James's success in the 400m and its tiny population, Grenada topped the per-capita medals table at both the 2012 and 2016 Olympics.

We reached Prickly Bay on the south coast of **Grenada** the following afternoon. After thanking Ted, John and Linda profusely (and apologising for all the vomit) I raced over to St Georges. From there I caught the ferry to nearby Carriacou Island, which is still part of Grenada. I wanted to press on to Saint Vincent and The Grenadines, just a few miles north, but no boats were going until the next day.

So I found a hammock on the beach and made myself comfortable for the night, taking a small panga boat over to Union Island in The Grenadines first thing the following morning, a journey that left me soaking wet from head to toe.

But still, **Saint Vincent and the Grenadines**! Sounds like a doo-wop band from the 50s.

After being stamped in I headed for the main sea port, hoping to catch an internal ferry to the capital Kingstown (not be confused with Kingston, Jamaica) on the island of St Vincent. Unfortunately, I missed the boat by five minutes, and there wouldn't be another until the next day.

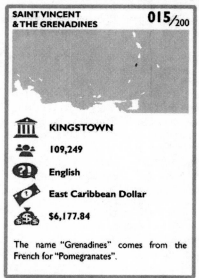

SAINT VINCENT & THE GRENADINES 015/200

🏛 KINGSTOWN

👥 109,249

❓ English

💵 East Caribbean Dollar

💰 $6,177.84

The name "Grenadines" comes from the French for "Pomegranates".

It was at this point that I realised that getting to every island nation in The Caribbean in just two weeks was a total pipedream.

But I have to admit, Union Island wasn't a bad place to be stuck for the night — weatherboard shacks, palm trees, warm breeze, white sand beach, tree covered hills, turquoise waters gently lapping at the shore and *The Best of Ennio Morricone* on the stereo. Lovely.

The next morning, bright and early, I boarded a rusty old hulk called the *Barracuda*. It arrived in Kingstown a little before noon.

Now, I knew there was no ferry service between St Vincent and Barbados, but what I didn't know is that no yachties[10] would be heading that way either. Apparently the wind would be against them. It was Friday afternoon and no cargo ships would be leaving until Monday. I was told that if I wanted to leave before then I'd have to hire a speedboat and a driver to take me.

'And how much would that be?', I asked, all sweet and innocent.

'$7,000.'

Bloody hell! I had budgeted $2,000 for the whole of the Americas.

'I think I'll wait till Monday.'

'Oh well,' I thought, 'might as well make the most out of a bad situation.'

---

[10] Editor's Note: Yachtie is slang in Australia and New Zealand for a yachtsman (or sailing enthusiast).

Friday night! Party time, right?!

Wrong.

The whole country seemed to shut down at sunset. There were thousands of people here earlier. Where did everyone go?

Apparently everyone had buggered off back to their cruise ships.

A quiet weekend then.

Mustn't grumble.

Now, some of the scenes from *Pirates of the Caribbean* were filmed on location on St Vincent, so on the Sunday I decided to get off my arse and visit one of the old sets. I took a public bus and got about halfway there before I was unceremoniously asked to alight to make way for a bunch of churchgoers. Not very Christian of them!

I walked a good mile or so up the road in the sweltering heat with my thumb out.

(Hitchhiking was okay so long as I didn't do it as part of the journey.)

Eventually a car stopped. The driver was a cockney geezer named Cisco. He had been living over in St Lucia for the last 3 years and, as luck would have it, was doing a bit of a tour of St Vincent himself. So we checked out the *Pirates* set, grabbed a bite to eat, and went on a drive through the green rolling hills. St Vincent is thankfully quite "undeveloped" — meaning it isn't covered in air-conditioned shopping malls and multiplex cinemas. Yet.

That evening I ventured into town to find myself some din-dins. I found a simple food shack by the side of the road. Not wanting to eat chicken, beans and rice again (my staple diet since Guyana) I opted for the fish. When it turned up I found it was a single soggy fish finger on a bed of beans and rice. I should have stuck with the chicken.

Monday morning I was up with the lark and headed over to the local shipping offices to find out about any cargo ships going to Barbados. It turned out there was only one: the *Melinda II*. The good news was that the boat would be stopping in Barbados for the day, and then heading straight to St Lucia, the next country I needed to visit. The bad news was that the captain didn't want to take me.

'Maybe you could talk to him yourself?', suggested Rochelle, the lovely Vincentian in the shipping office who seemed keen to help me on my way.

'Do you think it would help?'

'You won't know until you try', she reasoned.

So I marched down to the docks to find the *Melinda II*. It was a small tramp freighter, only 40ft long, if that. A gang of stevedores were busy loading big old nets of bananas into its hold. I asked around for Captain Ainsley Adams and was directed to a rotund man, small moustache, wearing sunglasses. He looked like he was in charge.

I introduced myself and explained the whole Odyssey project, and how great it would be if I he could take me with him to Barbados and St Lucia. He said he had no bed for me. I told him I'd sleep on the floor. He said the sea would be too rough. I promised him I didn't get seasick. He said that the crew didn't want me on board. I said I'd stay out of their way.

In the blazing heat, I bartered and begged to get on this banana boat to Barbados. I was just about to give up when Rochelle appeared on the quayside.

She took Captain Ainsley Adams to one side. I have no idea what she said to him, but a couple of minutes later, she walked over to me.

'You got your boat.'

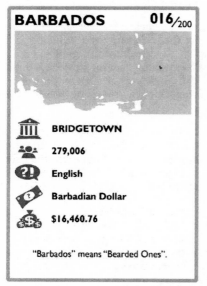

BARBADOS   016/200

🏛 **BRIDGETOWN**

👥 279,006

❓ English

💵 Barbadian Dollar

💰 $16,460.76

"Barbados" means "Bearded Ones".

I nearly leapt on her I was so damn grateful.

'You have to bring your own food and you have to sleep on the floor okay?'

'No problem.'

'And do yourself a favour, don't be sick.'

I rushed to town and stocked up on water, fruit, biscuits and about ten packets of seasickness tablets. *Barbados here I come!*

It was an overnight passage on the *Melinda II*. The cook gave me a cardboard box which I broke open to use as my bed for the night. I laid it out on the greasy metal floor of the tiny galley — my jumper for a pillow. Thank goodness that a side-effect of seasickness pills is that they also make you super sleepy.

I awoke at dawn, picked the cockroaches out of my tatty hair and went out on deck. There she was in the distance — **Barbados**. We arrived at the Port of Bridgetown at around 9am. Unloading and loading would take all day, so I headed into town. What a charming little capital!

Winding roads, rustic markets, quaint stone-built churches, ornate bridges — lovely.

And — oh my — the roti!

Wrap roti are the go-to hot snack all over The Caribbean. They're a bit like pasties in the UK or samosas in India. They're essentially curried meat and potatoes folded tightly in a type of pastry and they're bloomin' marvellous. For my money, Barbados makes them best.

That afternoon I headed back to the port. Captain Ainsley Adams was there giving me the evil eye. I sheepishly clambered on board and resolved to stay out of his way. We left before dark.

Next stop, **St Lucia**.

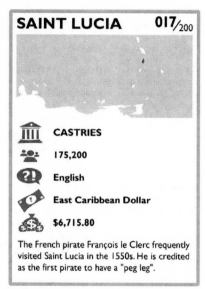

SAINT LUCIA   017/200

🏛 **CASTRIES**

👥 **175,200**

🗣 **English**

💵 **East Caribbean Dollar**

🛵 **$6,715.80**

The French pirate François le Clerc frequently visited Saint Lucia in the 1550s. He is credited as the first pirate to have a "peg leg".

The *Melinda II* pulled into Vieux Fort on the south-west coast of St Lucia around 4:30am. An unreasonable hour, and one that I refuse to believe exists. Consequently I stayed sleeping on the floor until 7:30am when the chap from the shipping company climbed aboard to sort out the formalities. Before disembarking, I presented Captain Ainsley Adams with a bottle of whiskey I picked up in Barbados. And do you know, he almost cracked a smile! *Almost.*

Before long I was on a minibus racing towards the capital Castries. I paid double so I could have the entire front seat to myself. After the *Melinda II,* I decided I deserved a little luxury.

When I reached the capital, the heavens opened. I bought an umbrella and made my way to the Rodney Bay yacht club in the downpour to find out if anybody was heading north in the next few days. 'Not in this bloody weather', was the almost universal response.

Feeling a bit dejected, I ordered a beer and explained my situation to the bartender. He asked me why I didn't just take the ferry.

Wha-wha?!!! Yes, ladies and gentlemen, let it be known. There are ferries that run between St Lucia, Martinique, Dominica and Guadeloupe. *C'est formidable!*

Even better, the ferry from St Lucia to **Martinique** only takes 80 minutes. I remember thinking 'if the rest of the Caribbean was like this, I'd be in Panama by now.'

Within the hour I was on the *L'Express Des Isles* catamaran to Martinique. Being a part of France, Martinique was not on my list of nations, but it was nonetheless a step in the right direction.

On the way I chatted with a pair of Austrians, Martin and Fabio. When we discovered that there was no onward ferry to Dominica until the next day they offered to let me crash on the floor of their hotel. A third night on the floor! Oh the glamorous world of international travel. Hey, I ain't complaining — it didn't cost me a bean. Thanks guys!

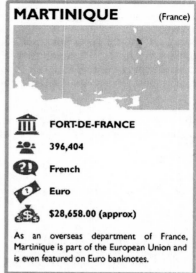

MARTINIQUE (France)

🏛 **FORT-DE-FRANCE**

👥 **396,404**

💬 **French**

💵 **Euro**

💰 **$28,658.00 (approx)**

As an overseas department of France, Martinique is part of the European Union and is even featured on Euro banknotes.

That night Martin, Fabio and I descended on the CyberDeliss restaurant in downtown Fort-de-France. After eating some of the most delightful food of the trip so far, we were treated to some free rum samples from the lovely owner (and rum connoisseur), Francois Xavier. Martinique you cheeky little monkey you, you know exactly how to rock my world.

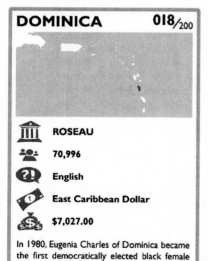

DOMINICA 018/200

🏛 **ROSEAU**

👥 **70,996**

💬 **English**

💵 **East Caribbean Dollar**

💰 **$7,027.00**

In 1980, Eugenia Charles of Dominica became the first democratically elected black female head of government in the world.

I was on the ferry to **Dominica** the next morning, nice and early. It took 90 minutes.

The ferry continued to the French island of Guadeloupe, but I was warned to steer clear because there was a general strike going on and I could end up stuck there for weeks.

After arriving in Dominica's capital Roseau I headed to customs to get stamped in, but the immigration officer was not happy with the fact that I had no onward ticket.

'It's okay — I'm booked on the *Eastpack* cargo ship heading for St. Kitts', I said.

I totally wasn't.

In fact, I had only heard the name *"Eastpack"* a few minutes earlier after receiving a text from Dino of Team Odyssey which read 'Vessel *Eastpack* leaving for St Kitts today, speak to Whitchurch and Co., shippers.'

But it did the job. I was stamped in.

Team Odyssey rocks.

I found the offices of Whitchurch and Co. (it was a short walk — Roseau is tiny!) and spoke to a shipping clerk. He picked up the phone and called Captain George Solomon of the *Eastpack* on my behalf.

The clerk didn't exactly go out of his way to sell this thing, so the captain unsurprisingly said no.

'Can I — er, can I speak to him?', I asked.

The clerk handed me the phone

I went straight into *bam-bam-bamboozle* mode with the old *I-can-sleep-on-the-floor-I-won't-eat-anything-you-won't-even-see-me-it's-for-charity-if-I-miss-this-boat-I-miss-all-my-connections-you-want-a-bribe-how-much-I'll-pay* routine.

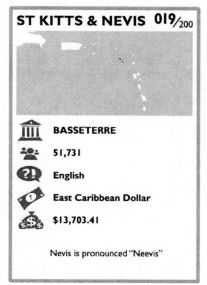

ST KITTS & NEVIS 019/200

🏛 **BASSETERRE**

👥 **51,731**

❓ **English**

💵 **East Caribbean Dollar**

💰 **$13,703.41**

Nevis is pronounced "Neevis"

He said yes, possibly just to shut me up. Good ol' Cap'n Solly.

I raced to Woodbridge Bay where the *Eastpack* was being loaded. It was an old tramp freighter, similar to the *Melinda II*. My bed for the night was a three-foot long wooden bench in the mess with my backpack for a pillow. I didn't mind since the next day I'd be in **St Kitts**.

We hit land on Friday afternoon. I thanked Captain George Solomon and the crew before heading off to find somebody to stamp me into the country.

There were no boats in the deep-water harbour and only three in the marina. *Where on Earth is everyone?*

I was about to leave the port when the shipping agent told me I would have to wait for customs at the entrance. I was a bit confused as I thought I had already been cleared by customs on the boat, but I did what I was told.

I sat on a concrete step next to the boom gate whilst some particularly ferocious ants feasted on my legs (through my jeans). I had nothing to drink and was pretty damn hungry.

The customs officer didn't return for another three hours.

Turns out I *had* been cleared for customs. But I was not yet free — I had to go to the airport to get my entry stamp.

'Can you call me a taxi?', I asked, plaintively.

'You can get one on the road', she said.

I started walking.

No taxis came.

Three kilometres.

In the dark.

In the muggy heat.

With all my bags.

When I arrived at the airport I had never been so thirsty in my life. I downed a two litre bottle of water without pausing for breath.

Once again, my lack of an onward ticket presented a problem. After a bit of discussion (and bargaining) the immigration officer told me that I had five days to get off the island and stamped me in (and out) of the country.

That was no problem – I hoped to be out of there the next day. However, the team back in the UK — John, Dino and Lorna — had no leads on getting to my next country, Antigua and Barbuda.

The following morning I headed to Basseterre's sailboat marina and tried asking around. It didn't take long. There were only five people there. I got chatting with Seamus (from Ireland), Derek (from the UK) and local guy called Wayne. They ran a glass-bottomed excursion boat. When I told them what I was attempting they offered me a beer.

'D'you fancy coming for a snorkel?', asked Derek.

It was the last day of January 2009. I had done well getting this far so quickly, 19 countries in 31 days. But my chances of getting to Canada in time to catch my ship on February 11th were now somewhat less than zero — I still had six countries in the Caribbean and ten countries in Central and North America left to go.

Sod it, I thought. *Let's take a moment to smell the roses.* Or at least get some salt water up my nose.

We headed out on the boat to a little cove and I plunged headfirst into the warm clear waters of The Caribbean.

That afternoon Wayne and Seamus insisted I come to the cricket with them. England was playing a warm-up match against St Kitts. Sun, beer, cricket and jerk chicken — how could I say no? Afterwards, Wayne took me under his wing and allowed me to stay with him and his family in their little home near the port.

One thing I'm going to keep coming back to again and again in the retelling of this story is the amazing kindness and generosity I received along the way.

I'd go back to St Kitts in a shot.

Sunday was a wash-out. But on Monday, Wayne and I returned to the marina with renewed vigour. Wayne asked the harbourmaster if he knew of any boats going to Antigua.

'Yeah — that one.'

He pointed to the *Vagrant*, a good-sized sailboat flying a Canadian flag.

We wandered over and spoke to the captain, an amicable chap by the name of Grant Gordon.

'How long will it take you to get your bags?' he asked.

'Five minutes, if I run.'

'Well you better start running. We leave in 10 minutes.'

I ran.

Having grabbed my things from Wayne's, I said my fond farewells and jumped aboard the *Vagrant*. I introduced myself to Jim and Freda, who were sailing with Grant, and before I knew it we were on our way to Antigua.

Now it's fair to say I don't really know much about sailing, but I know that when the wind and current are against you, it's going to take a long time to get anywhere. Having to "tack" (zigzag) all the way to Antigua meant that a 60 mile journey took all day and all night.

But at least I wasn't sick this time. I'll make a mighty pirate yet!

We arrived in English Harbour on the south coast of **Antigua** early the next morning. It didn't take long to clear quarantine, pass through customs, and get our passports stamped into the country. After a hearty handshake with Captain Grant, I set off to find a way of getting to country number 21, the Dominican Republic on the island of

Hispaniola.

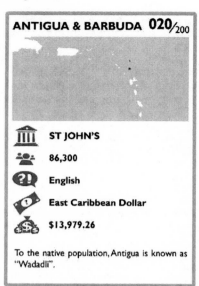

ANTIGUA & BARBUDA 020/200

🏛 ST JOHN'S

👥 86,300

💬 English

💵 East Caribbean Dollar

💰 $13,979.26

To the native population, Antigua is known as "Wadadli".

One teeny-tiny problem. The island of Hispaniola was over 500 miles away.

Unlike St. Kitts, which was fairly quiet, there were hundreds of yachts on Antigua. But finding a boat that was (a) going my way and (b) going to let me on board wasn't easy. It probably didn't help that I'm a scruffy ginger with no discernible talent when it comes to sailing.

Like many of the places I visited in the Caribbean, Antigua may be cheerful, but it certainly isn't cheap. Thankfully, Mandy had not only signed me up to the marvellous CouchSurfing.org, but had also found a local girl called Christal Clashing who agreed to put me up for the night.

Christal was not just a lovely person who allowed waifs and strays such as myself to stay at her place, she was also an Antiguan swimming champion who competed in the 2004 Athens Olympics, coached by her mum, Edith.

Even better, I didn't have to sleep on a couch. I got my own room. After five weeks sleeping on a variety of floors, benches, couches and coaches, having a big old bed all to myself was nothing short of heavenly. It was an incredible introduction to the wonderful world of CouchSurfing.

The next day, Christal and I hit the streets of the capital St John's looking for something reasonably buoyant and heading west. Not wishing to leave any stone unturned, Christal organised an interview on the national radio station. This resulted in the offer of a place on a ship heading to Puerto Rico — next door to the Dominican Republic. Perfect.

However, Puerto Rico is a US dependency, and US immigration had recently changed their visa rules. Anyone arriving on a cargo ship or private vessel must have a US visa in advance, something that requires an interview in an American embassy and costs $150. Not only that, but the process takes up to a month.

That'll be a no, then.

After a somewhat unsuccessful day, Christal cheered me up by taking me ballroom dancing. Later, her dad cooked up a gloriously tasty homemade meal. Travelling around the world can be an incredibly frustrating experience, but it does make you appreciate the little things.

The next morning I said my goodbyes to Christal and returned to the marina, determined to get on something, *anything* going west in the next few days. I asked everyone I could find, visited every clubhouse, every charter company, but it was slim pickings to be sure.

That afternoon I was hanging around outside the immigration office in English Harbour (it seemed like a good place to find people who were leaving the country) when I got a call from a guy called Andrew who worked at Superyacht Publications.

He told me that there might be a superyacht that could take me to the British Virgin Islands. The captain already agreed to let me on board, we were just waiting on confirmation from the owner. The boat would leave in the next half hour.

Holy flying monkeys!

I entered the immigration office for the usual departure formalities, but the lady behind the desk was nothing if not unhelpful. She wanted Grant, the captain of the *Vagrant,* to sign me off his crew manifest before she'd stamp me out. Getting signed off a crew manifest is an immigration technicality which formally states that I had officially left the ship. The problem was that Grant had flown back to Canada the day before.

Thus began a stand up row with the lady behind the desk, which culminated in me asking what would happen if I left Antigua without getting stamped out. She told me I would never be allowed back into Antigua.

'Suits me', I said all cavalier, before storming out of the building.

I ran in the hot afternoon sun, weighed down by heavy bags, sweating and panting, towards the marina, towards the superyacht. I was less than 50 metres away when my phone buzzed in my pocket. It was a text from Lorna in the UK.

'Sorry Graham — the owner of the yacht said no.'

Oh for the love of God!

I had one last roll of the dice. A rumour was afoot that a small sailboat called the *"Monparess",* was leaving the next day for St Martin, an island on the way to the Dominican Republic. The good people at the Waterfront Hostel allowed me to use their VHF radio to try and speak to the skipper.

'*Monparess, Monparess, Monparess.* Waterfront Hostel.' But there was no reply. Dejected and exhausted, I staggered into the bar and asked the barman to pour me a beer.

It was at that moment I realised I had also lost my wallet.

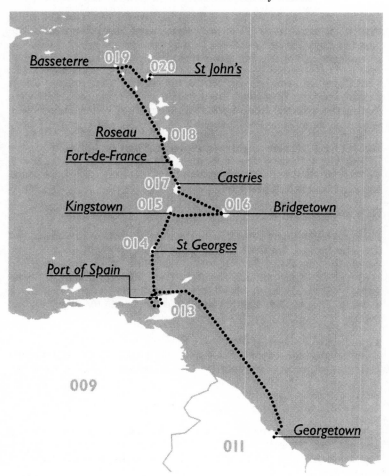

Chapter 4
The Long Dark Dingy Ride of the Soul

With no way of getting back to St John's that night without my wallet, I resigned myself to sleeping on a bench somewhere near the marina.

But thankfully, Joanne, a friend of Christal's, swooped in to save the day, offering me her couch for the night.

I headed back over to the immigration office first thing in the morning. 'I have something for you', said the lady behind the desk as she handed me back my wallet. 'You left it when you stormed out of here yesterday.'

I let out a huge sigh of relief. 'Thank you. Look, all I want is to be signed off the *Vagrant*. I'm trying to leave!'

'Then come back here with the captain of the *Vagrant*.'

'I already told you, he's flown out of the country.'

'Then I can't help you.'

Shoulders slumped, I left the building. As I made my way over to the shade of a great big tree to have a little cry, a middle-aged man with a British accent shouted, 'You found a boat yet mate?'

'Not yet! Still looking.'

'Well, you have now. We leave in two hours. We left a message for you at the Waterfront Hostel.'

'Are you the *Monparess*?'

'No — we're the *Mariposa*.'

No wonder the *Monparess* wasn't answering — it didn't exist! Damn you Chinese whispers!

The guy's name was Andrew and he was sailing with his wife Kerri. They were heading to the island of St Martin, which I hoped could serve as a stepping stone to the Dominican Republic.

But, ah, immigration.

'Would you mind coming to the immigration office with me?', I asked.

'Not at all', said Andrew, all chipper.

Thankfully, the unhelpful lady was no longer behind the desk, she'd been replaced by one of her colleagues, whose name was Jimmy. Andrew and I explained the situation. Jimmy explained that there was nothing to stop me leaving the country without signing off the crew list, but if I did so then Grant wouldn't be able to take the *Vagrant* out of the country when he returned the following week.

That would be a monumentally shitty thing to do to somebody who had kindly allowed me to hitchhike a free ride on his sailboat.

'Who are Jim and Freda?', asked Jimmy, scanning the crew list.

'They're an American couple, they came over with us from St Kitts', I replied.

'They can sign you off, you know.'

OMG.

Jim and Freda were staying on the *Vagrant*. All I needed to do is get in touch with them.

So as Kerri and Andrew of the *Mariposa* waited patiently at the harbour-side café, I got back on the VHF radio.

'*Vagrant, Vagrant, Vagrant...*'

No reply.

'I can't get them on the radio', I explained upon my return to the immigration office. Jimmy suggested I go to the boat itself. One small problem with that was that the *Vagrant* was not tied up on the quayside — it was anchored out in the water.

'Okay, we'll get somebody to take us over', said Jimmy. We headed out to the dock. As luck would have it, a woman was just pulling up in her dingy.

'Have you found a boat yet?', she asked.

Word had certainly got around.

'Yes, but...'

I explained the situation and I asked her really, really nicely if she'd take me and the immigration officer to the *Vagrant*. Thankfully, she said yes.

We put-put-putted over to the boat. 'Hello?! Jim? Freda?'

No reply.

'Hello?'

Nobody home.

Damn.

Kerri and Andrew were keen to get going — I couldn't really have them hanging about all day waiting for Jim and Freda to return. The ride back to shore seemed to take an eternity. It was all I could do to hold myself together.

As we came into dock something rather unexpected happened. Jimmy tapped me on the knee.

'It will be all right.'

I followed Jimmy back to the immigration office. He had words with the stern lady who returned my wallet earlier. She beckoned me over.

'You have a boat? You're leaving, right?'

'Yes, on the *Mariposa.*'

'Okay — we'll take you off the other list.'

'What? Really?'

'You can go.'

And with that, she took my passport and stamped me out.

If she hadn't been such a nightmare over the last 24 hours I would have kissed her.

Within half an hour, I was aboard the *Mariposa.* Kerri was from New Zealand and Andrew was British, but had lived in South Africa for many years. That night we slowly (but surely) made our way towards **Saint Martin**.

Or is that Sint Maarten?

I've always been a fan of geographical quirks and oddities, and the entire island of St Martin is, in itself, quite an oddity. It is the smallest landmass in the world to be shared between two sovereign nations — France and the Netherlands, which it has been (on-and-off) since 1648.

The island itself is called St Martin, the Dutch half is called Sint Maarten and the French half is called Saint-Martin.

Confused yet? I'm just getting started.

They have two languages and three legal currencies, even though "back home" France and the Netherlands use the same currency, the Euro. Cars from Saint-Martin have different licence plates to those from Sint Maarten, residents have different passports and there are even different plug sockets and voltages depending which half the of the island you're in. The governing councils, civil bureaucracy and emergency services are entirely separate.

All on an island five times smaller than the Isle of Wight.

If you want to call your friend in the Dutch half from a phone in the French half, you have to dial an international number. If you cross over into the Saint-Martin side with a Sint Maarten SIM in your mobile, you'll be smacked with international roaming rates. Not that you'd know when you cross the border as there isn't a helpful white line running horizontally across the island, just occasional road signs that say "You're now entering the French side".

SAINT-MARTIN / SINT MAARTEN	(France) (The Netherlands)

🏛 **PHILIPSBURG**

👥 **77,741**

❓ **French / Dutch**

💵 **Euro / US Dollar / Netherlands Antilles Guilder**

💰 **$15,400 (approx)**

The border between the two territories that make up the island of Saint Martin was determined by a (slightly tipsy) walking contest.

Put bluntly, St Martin is a little silly. Still, I can't help but feel it's a great example of how arbitrary and bonkers borders are in general.

Like Martinique, St Martin is not a sovereign nation so it wasn't on my list. But it was in the right direction if I wanted to get to the Dominican Republic via The British Virgin Islands, The US Virgin Islands and Puerto Rico. As for that cargo ship from Canada to Iceland, it left in four days. Maybe I'd be able to take the next one in a month's time.

We arrived in Simpson Bay on the Dutch (south) side of the island on the morning of February 7th, Day 38 of *The Odyssey Expedition*.

Dino over at Team Odyssey had found an excellent way of getting me one step closer to the Dominican Republic, by helping to return a charter sailboat. Like with hire cars, sometimes people don't want to do a round trip, they'd prefer to get from A to B and then leave the thing at B. I'd be assisting the process of returning the yacht to A, which in this instance was the British Virgin Islands.

It left the next day and Kerri and Andrew kindly agreed to put me up for one more night on their boat, now at anchor in the lagoon.

That night we talked strategy for getting to the remaining 5 countries of The Caribbean — the Dominican Republic, Haiti, Jamaica, Bahamas and Cuba.

First of all, they explained how best to get myself on a sailboat. What I did in Antigua was all wrong. What I should have done was, rather than asking random people if anybody was going to the Dominican Republic like some terrible mooch, was just to sit down in the bar and chat with people about what I was doing, strike up a bit of rapport and allow them to invite me on board if they happened to be going the same way as me.

Kerri explained that for many "cruisers" their boat is not just some means of transportation, it's their home. So turning up at the harbour with a piece of cardboard with "Jamaica" written on it would get me nowhere — in hindsight, this made a lot of sense.

Afterwards they got out the sailing charts and persuaded me that it would be best to attack The Bahamas from Florida rather than the Dominican Republic because there are day trips that leave from Fort Lauderdale. Okay, that's The Bahamas sorted — what about Cuba?

Ah yes. Cuba. Well, good luck with that.

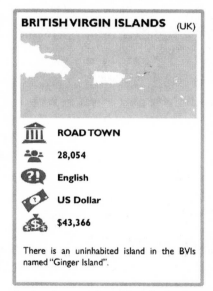

BRITISH VIRGIN ISLANDS (UK)

🏛 **ROAD TOWN**

👥 **28,054**

❓ **English**

💵 **US Dollar**

💰 **$43,366**

There is an uninhabited island in the BVIs named "Ginger Island".

The sailboat to the **British Virgin Islands** was called the *Vivo Libre*. I was aboard with Sylvie, our captain who was from France, Terry, an Irish skipper who had lived in St Martin for seventeen years and Cyril, who was a fellow freeloader, like me. The sea was choppy and the boat rocked and rolled all the way to Tortola, the main island of the BVIs.

As I mentioned in the last chapter, if I entered the USA on a private sailboat or cargo ship I'd need to buy a visa. I could however enter the Land of the Free™ on a public ferry without having to pre-arrange permission. Wonderfully enough, there are ferries that run from Tortola (in the British Virgin Islands) to St Thomas (in the **US Virgin Islands**). Even better — they only take 50 minutes.

On the Road Town Fast Ferry over to St Thomas I discovered that, back on Tortola, there was to be a full-moon party that night on one of the beaches. I was offered a couch to crash on if I fancied attending. I decided that if I was not successful at getting off St Thomas that day, I'd get the ferry boat back to the BVIs because this shindig sounded epic!

Once stamped into the USVIs I was just one island away from the

Dominican Republic; that island being Puerto Rico, another territory of the United States. I assumed that ferries over to Puerto Rico would be a once-a-day thing, but it turned out to be more like a once-a-fortnight thing, which wasn't exactly helping me on my way.

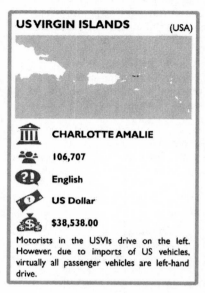

US VIRGIN ISLANDS (USA)

🏛 **CHARLOTTE AMALIE**

👥 106,707

❓ English

💵 US Dollar

💰 $38,538.00

Motorists in the USVIs drive on the left. However, due to imports of US vehicles, virtually all passenger vehicles are left-hand drive.

But Team Odyssey's Lorna had a plan. She was trying to get me on a cruise ship that was skipping Puerto Rico and heading straight for the Dominican Republic — it left later that day.

By midday we had a thumbs up from the ship's PR company in the UK and were just waiting for email confirmation from the captain.

It was a long, hot walk from the ferry dock to the cruise ship terminal. Once there, I sat in the car park alongside the ship and waited. And waited. And waited.

After several hours sitting the blazing tropical sun, I went to the ship to ask if the captain had checked his emails. Not yet, apparently. 'Oh, hang on, yes, he just sent us a message.'

'The captain says no.'

Apparently there wasn't enough time for me to clear security. Of course, there would have been time five hours ago — when I started waiting.

I looked at my watch — 5:30pm. I checked the ferry times back to the BVIs. The last boat was due to depart — at 5:30pm. Buggeration.

I ran as fast as my legs could carry me to the ferry dock. But the ferry had disappeared into the wild blue yonder taking with it not only my chance to go to the full moon party but also my accommodation for the night.

I went to a bar near the harbour and started looking for an emergency CouchSurf. By 11pm, I'd still had no replies. I had nowhere to stay, nowhere to go. The hotels that weren't ludicrously expensive were full. I wandered the streets for hours. Eventually I found a resort type place with sun loungers outside. There didn't seem to be anybody around so I stuffed my bags under one of the loungers and fell asleep, praying that my stuff would be there in the morning.

It wasn't until afterwards that I learnt that the US Virgin Islands has one of the highest murder rates in the world. Sometimes, ignorance is bliss.

A heavy dew formed on me and my bags in the night. The following morning, the "Beans, Bytes and Websites" café was just what I needed — hot drinks and internet access.

But as the day wore on, it became more and more obvious that I was to spend a second night in the US Virgin Islands. Puerto Rico lay just 50 miles to the west, but without a boat that would take me there, I might as well have been trying to get to the moon.

Uncle Sam bought St Thomas from Denmark about a hundred years earlier, and since then it has suffered from a lot of insensitive development. In 2007, St Thomas ranked bottom on National Geographic's list of the most appealing islands in the world. However, I found the old town really quite pleasant. Although the plethora of jewellery shops that adorn the old arcades is admittedly a bit tacky, the streets still have their old Danish names and they retain a modicum of Nordic charm.

The shopping malls down the promenade, though — urgh — I find it hard to believe that people travel halfway around the world to a sun-kissed tropical island to admire the concrete.

That evening, Sarah, the barista at the Bytes, Beans and Websites café, offered me a couch to sleep on. The next morning there was a message waiting for me from Lorna of Team Odyssey. The subject line was "Costa Cruise to Dom Rep sorted for today!"

I physically jumped up and down with glee. Sarah thought it was hilarious.

Once on board the utterly gargantuan *Costa Fortuna* (it didn't cost a fortune, in fact it was free!), I was shown to my cabin — a TV, crisp folded sheets, a hot shower all to myself. A bit of a step up from the greasy metal floor and friendly cockroaches of the *Melinda II*.

I dumped my bags and went for a bit of exploration. Blimey, I thought cargo ships were insanely big. This place had multiple restaurants and casinos and shops and swimming pools and all sorts. I could see why some people don't even bother leaving the ship when they come into port.

I was mooching about in one of the (many) bars when my name was called out on the public address system, asking me to come to reception. The naughty schoolboy in me thought 'Oh crikey — what have I done?'

Maybe I was in detention.

But I needn't have worried. I had been summoned to the bridge for our departure! I have to admit I was feeling a bit nervous, probably because with my scruffy old jeans and beat-up old backpack I felt a little out of place amongst the tuxedos and the ball gowns.

But Captain Claudio made me feel like an honoured guest. He told me that I was the first civilian allowed on the bridge during departure since the 9/11 terror attacks. Serious business, to be sure.

PAAARP!! PAAARP!! PAAARP!!

The ships horn blasted three times and the captain beckoned me over to see the "all clear" signal from the dock.

Far below us, two excitable young women ran from the sushi bar on the quayside and flashed us their boobs.

'All clear', said the captain, beaming, 'let's go!'

That night I enjoyed a beer on the top deck, watching the lights of St. Thomas disappear into the distance and wondering quite how on Earth Lorna had managed to wangle this little caper.

The island of Hispaniola is split between two sovereign nations: The Dominican Republic and Haiti. With a long and turbulent history dating back to the arrival of Christopher Columbus in 1492, the **Dominican Republic** has cast off the shackles of the past to become one of The Caribbean's most vibrant and exciting destinations. Haiti, on the other hand, is the poorest country in the Americas, a situation that seems unlikely to improve in the near future.

The *Costa Fortuna* arrived in the port town of La Romana around 8am. I said my goodbyes to the staff and headed to the capital, Santo Domingo. Brightly painted buses, crazy drivers, deafening music and baseball. No doubt about it, after a month bumming my way up the Lesser Antilles, I was finally back in Latin America.

DOMINICAN REPUBLIC 021/200

🏛 **SANTO DOMINGO**

👥 9.884m

❓ Spanish

💵 Dominican Peso

💰 $4,844.97

Santo Domingo is the oldest European settlement in the Americas.

From Santo Domingo I took a coach straight up to the city of Puerto Plata, close to the border with Haiti and from where I hoped to find a yacht heading west.

Mandy had arranged for me to CouchSurf in Puerto Plata with an Iranian national named Mehrdad, who I believe was the only Persian sushi chef in the Caribbean.

The next morning Mehrdad took me to the local marina to look for anything that might be going to Cuba or Jamaica, two of the last three island nations of the West Indies I needed to visit. Nothing.

I reluctantly decided to stick a pin in that for now. Mehrdad went off to work and I took the bus to the border with Haiti.

If you cross into **Haiti** from Dajabon in the Dominican Republic to Ouanaminthe on Market Day you don't need a visa. Hell, you don't even need a passport. However, the Lonely Planet specifically warns not to cross this particular border on Market Day, citing security concerns.

I had left my valuables with Mehrdad, just in case.

The crossing may have been a throng of people going to and fro, goods on their heads, bags packed to the brim, but the presence of UN peacekeepers made me feel safe.

Haiti is a long sad story, from its founding as a slave colony to its independence from France, through dictatorship after dicta-

HAITI 022/200

🏛 **PORT-AU-PRINCE**

👥 **9.765m**

❓ **French**

💵 **Haitian gourde**

💰 **$674.30**

Between 1804 and 1915, Haiti was ruled by 70 different dictators

torship, tyranny after tyranny. Even now, Haiti ranks exceptionally low on the Human Development Index and its GDP per capita is six times less than neighbouring Dominican Republic and *sixty* times less than the British Virgin Islands.

Haiti also suffers from severe deforestation, overpopulation, and a lack of basic sanitation.

But as a taste of what was to come once I hit the nations of sub-Saharan Africa, I didn't find it grim or intimidating — just a lot of people going about their business. It's worth bearing in mind that Haiti, for all its woes, has a lower murder rate than Louisiana.

On the way back to Puerto Plata I dropped into the small port town of Luperon to see if there were any yachts heading west in the next few days, but again I came up short.

That night Mehrdad and I hit the town. I ate sushi, sang karaoke, and tried not to think about the fact that the next day would be Valentine's Day. Mandy was far, far away — and at this rate I'd be lucky to see her again before the end of the year.

Our last roll of the dice was "Ocean World" on the north coast, a nearby marina with more than its fair share of superyachts. It was a long shot at best, but the only movement in the next few days was not west, but north to Turks and Caicos, a British territory and not on my list.

With the global recession, the recent murder of an Australian skipper on Antigua, and the general strike and riots in Guadeloupe, this was not a great time to be hitchhiking around the Caribbean.

Another problem was that US citizens were not allowed to go to Cuba, except in exceptional circumstances. Under the "Trading with the Enemy Act" of 1917, Americans faced a large fine or even a jail sentence if they spend a single dime in Fidel Castro's back garden. The fact that the Berlin Wall came down 20 years earlier didn't seem to faze the US government and as of 2009 Cuba was still on its list of "enemies". As a consequence, very few sailboats were travelling to Cuba.

And so I made the executive decision to concentrate on getting to Jamaica first and worry about Cuba later. My best chance of finding a ship to Kingston would be to return to Santo Domingo, so that's exactly what I did.

I arrived on the morning of February 15th. After meeting my new CouchSurf host Ken and his flatmate TJ, I headed to the port to make a note of the names of the cargo ships in dock, and to see if I could find out where they were going.

Along the old waterfront on a sunny, Sunday afternoon, kids were running about, young lovers were staring out to sea, and old folks were playing dominoes. I ambled through the lovely old colonial town as the sun set. Once again, not a bad place to be stuck for a few days. But I was not there on holiday — I was trying to set a new Guinness world record. And I was going nowhere fast.

The next day Ken and TJ took me to their place of work — the offices of DR1.com, an English news site for the Dominican Republic. I was given a desk and a nice fast internet connection to help me on my way.

Believe it or not, this entire time I had been regularly editing and posting videos of my journey to YouTube. Around lunchtime a local guy called Román Cid dropped by. He had seen my YouTube videos and wanted to meet me and help me on my way. Amazingly, he had printed out that week's shipping timetables for the entire country – every ship in and out. Wow.

The way in which people supported *The Odyssey Expedition* is something that leaves me humbled to this very day.

The good news was that there was a cargo ship leaving Santo Domingo for Jamaica on Thursday. The bad news was that there was a cargo ship that left for Jamaica today — from the place I just came from, Puerto Plata. Argh!!

I spent that afternoon online with my friend Hugh Sheridan, the guy who taught me how to sail (kinda). He made phone calls and sent emails. Thursday's ship to Jamaica was called the *Linge Trader* and it would be travelling via Port-au-Prince in Haiti. Not only that, but there was another ship called the *Pamplona* which would be going from Jamaica to Puerto Limon in Costa Rica – pretty much as soon as the *Linge Trader* arrived in Kingston. Perfect.

I drew up a rough calendar. It was February 17th. The next Eimskip cargo ship across the Atlantic from Canada to Iceland departed on March 8th. If I could just get on the *Linge Trader* to Jamaica, the *Pamplona* to Costa Rica, make every bus connection from Panama to Florida, a daytrip to Cuba and back on a speedboat (with special permission I was waiting on from the US government), another daytrip to The Bahamas, travel from Florida to Halifax in less than two days *and* if Eimskip were still willing to take me — I might just make it.

It was a lot of "ifs".

The next day I received an email. I was to be allowed passage to Jamaica on board the *Linge Trader*. As I was reading the message, Skype rang. It was another friend of mine from the UK, Mary Dowrick, calling to let me know that the *Pamplona* had also granted me permission to travel with them from Jamaica to Costa Rica.

'Hell yeah!' I thought, 'I may just make it out of the Caribbean yet.'

The *Linge Trader* arrived in Port-au-Prince on the afternoon of the 20th.

JAMAICA   023/200

🏛 **KINGSTON**

👥 **9.765m**

💬 **English**

💵 **Jamaican dollar**

💰 **$4,521.92**

It's not just ska and reggae: hip-hop, rap and grime all owe their origins to Jamaican music.

I tried to go for a mooch around the city, but the Haitian authorities wouldn't let me out of the port. That night we slipped off into the darkness towards country number 23, **Jamaica**.

We arrived two days later in Kingston. The *Pamplona* to Costa Rica was scheduled to leave the next day. That night, Mandy had arranged for me to stay with a local girl called Diane who was going to teach me how to play the steel drums. It was perfect. *A little too perfect...*

You know how in Homer's Odyssey, Odysseus's greatest nemesis is Poseidon, the God of the sea, and he is always making trouble for him? Well...

First of all, the port authorities wouldn't let me out of the port without an onward ticket — this meant I'd have to book a flight out of Jamaica even if I had no intention of using it. But that issue became moot when I learnt that the *Pamplona* was leaving early — at midnight.

So I ambled over to the *Pamplona* to speak to the captain. He didn't have good news for me. Although the charterers (the company in charge of everyday activity of the ship) had given the go-ahead, permission hadn't come through from the actual owners of the vessel.

Without that permission there was no way I was getting on his boat.

I returned to the *Linge Trader* with my tail between my legs. Captain Van Der Plaats suggested I simply remain on board his ship instead. The *Linge Trader* was heading to Mexico next.

Although it would mean being dropped off over 1,000 miles from where I wanted to be, it was still a great offer. Once I was back on the continent, getting around would be a piece of cake — overlanding is my speciality.

I thanked Captain Van Der Plaats for his kind offer. Next stop: Mexico!

I returned to my cabin and checked my notes. There was no way on Earth I'd make the March *Eimskip* boat now. I curled into a ball and, as I have a tendency to do when things are not going my way, fell fast asleep.

At 5:30am my cabin phone rang. Groggy as hell, I answered it. 'Hello?'

It was Captain Van Der Plaats.

'I'm very sorry, but you have to get off this ship. Now. We will not take you and the ship leaves in ten minutes. Get off!'

You've *got* to be kidding me.

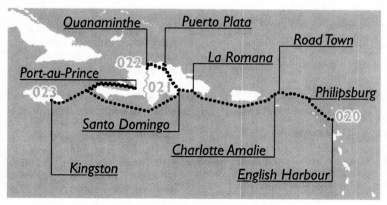

Chapter 5
Halcyon Days And Halogen Nights

In a somewhat quixotic attempt to force fate to allow me to stay on the *Linge Trader*, I hadn't packed my bags. My crap was spread out all over the cabin. I hurriedly stuffed everything into my backpack and trudged downstairs like a man condemned.

I entered the ship's office. The port agent, Junior, was finishing up the ship's paperwork.

'What are you doing?', asked Junior.

'I have to get off the ship, the captain says...'

'No, no, no — you can't get off here, they won't let you.'

'What?'

'Immigration say you cannot get off the ship without an onward ticket. Let me speak to the captain.'

A fraught phone call ensued.

The outcome being, by virtue of the port authority of Jamaica not wanting to let me into the country, that I got to stay on the *Linge Trader* all the way to **Mexico**. Woo! Thanks, Jamaica — your stubborn unwillingness to let me visit your country ensured my passage out of The Caribbean. Ha!

That night, out to sea, a hundred miles from Kingston, I went up on the bridge while the first

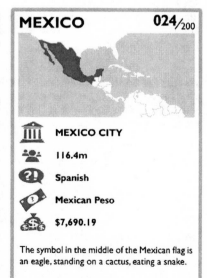

MEXICO 024/200

🏛 **MEXICO CITY**

👥 116.4m

💬 Spanish

💵 Mexican Peso

💰 $7,690.19

The symbol in the middle of the Mexican flag is an eagle, standing on a cactus, eating a snake.

mate Alexander from Ukraine was on watch. The control room was bathed in darkness to allow the officer on duty to see the murky waters around the ship a little better. The panels were dimmed and a solitary light bulb illuminated the coffee pot, essential for these graveyard shifts.

On either side of the bridge are external platforms called wings. Perched several storeys above the poop deck (the "ground" floor, nothing to do with changing nappies), they're used by the captain to gauge how close the ship is to the dock when coming alongside. There was no moon, no clouds and the sky was littered with bright, clear stars.

Mandy would love this.

I'd point out Puppis, the constellation of the poop deck, because that totally exists but nobody would want it as a star sign. I'd tell her it used to be part of the constellation Argo Navis, Jason's ship immortalised in the firmament, but that in the 1930s it was officially split in three: Vela (the sail), Carina (the keel), and poor old Puppis.

But Mandy wasn't here to put a blue ribbon on my brain, so I turned on my phone light and continued to read a book of Greek legends I had found a couple of days earlier in the ship's TV room.

Ceyx was the son of Lucifer (the bringer of light, not the devil) and he loved Alcyone, but one day he went to sea. Seized by a premonition of doom, she called out for him not to go, but he went anyway. He had her name on his lips as the storm waters closed over his head. Eventually, Morpheus (the god of dreams) sent Alcyone a vision of her beloved, Ceyx — soaking wet — informing her that he was dead.

She ran down to the rocks where she had watched his ship depart. There she found Ceyx's body washed up on the shore, but the gods were kind. They turned her and Ceyx into birds and they flew out together, flying and riding the waves.

Every year there are seven days when the sea lies still and calm; no breath of wind stirs the waters. These are the days when Alcyone broods over her nest floating on the sea. After the young birds are hatched, the charm is broken. Each winter these days of perfect peace come and they are named after her, Alcyon, or more commonly, Halcyon days.

Why am I telling you this? Because in less than 72 hours I would be turning 30 and I wanted to write something more eloquent than "ARRRRRGH!"

Slowly but surely we approached the Mexican port of Veracruz.

We arrived on the afternoon of February 26th. Since we had made landfall 1,000 miles northwest of where I had hoped to be, I'd have to take a series of buses down to Panama via five other countries: Guatemala, El Salvador, Honduras, Nicaragua and Costa Rica; and then back up again, calling into Belize along the way. I'd be doing this all without a map or a guidebook. My Lonely Planet's *Central America* was sitting in a Fed-Ex office in Kingston.

I left the ship with Raymundo, the local shipping agent. He ensured I was stamped into the country and even dropped me at the bus station. Top bloke.

The bus to Guatemala City was new and clean and fast, although a bit too well air-conditioned for the all-important comfort of my testicles. In the arm rests were mini-jack sockets for headphones. I plugged myself in and got to listen to the bus company's surprisingly good playlist, which consisted mostly of rock classics, but in Spanish. It was all tremendously Wes Anderson.

GUATEMALA 025/200

🏛️ **GUATEMALA CITY**

👥 13.99m

❓ Spanish

💵 Guatemalan quetzal

💰 $2,697.38

The ancient Mayan city of Tikal doubled as the Rebellion's Yavin IV base in Star Wars.

The next morning I switched buses in the town of Tapachula near the border with **Guatemala**, and before I knew it I was in country number 25.

A 24-hour bus journey is something that many people would approach with a sense of foreboding and trepidation. Not me — I was simply relieved to be back on the road and clocking up countries again. Over

the next three days I'd tick a total of *seven* new countries off my list — more than I had managed in the preceding three weeks.

El Salvador is the murder capital of the world, an unenviable accolade that occasionally transfers to neighbouring Honduras. How countries are damned or blessed by geography became a theme through the course of my travels. Bolivia and Paraguay are poorer than their neighbours simply because they're landlocked. Much of Central America is insanely dangerous because they have a virtually unlimited supply of guns coming down from the USA and drugs

EL SALVADOR 026/200

🏛️ **SAN SALVADOR**

👥 6.183m

❓ Spanish

💵 US Dollar

💰 $3,341.32

El Salvador once went to war against neighbouring Honduras over a football match.

coming up from South America. It's no surprise that the countries stuck in the middle bear the brutal brunt of gang violence. The murder rate in El Salvador is over NINETY TIMES that of the UK.

After a butt-clenching *oh-dear-it's-dark-and-I-have-no-map-where-the-hell-is-an-ATM-when-you-need-one* walk around the capital city of San Salvador, I found a bus that was going through Honduras, Nicaragua and ending in San Jose, the capital of Costa Rica. The only problem was that it left at 3am, which is officially the most inconvenient time for anything to happen, ever. You can either waste money on a hotel room for just a few hours of sleep or you can stay up all night drinking. I threw my bag in the bus station office and headed out to the pub.

I found an Irish bar (there's always an Irish bar) and got chatting with some locals; Jorge, Rene and Memo. Upon learning that I would be turning 30 at midnight, they demanded I come and have some sushi at their mate's restaurant. After stuffing my face with raw fish (and successfully pulling off a wasabi challenge), my new buddies invited me to the beach. We piled into Memo's car and half an hour later were drinking cold beers on the sandy shores of the Pacific Ocean. There was a wooden shack serving alcohol, as well as music, hammocks, and people dancing in the cool night air.

At midnight, I placed my hands in the ocean and screamed.

At 2am it was time to go. I had a bus to catch, and it was leaving soon. Memo drove like a maniac. But he drove like a maniac to the wrong bus station. San Salvador has no central bus station; every bus company has their own garage. Some, annoyingly, have two.

As the seconds ticked away, we drove around the empty city streets, desperately trying to find the correct bus station. Luckily for us, I recognised a billboard — the bus station was just around the corner! Unluckily for us, at that very same moment the police pulled us over.

Memo was outraged. He had to get his ginger gringo friend to his bus, goddamnit! After searching us and the car for drugs or bombs or whatever, the police continued talking to Memo, who — like me — was getting increasingly infuriated with their intransigence — my bus was leaving in less than five minutes!

'Will this make you go away?', I asked as I passed over a 20-dollar bill.

An awkward moment. Was I to spend the rest of my birthday in a prison cell in El Salvador for attempting to bribe a policeman?

The policeman smiled and stuffed the twenty in his pocket. Before he could say adios, Memo was tearing down the highway towards the bus station.

Only to get there five minutes late. The bus had gone.

But all was not lost. Memo spoke to the people in the bus station and they said there was another company's bus that does the same route down to Costa Rica, and it leaves at 4am.

Slam dunk the funk.

Only one problem. My bag was in the station office, and the only guy with a key had gone to bed in the hotel upstairs and the night manager was adamant that he wasn't going to wake him up.

I took out another $20.

Memo and I made it to the King Quality bus station at 4am, just in time. After thanking Memo profusely for such an excellent birthday adventure, I plonked myself down on the back seat of the bus next to an Argentinian girl named Sophia. Sophia apologised for spilling her bottle of water on my seat, something I wished she had warned me about before I sat down.

Skint, exhausted, wet arse. I couldn't think of a more fitting way to begin my fourth decade on Planet Earth.

These "King Quality" buses were missing a "Fuc-" at the start of their name. The bus was brand new, tons of leg-room, free food, drinks, flat-screen TVs — and a good selection of films. Like flying first-class but with more interesting things going on out of the window.

HONDURAS 027/200

🏛 **TEGUCIGALPA**

👥 **7.47m**

❓ **Spanish**

💵 **Honduran lempira**

🏍 **$1,952.85**

The Honduran currency gets its name from Lempira, an indigenous chief who fought to the death against the Spanish conquistadors.

We hit the border with **Honduras** around 7am. I bought a bottle of whiskey from Duty Free. When I got back to the bus, Sophia and her friend presented me with a madeira cake, used a cigarette as a candle and sang *Happy Birthday* in Spanish. We made the bold decision that it was in no way too early to start drinking.

While it's fair to say Honduras suffers from a bad reputation (the hostels in the capital Tegucigalpa are surrounded by razor wire), **Nicaragua** is a much more chilled out place and well-regarded in backpacker circles as cheap and cheerful with some incredible coastlines, unspoilt jungle and terrifyingly active volcanoes. I hope to get to experience them myself one day.

By the time the bus arrived in San Jose, the capital of **Costa Rica**, I had travelled through six countries in less than 36 hours — even better, I only had six countries of The Americas left to go.

Sophia's friends wanted us to stay at a guest house recommended by our taxi driver. My objections (I never trust taxi drivers) were overruled and I was too tired (and drunk) to argue. I had to be up at 4am for my next bus anyhow.

We shared a dorm room that was about four cubic metres big. My bed consisted of just three planks of wood haphazardly plonked on an empty frame with a wet sponge on top pretending to be a mattress. The floor of the *Melinda II* was more comfortable.

It's not uncommon when crossing land borders for the powers that be to demand an "onward ticket" as proof you're actually going to leave the country at some point.

Just in case, I had bought a flight out of New York, printed out the itinerary and cancelled it. I had used my phony "flight" a few times around The Caribbean to show I would (eventually) be leaving the area. It usually sufficed, but the guards on the Panamanian border wanted to see evidence that I would be leaving **Panama** itself before giving me a stamp into the country.

NICARAGUA 028/200

🏛 **MANAGUA**

👥 **5.743m**

❓ **Spanish**

💵 **Nicaraguan Córdoba**

💰 **$1,459.21**

Lake Nicaragua is home to the only freshwater sharks in the world.

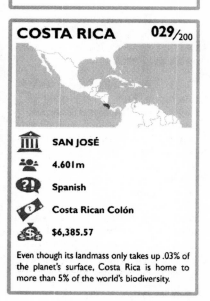

COSTA RICA 029/200

🏛 **SAN JOSÉ**

👥 **4.601m**

❓ **Spanish**

💵 **Costa Rican Colón**

💰 **$6,385.57**

Even though its landmass only takes up .03% of the planet's surface, Costa Rica is home to more than 5% of the world's biodiversity.

I asked if I could cross the border and find somewhere to buy a bus ticket back out. Bizarrely, they said 'sure!'

So I crossed the bridge at Paso Canoas, got a photo next to the *Bienvenidos a Panamá* sign, bought myself a can of Coke from the petrol station, spun around 180 degrees and walked straight back to Costa Rica.

'Oh well', I said to my camera, 'I'll be back one day.'

Five years later I won a private island in Panama on a game show.

It's funny how things turn out.

Since I had missed the country of Belize on the way down from Mexico, I'd have to hit it on the way back up. My plan was to then head up through Mexico, into Texas and over to Florida; from there I would have to find my way to The Bahamas and Cuba. *Somehow.*

On the bus back up north I got chatting with a remarkable guy from Texas called John, who

PANAMA   030/200

🏛 **PANAMA CITY**

👥 **3.616m**

💬 **Spanish**

💵 **Panamanian Balboa (Tied to US Dollar)**

💰 **$7,169.86**

"Caledonia", a Scottish colony in Panama, was backed by up to 50% of *all* money circulating in Scotland at the time. Its failure in 1699 led to the dissolution of the Scottish Parliament.

was — like myself — backpacking around Central America. Why was he remarkable? Because he was 86 years old.

Late the following night I arrived back in San Salvador. I was told that a bus would be heading north to Guatemala City at 3:30am. I booked a ticket and made my way to a nearby hostel. Since there was little point checking in for just a few hours' sleep, I just asked if I could take a shower instead. It cost me $2, which was a bit extortionate considering it was an icy cold dribble, but then judging by the state of the electrical wires sticking out of the showerhead, the lack of hot high-pressure water was possibly for the best. After drying myself, I headed to the Irish pub, hoping for it to be the start of some wacky adventure, but it was not to be; I just sat there on my own writing up my blog.

I left the pub at 2:30am and began looking for a taxi. The streets were dead. I walked and walked. Soon it was past 3am and I was getting worried. I was on my own with no map and carrying all of my belongings: credit cards, money, camcorder, laptop, testicles etc. in San "holy shit" Salvador, one of the murder capitals of the world.

I saw a bright white halogen lamp down the road and made my way towards it like a big ginger moth. The light was coming from a 24-hour petrol station. A couple of policemen were filling up their patrol car. I asked them where I could find a taxi. They shook their heads. 'No more taxis tonight.'

Maybe El Salvador had some kind of curfew?

One of the policemen asked me — in broken English — where I was going. I told him the bus terminal. 'No problem', he said, and motioned for me to get in.

The Salvadorian police dropped me at the bus station just in time for my bus. I thanked them profusely and entered the bus station. It was then I discovered that the 3:30am bus didn't actually exist. It was more like a 6am bus.

To make matters worse, the bus station was *freezing*. There was nowhere to go and nothing to do but huddle in the corner. Sit there, wait, and shiver.

But by 10am I was back in Guatemala City. I hopped off my bus and took another to Puerto Barrios on the Caribbean coast. From there I could take a short ride in a fibreglass boat to Punta Gorda in Belize.

Unluckily, I arrived in Puerto Barrios too late for a boat to Punta Gorda, but luckily I had spent most of the journey from Guatemala City chatting to a friendly guy from Livingstone — a Guatemalan town halfway between Puerto Barrios and Punta Gorda in Belize. He invited me to come to Livingstone with him, and said he'd put me up for the night. His name was Ismael, so I called him Ismael.

Ismael was Garifuna, a descendent from the offspring of the indigenous Caribs (from where we get the word 'Caribbean') and African slaves brought over by the British, French, Spanish and Dutch. Ismael's people originated from St Vincent and the Grenadines, where the Garifuna led a series of revolts throughout the 18th century. Afterwards the Garifuna were deported to an island off the coast of Honduras where they were not expected to survive. But they didn't just survive, they thrived. There are now around 600,000 Garifuna people living in and around Central America, with their own language, rituals and traditions.

Ismael's place was pretty basic — no electricity or running water, but it had a hammock, which is all I need. I dropped my gear and we headed to Livingstone's main street for drinks and fried chicken.

Like Guyana, **Belize** is more closely affiliated with the Caribbean than with Latin America. The people of former British Honduras speak English, play cricket and even have the Queen on their money.

Belize was founded by a group of shipwrecked English and Scottish seamen back in 1638.

BELIZE   031/200

🏛 **BELMOPAN**

👥 **301,016**

❓ **English**

💵 **Belize Dollar**

💰 **$4,441.48**

The famed crystal skull of the Mayans was found in Belize. It was a total hoax, although that didn't stop George Lucas making a god-awful Indiana Jones film about it.

Naturally, the Spanish weren't too pleased when they discovered that the Brits had set up a colony in what was regarded as Spanish lands. But in 1859, after decades of fraught relations and occasional open warfare, the British promised to build a road from Guatemala to Punta Gorda in return for formal recognition of Belize by the Guatemalan government.

To this day, that road has still not been built, and as a consequence the southern half of Belize is still claimed by Guatemala, in a startlingly similar situation to Venezuela's dispute with that other former British colony of Latin America, Guyana.

Once I arrived in Punta Gorda on the morning of March 4th it was decision time. I could either continue north through Belize, travel to Cancun in Mexico and ask about a ship going to Cuba or else head back to Guatemala City and continue up the Pan-American Highway to the USA.

I had recently watched the Michael Moore documentary *Sicko* in which he hops on a speedboat in Florida and ends up in Cuba, no problemo. So I chose the USA option.

Big mistake.

By 1pm, I was back in Puerto Barrios and from there I took the bus to Guatemala City. I then took an overnighter to the border with Mexico.

By this stage of my Herculean bus ride, it had been a week since I'd last had a hot shower and even longer since I had last slept in a decent bed.

But whatever, soon enough I was excited to be back in Mexico. I found that nobody in Latin America or The Caribbean takes food as seriously as the Mexicans. And one of the great joys of travel is *food*. Enchiladas, nachos, burritos, fajitas, quesadillas... *si por favor!*

As I sat on the bus that afternoon all I could think of was just how many spicy tasty delights I was going to stuff into my face come dinner time.

But the bus didn't stop. It just kept going. It kept going until midnight. And then finally — *finally* — it came to a halt beside a grotty little roadside café lit by humming florescent tubes. As I staggered towards salvation, I was more than ready for some total chili con carnage.

I stacked my plate with food, paid, sat down, and forked as much of Mexico's fine cuisine into my mouth as I could, only to find that I couldn't swallow.

What the hell?

Being a total boy scout, I had been taking an anti-malarial pill each day of my adventure thus far.

Being a total idiot, I hadn't listened when I was told to never take them lying down, on an empty stomach or without lots of water.

As a consequence, my oesophagus had become ulcerated — super sore and horribly restricted. That yummy yummy Mexican street food was not going down without a fight.

Crying while eating is never a good look.

I awoke the next day around 7am as the bus arrived in Mexico City. A well-timed bus left the capital for the town of Nuevo Laredo on the US border about 90 minutes later.

This bus was the best of the lot — cheap, fast and it showed a load of great movies — including *Leon (The Professional), The Boy In The Striped Pyjamas* and *Babel* — making a change from the 1980s action movies that tend to dominate this sector of captive audience entertainment. Although I still don't understand why Latin American bus drivers insist on setting the air conditioning to zero degrees Kelvin.

Outside, the landscape became more and more arid and dry — lush equatorial greenery gave way to cacti and dust. Before I knew it, we had hit the border with the **United States of America.**

I had two hours to get across the border before the bus left for San Antonio in Texas. It was 2am, nobody was there so I had plenty of time. A good job too — crossing this particular frontier took ages. The Yanks kept me talking for an hour while they searched my bags three — *yes three* — separate times. I must fit some kind of profile. Thankfully, no rubber gloves were involved.

US immigration finished with me around 3:30am and it was a sprint to the Greyhound bus station.

Oh boy. The Greyhound.

USA 032/200

🏛 **WASHINGTON DC**

👥 306.8m

❓ English

💵 US Dollar

💰 $47,001.43

While it's fairly easy to purchase an assault rifle in the US, Kinder Eggs, haggis and various French cheeses are illegal.

Make no mistake, I'm looking back on this adventure through the prism of somebody who has slummed it on the cheapest form of land transportation to over 200 countries and I have got to say, hand on heart, that Greyhound buses are, without a shadow of a doubt, *the worst.*

On the entire planet.

If it was just that the buses themselves were old, grotty and showed no films, that would be bad enough. If it was just that the bus stations are always located in the absolute worst part of town, and here you are arriving with all your worldly possessions in a country with an embarrassingly high murder rate, it would be a bit shit — still nothing particularly out of the ordinary for somebody who has travelled to as many developing nations as I have.

No, it's the employees that make Greyhound the absolute pits. Aggressive, condescending, grumpy drivers, ticket staff so surly it borders on psychopathic and ancillary personnel who survey the outside world with such loathing one can only imagine they just found out that their wife had left them for their oldest and most trusted friend.

On the way from Texas to Florida I had one driver pulled over for speeding. Another driver stopped the coach on the chevrons of a run-off lane on the *actual freaking freeway* in order to march down the aisle and verbally berate a passenger for the crime of allowing his mobile phone to audibly ring. Like, once.

A simple enquiry to a chap in a hi-vis vest, 'Is this the correct line for Orlando?', was met with a 'Do I have "information" written on my back? Piss off!'

Charming.

Having just come from the air-conditioned, hosted, coffee-and-snacks-included, European-arthouse-film-screening Latin American buses, Greyhound buses were nothing short of shocking. I couldn't hitchhike as part of my journey, but given the choice I'd have much preferred to spend eight hours travelling across Texas in the company of a big hairy trucker (and possible serial killer) who sang along to Christian rock and demanded I call him "Clarabelle".

I can only imagine that Greyhound is owned by an oil giant in order to persuade people to waste petrol and kill the planet by driving across America instead of taking public transport. If that's the plan, they're doing a bang-up job.

From San Antonio to Houston, I had the pleasure of chatting with Jackie, a girl from Nicaragua who had been living in Texas for the last few years. She told me that if I fancied a McDonald's in the Lone Star state I could ask them to "Texas-size" my meal — that's double XL to me and you.

From Houston to Baton Rouge in Louisiana the seat next to me lay empty. But given the significantly high proportion of nutters and weirdos on these buses, that was probably for the best. My heart went out to the poor teenager in the seat in front of me — the grizzled-looking vagrant sitting next to him spent two hours explaining over and over again how he'd done "every drug in the world" but had now found Jesus and cleaned himself up.

I couldn't help but think we'd all be a lot more comfortable if he had found soap and cleaned himself up with that instead.

A change in New Orleans saw me board my fourteenth long-distance bus of the last nine days.

The following evening I arrived in Fort Lauderdale and checked into the Bridge II hostel.

In less than a week I had travelled overland from Panama to Florida via Costa Rica, Nicaragua, Honduras, El Salvador, Guatemala, Belize, Mexico, Texas, Louisiana and Alabama. But the night was yet young!

So I went to see the movie *Watchmen* at the cinema with Robbie, a bomb disposal expert who was also staying at the hostel. Afterwards, we hit the town so hard it hit us back, ending up in one of those fine drinking establishments that I thought only existed in movies, ones where girls get up and dance on the bar in hot pants for some reason. Who knew?!

So then. 32 countries of The Americas ticked off the list, three to go. There were daily cruises over to The Bahamas and, aside from having to travel on the infernal Greyhound bus again, getting into Canada would be a doddle.

That just left Cuba — only 100 miles from the southern tip of Florida. A few hours in a speedboat. An overnight sail. But as I was about to discover, it wasn't going to be as easy as all that.

In fact, it wasn't going to be easy at all.

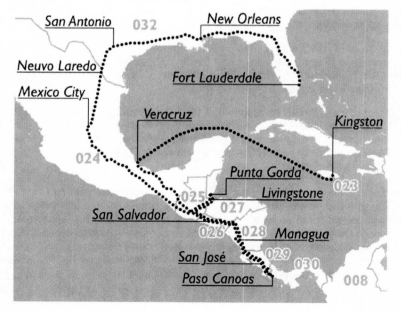

Chapter 6
Trading With The Enemy

Things may have changed in the last few years, but when I was travelling in 2009, the restrictions against US citizens travelling to Cuba were still in full effect.

Americans could not spend money in Cuba. To do so would invoke a fine of up to $250,000 and a possible prison sentence.

American-registered boats could not go to Cuba. If they did, they were likely to be impounded by the US Coastguard on the return journey. American captains could lose their license if they, for instance, took me over there, even if I spent money and they didn't. If I went to Cuba without permission, Uncle Sam wouldn't let me back into the US for 6 months.

So, Fortress Cuba. How to get in?

There was one possible back door: an OFAC (Office of Foreign Asset Control) license that I could apply for from the US Treasury Department. Dispensations were given for journalism and charity. As my expedition was for charity and I'm a journalist (kinda), getting permission didn't seem too unrealistic.

John, my lawyer, put in the application while I was travelling around the Caribbean. He had been badgering The Treasury for a reply ever since. Up to this point we had heard nothing back. That being the case, I booked a day cruise to the island of Grand Bahama, 100 miles to the east of Fort Lauderdale.

It was an inconveniently early start. Even more inconvenient was the fact that it was Spring Break and the cost of the cruise had tripled. Still, it was a hell of a lot cheaper than paying for my own boat.

The "cruise" ship was so 70s it might as well have been wearing tie-dyed flares. Dented plastic panelling on the ceiling, tacky little golden lights set into them failing to adequately illuminate the garish candy-coloured seats. Strip mirrors on every wall, bent and distorted with time. Not enough sun-loungers outside, the air-con set to "Arctic Tundra" inside. For entertainment, a soul-destroying casino and an old CRT television in the corner of the bar showing fuzzy basketball games. A small pool, but too cold for anyone to bother swimming. That and the constant humming and vibration of the engines made me thankful I'd only be aboard for a few hours and not a few days.

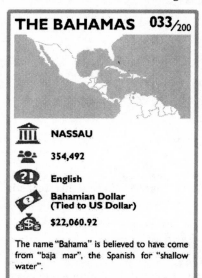

THE BAHAMAS 033/200

🏛 **NASSAU**

👥 **354,492**

❓ **English**

💵 **Bahamian Dollar (Tied to US Dollar)**

💰 **$22,060.92**

The name "Bahama" is believed to have come from "baja mar", the Spanish for "shallow water".

Grand Bahama was a lot like many of the Caribbean islands I visited — the place had obviously benefited economically from being on the doorstep of the world's richest nation, but at the price of its soul. Concrete strip-mall style buildings, a-bit-too-perfect avenues of palm trees, beaches teaming with sunbathers and party-goers, overloaded sound systems and strawberry daiquiris.

Being all ginger and freckly I don't know what to do with beaches — I could sunbathe for 10 minutes before being burnt to a crisp. Or I could go for a swim for 10 minutes before being burnt to a crisp. In a stand-up fight between me and the sun, the sun is always going to kick my ass. What I need is some shade and a hammock. And maybe a copy of Hemingway. But this wasn't that kind of place.

That evening I was back in the USA with only two countries of Western Hemisphere left to visit. Funnily enough, both began with "C" and ended in "A".

I spent a good few frustrating days in Fort Lauderdale waiting to hear back from the Treasury department, but there was little to be done to oil the wheels. So I elected to do something I had wanted to do since I was a child — watch a space shuttle blast off into outer space. Luckily, one was scheduled to do exactly that at the weekend.

So I jumped on a (horrible) Greyhound bus up to Titusville, the nearest town to Cape Canaveral.

I checked into the Three Oaks Motel. It was one of those classic American motels were you park outside your bedroom door (presumably whilst on the run from the cops or the mafia).

I looked for somewhere to get a bite to eat, but Titusville seemed dead. After 30 minutes of wandering about, I found a tremendously inconvenient convenience store. It sold nothing that would constitute an actual meal but I was not so desperate that I would consider eating American "chocolate".

Eventually I found a pizza place, but it was delivery only. I had to call the number on the door and have it "delivered" to the parking lot, a service for which I was charged $2.

The closest that Joe Public can see a rocket taking off from Cape Canaveral is the NASA Causeway, around a mile from the actual launch site. If that seems excessively cautious, bear in mind that if you get much closer and the thing blows up on the rig, there's a good chance it'll take an unhealthy portion of your skin with it.

Tickets for the Causeway usually sell out months in advance, however this particular launch (STS-119) had been postposed three times already, meaning that there was a good chance that resale tickets would be on sale in the morning.

Needless to say, I was first in line.

Causeway ticket in hand, I spent the day touring the Space Centre, my inner geek running riot over my otherwise cool ginger-haired four-eyed freckle-faced exterior. I was mildly apprehensive that lift-off might be postponed again — this would be one of the last few shuttle launches — for me, it was now or never.

That evening I took the courtesy bus to the Causeway, plonked myself down on the grass behind the yellow rope and set up my camcorder.

At 7:34pm, there, in front of me, was the biggest explosion I had ever seen with my own eyes. The ground shook, the shuttle blasted off and there was much cheering and whooping. It was twilight, the last of the night launches, but when the rocket got high enough, the exhaust plume was lit by the multi-coloured rays of the sun below the horizon — it looked unreal. I found myself pondering whether it was easier to send an American into space than it was to get one to Cuba.

Speaking of Cuba, it was time to head south. One way or another, country number 34 was getting ticked off the list.

The Florida Keys are a string of islands that run down from the southern tip of mainland Florida. They're connected by a series of causeways (one is seven miles long) and they seemed like the best bet for getting a boat to Cuba. Key West, the most southerly you can get to by road, is just 90 miles from Havana.

I took an overnight Greyhound Bus (urgh) from Orlando to Miami. There, while attempting to board the bus for the keys, I was informed by driver that I was too "scruffy-lookin'" to get on "his" bus.

I took a deep, exasperated breath.

I enquired, in my best British accent, what in heavens I could possibly do to further mess up his filthy knackered old bus that stunk of effluent and historic cigarettes.

'Oh, you're a tourist?', asked this mouth-breathing embodiment of everything everybody secretly hates about Americans.

'Yes I am. And furthermore, if I am looking a little worse-for-wear it's because I spent last night sleeping on one of "your" Greyhound buses from Orlando. It was filthy. As you can see.'

I could see the driver wanted to say something along the lines of an apology, but that was well beyond his pay-grade. He just grunted and I got on the bus.

Happily, when I met my CouchSurf hosts, Tom and Midge of the *Mariposa* retreat, my up-to-that-moment negative view of Floridians improved somewhat. They were lovely, and really got behind me on my mission to get to Cuba.

Early the next morning Midge set me up to talk to Captain Finbar of the Schooner *Wolf*, the flagship of The Conch Republic[11].

The Conch Republic was founded in 1982 as a response to the US government setting up border controls between the most northerly Key and mainland Florida. It was a grand plan of the Reagan administration to stop drugs and refugees entering "mainland" America. But hang on — if you have to show your passport to visit Miami, does that mean that the Florida Keys are a separate country?

Captain Finbar and his friends thought so, and in response they seceded from The Union and declared themselves an independent state — "The Conch Republic". Then, inspired by the Peter Sellers comedy *The Mouse That Roared*, they declared war on the USA. A flotilla of ships set out, led by the newly christened *"HMS" Wolf*[12], and attacked the US Coastguard with water balloons and stale Cuban bread. The aim was to lose the battle, surrender unconditionally and receive a billion dollars in aid from the US Government.

Unfortunately for the Royal Navy of The Conch Republic, they won. The Coastguard retreated. But the good people of The Conch Republic had made their point. They never got their billion dollars, but the border post was scrapped.

Captain Finbar was a proper old-school seadog. He told me that if the *Wolf* wasn't getting fixed up, he'd have given me a lift to Cuba and told the US Treasury to shove their "permission" where the sun don't shine.

Finbar put me onto a few different sailors who might be up for the journey. A good few of them told me that if the US Treasury gave me the

---

[11] Author's Note: Pronounced "conk".
[12] Author's Note: Apparently, The Conch Republic had a king.

thumbs-up we could leave the next day. So now we played the waiting game.

One of the benefits of having red hair and a funny accent is that a lot of Americans naturally assume I'm Irish. This is great because everybody seems to like the Irish. Even better, it was St Patrick's Day and Key West was gearing up for some rather epic nocturnal shenanigans.

For the love of the *craic* I threw myself into the Beer Vortex with reckless abandon. Along the way I stumbled upon a book for sale in Harpoon Harry's bar called *CUBA: The Definitive Guide to getting there Legally and Illegally.* I left my contact details with the bar staff, hoping to speak to the author, who (I was told) was a local.

Later I met St. Patrick himself. He carried a staff with a snake wrapped around it, and when he pressed a secret button Jameson's Whiskey came forth from out of the snake's mouth. I then met a couple of swingers who wanted to take me home with them, but I ended up at a "clothing optional" disco instead.

I woke up on a pirate ship, a little bewildered as to how the hell I got there. Incredibly, I still had my hat, laptop, video camera, wallet, phone and passport. I don't think pirates are quite what they used to be.

Stumbling from my berth, I staggered out onto deck. I was greeted by stingingly bright sunshine and loads of young fresh-faced Spring Breakers queuing for a jolly excursion on the pirate ship. As I disembarked I tipped my hat down over my eyes and headed for an internet café to see if the Treasury Department had been in touch.

I had barely booted up my computer before Mandy popped up on Skype.

'Bad news babe.'

I braced myself for the worst.

'They've denied your application.'

Good job I was as hungover as a dog, otherwise I might have blown a gasket. The swines. The complete and utter *hijos de puta.*

Land of the free, my arse.

So, I couldn't charter an American boat and captain to take me to Cuba and back. Also, I couldn't charter a foreign boat and captain to take me because you need a visa to enter the US on a private vessel, even if you left from the US in the first place.

It was back to square one. My options were as follows:

- Travel all the way up to Canada and wait for a cargo boat headed for Cuba. Blag my way on board. Estimated travel time: 28 days. Odds: 1 in 3.

- Travel back to Mexico, get to Cancun, find someone who'll take me to Cuba and back on a private yacht. Estimated travel time: 14 days. Odds: 1 in 5.

- Travel back up to Fort Lauderdale, get the boat back over to the Grand Bahama, wait for the mail boat for Nassau (twice a week), catch a lift off a yacht to Cuba and back, wait for the mail boat back to Grand Bahama, then ferry back to Fort Lauderdale. Estimated travel time: 21 days. Odds: 1 in 10.

- Find an American with a private yacht who's leaving tomorrow and simply doesn't give a damn because he's never coming back to the US ever again. Persuade him to take me to Cuba then drop me off in Mexico. Estimated travel time: 7 days. Odds: 1 in a million.

As I pondered my options I walked to the southern tip of the continental United States and looked out over the water towards Cuba, less than 100 miles away.

My phone rang.

It was Michael Bellows, the author of *CUBA: The Definitive Guide to getting there Legally and Illegally.*

'I believe you're trying to get to Cuba on a boat.'

'Indeed I am!' I replied.

'Meet me at Harpoon Harry's in an hour.'

We sat down and I explained my predicament. Michael said he couldn't promise anything, but he had heard of a yachtie who was leaving for Mexico the next day. Even better, he wasn't planning on coming back to the US and wouldn't be averse to the idea of dropping into Cuba along the way.

It all sounded too good to be true.

Mike drove me over to Safe Harbour where I met Captain Johnny — a young skipper, same age as me, originally from Indiana. He shook my hand and told me he was leaving in the morning, could do with another pair of hands on board and was happy to drop into Cuba along the way.

It took me a few moments to gather my jaw up off the floor.

With a little help from the good people of Key West, I had snatched victory from the jaws of defeat. I love this town!

The next morning, Midge drove me to the marina. I threw my kit on Johnny's boat, a 40-foot Morgan Outland Sloop called (somewhat appropriately) the *Bootlegger*. We bought supplies, cleared customs, checked out of the marina, and by 2pm we were barrelling over the waves en route to Cuba, and there was nothing the US Treasury department could do about it.

Key West had been a real blast; gorgeous old buildings, art shops you can browse for free, great bars and clubs, relaxed atmosphere, friendly people and a crazy/bohemian air to the place. Part of me was sad to see it go.

We couldn't go straight to Havana — it would be too obvious if anyone was tracking us — so we set a course to a town on the west coast of Cuba called María la Gorda (Maria the Fat), named after a popular prostitute from back in the day. It would take three days to get there.

Captain Johnny's boat didn't have an autopilot, so we took turns skippering while the other got some much needed shut-eye. As I stood out on deck piloting the yacht under the twinkling stars, I strengthened my resolve. *The Odyssey* may well be stopped by war, illness or accident, but it will not be stopped by bureaucrats, goddammit!

It was now March 20th. If all had been going to plan I'd be in Africa by now, having already stepped foot in every country in The Americas and Europe. And yet here I was, spending three weeks trying to reach one little country.

The next day we rolled over giant swells, slowly making our way across the Gulf of Mexico. Captain Johnny's endgame was to sail to his wife and kid in Fiji, so this was just the beginning of a much longer trip for him. The *Bootlegger* was a proper piratey affair, lashed together with bits and bobs purloined and plundered from less worthy vessels.

All was going swimmingly until around 2am when Captain Johnny decided to take down the spinnaker sail in the dark, which resulted in the sail making its way under the boat. It was up to us two hapless buccaneers to try and rescue the damn thing from the vile clutches of the Gulf Stream while the good ol' *Bootlegger* swayed to and fro like a drunkard on a revolving bouncy castle.

Sailing with Captain Johnny was a lot like working Saturday mornings at my Dad's garage as a kid, in that he would point in a vague direction, scream at you to grab the thingymabobajig and when you try to confirm what in fact a thingymabobajig is, he will continue to point and scream *THE THINGYMABOBAJIG!! The bloody THINGY-MA-BOB-A-JIG!! IDIOT!!!!!*

At this point he'll down tools, walk over, violently pick up a random object (which is now *obviously* the thingymabobajig), hold it in front of your face and say 'THINGYMABOBAJIG! Moron!'

I perhaps exaggerated my sailing capabilities a little.

On our third day at sea, I was behind the wheel while Johnny was adjusting the mainsail. All of a sudden something went TWANG and clobbered my forehead so hard I saw stars. Blood spurted from the wound.

I thought it was the boom (the ruin of many a sailor) but it was a metal hook, big enough to cause me a modicum of discomfort, but not enough to cause any serious cranial damage. I was lucky. Having a yacht captain use a fish hook to put stitches in your head with no anaesthetic other than a bottle of scotch while your boat smashes through the choppiest waters this side of Cape Horne doesn't bear thinking about — landfall was still a day away.

Johnny bandaged up my head and that night I helmed the *Bootlegger* while *El Capitan* slept. It was a full-time job trying to keep a steady course against the wishes of the Gulf of Mexico. As the boat bowed and pitched its way through the inky black water I felt like a proper adventurer, one of those chaps involved in daring of do and the buckling of swashes.

The next morning Johnny called me on deck — he'd been chatting on the VHF radio with a passing yacht that had just left María la Gorda. A yacht called the *Mariposa*.

Remarkably, it was the very same *Mariposa* that rescued me from Antigua!! I got on the radio and said hello to Kerri and Andrew, laughing that maybe I should have stayed with them after all.

Johnny and I swung into the sleepy little bay of María la Gorda just before noon. It was a gloriously sunny morning, but storm clouds were approaching. There was no port to speak of, just some mooring buoys off the shore, and two other boats beside ours. We dropped anchor, hoisted the quarantine flag, then called the port attendant on the radio.

'Can we come in?'

A voice crackled over the VHF. 'Yeah sure, why not?'

Within half an hour, we were boarded by Customs and Immigration. The guy from immigration wasn't too impressed with my Cuban visa and the terror of making it all the way to Cuba only to be knocked back 100 metres from dry land flashed through my mind.

But no fear, I slipped him twenty bucks and got my entry stamp (on a piece of paper so as not to upset the Americans).

The reason why US citizens are so strongly discouraged from visiting Cuba is that the US government doesn't want them "trading with the enemy".

And yet the first thing I saw as I stepped onto the jetty was a big sign for Coca-Cola.

Go figure.

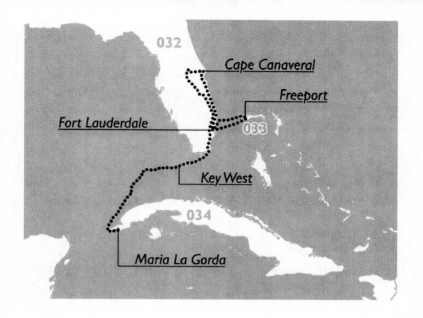

Chapter 7
We're Gonna Need A Bigger Coat

Once on dry land, Johnny and I exchanged some dollars for pesos and headed to the bar for a well-deserved beer.

There we got chatting to some of the rather lively locals. I asked them what they thought of all the rules concerning travel and tourism in **Cuba** — such as the fact that Cubans are not allowed to leave the country without permission and it being illegal to have a foreigner stay in your home or to even give them a lift in your car.

One of the guys said that he loved his country and never wanted to live anywhere else, but would like to pop over to Mexico at some point in his life — he had family over there. Another guy said that he feels like he lives in a prison — a very big and an exceptionally

CUBA 034/200

🏛 **HAVANA**

👥 **11.29m**

❓💬 **Spanish**

💵 **Cuban Peso**

💰 **$5,499.12**

The CIA tried to assassinate Fidel Castro an estimated 638 times, using increasingly desperate methods – including a poisoned wetsuit and an exploding cigar.

beautiful prison, but a prison nonetheless. Again, not that he wanted to "escape", but he too thought it unfair that he wasn't allowed to go on holiday someplace else without the nod from the powers that be.

They knew the American government made it very difficult for US citizens to visit Cuba, and appreciated Johnny's efforts getting over there, almost as much as I did.

I got a wonderful vibe from Cuba. The people I met were super friendly and the coast was spectacular — not overdeveloped, miles of deserted beaches with a lush tropical interior. Sweet.

That afternoon the heavens opened. As the rain lashed down we planned what to do next. Being several weeks behind schedule, I was keen to press on to Mexico. However, with no weather charts available, if we left immediately, we could end up ploughing straight into a storm.

Eventually, the rain abated and Johnny decided (possibly after a few too many shots of Havana Club) that we should leave that night. And so off we went.

As we barrelled over the Caribbean swell, the madness of leaving at sunset, drunk and without a weather window became increasingly apparent. With distant electrical storms illuminating the night sky all around, I was acutely aware that we were floating in the middle of the ocean inside what is effectively a giant lightning conductor.

The following morning there were nasty looking storm clouds congregating directly ahead of us, so we dropped sail and threw out the sea anchor — basically a big yellow bag that drags behind the yacht, hopefully slowing us down. Only this was the Gulf Stream; the damn thing is like a conveyor belt. Even with no sail, no engine and a sea anchor deployed, we were still bumbling towards the storm at a good four knots.

Captain Johnny mocked me for hurriedly putting my gloves on. 'You think that a tiny bit of fabric is going to save you if we get struck by 100 million volts, sailor?'

'Er, won't it?'

The laughter followed the captain as he made his way below decks to eat a banana.

Luckily the storm passed harmlessly to the side of us.

It was dark when we reached Isla Mujertas, a little spit of an island a few miles off the coast of Cancun. Captain Johnny, fancying himself a piratey buccaneer, decided we would try a night entrance to the marina.

Most countries around the world have red buoys to the left and green to the right when coming into port, so you stay in deep water and don't run aground. For some reason, the Americas do it the other way around.

Even if you know which side is which, it can still get a little confusing, especially if the channel snakes from left to right. Hell — it's hard to judge distance in the dark.

'Aren't we a bit close to shore?'

THUD!

Oh dear.

We were more grounded than a naughty teenager. I mean, I was happy to hit Mexican soil, but this wasn't quite what I had in mind!

For the next half-hour we went a little crazy trying to free the yacht from the shallows. We put the sails up and Johnny damn near blew the engine but eventually we managed to shift ourselves back into the channel. Phew!

After all that excitement, Johnny thought it best we just drop anchor there and then. So that's what we did, taking shifts to ensure nothing else went bump in the night.

In the morning, all those years of never going to the gym finally paid off big-time as I made a huge arse of myself by failing to pull up the anchor — Johnny had to do it for me. But before too long we had successfully manoeuvred into the anchorage and found ourselves a parking space between two much bigger yachts.

We had been informed that Mexican customs and immigration could take a couple of days, so Johnny hopped into his trusty dingy and shot off to find out more. I just had time to drop a (long overdue) dreadnought in the ship's toilet and pack my stuff before he returned to say it all looked quite straight-forward. No medical, no sniffer dogs; just head over to the immigration office, get stamped in, then see the port captain and get stamped off the crew list and we were done.

And so it was time to say goodbye to the mighty *Bootlegger* — she held together magnificently on our little jaunt; save a broken cleat, a broken griller, two torn sails, the main sail slipping off the mast, a couple of damaged ropes and a host of other major and minor technical issues. Actually, it's a miracle she made it in one piece — there are just so many things that can — and do — go wrong on a sailboat. Scares the bejesus out of me. Why people do this kind of thing for fun is beyond my programming.

A bus left for Mexico City at 6pm from Cancun so we jumped on one of the frequent ferries, squeezed onto a local bus, downed a few last beers at a bar opposite the bus station and bid each other fair winds on our respective journeys. Maybe I'd see Captain Johnny again in Fiji, who knows?

It would take five days, several buses and a train ride to get from Cancun to the port of Halifax in Canada. I hadn't had a shower since Key West. I pitied the poor souls sitting next to me.

Twenty-three hours later I arrived in Mexico City. After a quick change of buses I was making my way up to the border at Nuevo Laredo for the second time.

Leaving Mexico was a doddle, they just ran my passport through the computer and off I jolly well popped. I don't think they even stamped me out.

US immigration was another matter entirely. When I explained that I had sailed from Key West to Cancun, the immigration officer got rather excited. Seems he was a keen sailor himself — just my luck. He quizzed me over what a knot was, what a sheet was, what a head was, maritime law concerning sailing at night, whether we caught any fish, what type of fish we caught and if I had seen any Cubans along the way?

My answers were, respectively: one nautical mile an hour, a rope, a toilet, if you're not at anchor you must have somebody on watch, yes, mahi mahi and erm, no?!

'Can I come in now?'

The whole process took 30 minutes, before the magic stamp came down and I was officially free to enter the United States of America again.

So then it was off to the Greyhound bus station to buy my 30-hour bus ride to New York.

I actually managed to get quite far this time before the overwhelming awfulness of the Greyhound bus company just couldn't help rearing its ugly head. The lady driver took to the bus's loudspeaker to berate me — for filming out of the window.

That is forbidden, apparently. You know, *like in North Korea.*

We drove into the night; Texas, Louisiana, Mississippi, Alabama, Georgia... looking out the window, all I saw were boxes. All along the freeway — box after box after box. The names changed, the boxes remained the same. Best Buy, PetSmart, Starbucks, Arby's, Home Depot, CVS Pharmacy, Wendy's, Pre-Owned Sales, IKEA, Rentacar, HT Fitness, Multiplex Movie Theatre, Late Nite Comedy, 1-800-Lawsuit, Budweiser, Denny's, Pizza Hut, Waffle House, Taco Bell, Wing Shack, Subway. There was a Pentecostal church in a warehouse. A funeral home in a shed. Nobody seems to want to build nice things any more. At least not at the side of an American freeway.

When it came time to change buses in Atlanta, I made a fatal error — I didn't push to the front of the queue like a twat. Consequently, the bus I was supposed to be on filled up and left. Myself and fifteen other unfortunates were shunted onto an "overflow" bus, a bus that didn't leave for another hour.

From Atlanta to New York I was supposed to have just one more change of bus. As things turned out we had *seven*. I was rudely awoken at 1am, 3am, 4am, 6am and 8am to stand like a lemon in one of several Greyhound bus terminals while the Greyhound staff flat refused to tell me what was happening and why.

When we finally rolled into Manhattan around 7pm that day I really should have been far too tired to go out partying all night.

Should.

I headed over to Central Park to meet my friend Monica Ibacache. Monica and I met over a "happy" pizza in Cambodia back in 2002 and the offer of a floor on which to crash if I was ever in the Big Apple had been open ever since. After taking a much-needed shower at her apartment, washing off 10 days' worth of sweat, sea-salt and bus slime, we trotted out to see what New York had to offer a boy from Liverpool on a Saturday night.

We ended up in a burlesque club called The Slipper Room on the Lower East Side. Dancers, acrobats, strippers, a man-monkey and an evil superhero called Doctor Donut. I drank way more than was practical considering I needed to be up early to catch the bus to Canada. Afterwards we stuffed our faces with — hats off to you, NYC — the BEST pizza I have ever eaten, and I've eaten a lot of pizza. You can probably tell.

At about 4am I found myself negotiating New York's Subway system in the dead of the night, drunk, and on my own, with instructions on how to get back to Monica's friend's apartment scrawled on my hand. I didn't even die.

I ♥ New York.

I set my alarm for 6:30am to give me loads of time to wake up and get to the bus station for 8:30am when the bus left for Montreal.

Only I somewhat heroically didn't wake up until 8:00am.

Oh dear.

Up and out of the apartment before you could say "Crikey!" in a silly voice, I pounded down the stairs and emerged onto the streets. When I was a kid I learnt to whistle through my fingers for this one and only purpose — grabbing a cab in an emergency in New York City.

'The bus station please and STEP ON IT!'

#LifeGoals.

I was on 109th Street. The bus station was on 45th Street. That's 64 streets between me and the bus.

Luckily, it was Sunday morning, and the streets were (relatively) empty — my driver hurtled down Central Park West like a bank-heist maniac, switching lanes and honking at those crazy fools who dared to drive slower than us.

There was a sprint to the finish, but by 8:29am I was on the bus to Canada.

There was snow on the ground as we passed American border control.

A harsh winter chill lingered in the air. Quite a contrast to the dust and heat of Mexico I had experienced just a few days earlier. My leather jacket was not going to cut the mustard. I put on an extra pair of socks.

Considering how obsessed Americans are when it comes to immigration, it's a bit weird that they rarely stamp you out of the country. But at least the Canucks on the other side were friendly enough. And so there I was. **Canada**. March 29th. Day 88. The 35th and final nation of the Americas.

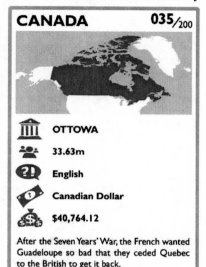

CANADA 035/200

🏛 **OTTOWA**

👥 **33.63m**

💬 **English**

💵 **Canadian Dollar**

💰 **$40,764.12**

After the Seven Years' War, the French wanted Guadeloupe so bad that they ceded Quebec to the British to get it back.

Arriving in beautiful old Montreal at 5pm, I had just 60 minutes to race across town to catch the 20-hour "Ocean" train to Halifax. This would be my first train ride of *The Odyssey Expedition* — and what a way to get started!

The train had tons of legroom, electrical outlets (power was something that had been in short supply over the previous fortnight) and a dining car.

Meanwhile, outside looked *cold*. Bloody cold. Everything around us was blanketed in pure white snow. I couldn't tell where the roads ended and the fields began. Even the trees looked cold, like they were huddling together in a vain effort to keep warm.

From the observation car of the train it was all quite beautiful. A picture postcard of winter that stretched for hundreds of miles in every direction.

The next day, as the train crossed from New Brunswick to Nova Scotia, we hit a blizzard. Had this been the UK I'm fairly certain that this would have caused something of a delay, but Canada likes to take these things in its stride. The train arrived in the port town of Halifax bang on time.

I checked into the Halifax Backpackers and got online. While I had been travelling up from Cancun, Team Odyssey — in this case, my friends Dino and Lorna — had been communicating with Eimskip, the Icelandic shipping company that had agreed to take me across the Atlantic two months earlier. With a little help from my Danish cousin Christian (speaking Danish helps when chatting to our Icelandic friends), I had been granted passage on a container ship that was scheduled to leave Halifax in one week's time. Amazing.

At first I was a bit miffed that I hadn't taken the opportunity to spend more time in New York, but Halifax grew on me. That night I was invited to a gig — an open mic night that was being held in somebody's house, in their living room.

Three things I like:

1. Live Music
2. House Parties
3. Backpacking

So I went along with fellow backpackers Travis the Canadian, Toby from Australia, Patricia from Germany and Seppe, also from Germany. Seppe was good enough to lend me his big coat because holy shit it was cold.

Needless to say the gig was very much up my street and very, very Canadian. Throw in some poutine, maple syrup, a moose and a game of hockey and you'd hit Peak Canada.

A few days later most of my Halifax Backpackers gang had moved on. That night I shared the dorm with a young couple who, thinking I was asleep (I wasn't) started "quietly" going at it on the lower bunk. I lay on the top bunk in that horrible state of quintessentially British paralysis — do I cough or what?

The next day I sent an SOS to James, the CouchSurfing ambassador for Halifax. He told me no problem — I could stay with him for the next few days.

James was a member of Engineers Without Borders, an international organisation involved in setting up essential infrastructure, much like WaterAid, the charity that I was supporting on *The Odyssey Expedition*.

James also reminded me of Brian Blessed.

His house was a little out of town on the banks of a frozen lake. In the night you could hear the ice cracking as the spring thaw kicked in.

That weekend James and I took his dog Rocky for a trip to Liverpool. Not my hometown of Liverpool, but Liverpool Nova Scotia. On the way, we stopped at Peggy's Cove, a picture-postcard fishing village complete with lighthouse and waves crashing against rocks.

We found a charming little restaurant and I picked a lobster from the tank, named him "Oscar" (James' suggestion) and had the chef throw him in a big pot full of boiling water for my evil pleasure.

The east coast of Canada is famed for its lobster, and with good reason — it's delicious.

Over lunch, James told me the story of the crash of SwissAir Flight 111.

On September 2nd 1998 a McDonnell Douglas MD-11 flying in from New York hit the ocean just five miles from Peggy's Cove. All 215 passengers and crew were killed. James told me that a lot of locals swore off lobster for a few years after that — there was no way of knowing what the lobsters had been eating.

I looked at Oscar, currently in pieces on my plate.

'How long do lobsters live?', I asked.

'Forever, I think. Unless something eats them — they just keep growing', smiled James. 'Are you going to finish that?'

After lunch, we continued to Liverpool. It was a remarkably pleasant little town by the sea. The houses were old and quaint and made of wood, and there were little cafés and gift shops. It reminded me of the seaside towns in Wales I visited as a kid — Llandudno and Colwyn Bay.

The ship to Iceland was scheduled to leave the next day, but when I returned to the Halifax Backpackers, I discovered that the ship – the *Reykjavoss* was delayed until Wednesday morning. So I went for a few drinks with Seppe, the German guy who lent me his coat the week before. He was also waiting for a cargo ship to take him to Cuba, funnily enough, but it kept getting delayed, meaning he was now stuck in Halifax for another week.

On the Tuesday evening I spoke to Mandy via Skype. Because of the time difference it was Wednesday morning in Australia — the morning of her 33rd birthday. After three months the pain of her not being with me may have been less immediate, but that didn't make it any less piercing. On the plus side, the idea of seeing her again didn't half spur me on.

Afterwards, Justin, a guy from Queenstown in New Zealand (The Bungee Jump Capital of the World), tried to convince me to come out and drown my sorrows.

'But I've got to be up at seven to meet the port agents for the boat', I said, 'and the next ship isn't for another month.'

'Let's just go for a quick game of pool', said Justin.

It sounded harmless enough.

One game turned into two, then three. Eventually Justin and I ended up in some place that had a live band doing covers. Somebody must have been buying me drinks because I have no recollection of getting back to the hostel or going to bed.

I woke up with thunder crashing in my head. I looked at my watch. It was 9am. I had overslept.

Bugger.

Pants on, backpack slung over shoulder, I ran downstairs. Samme the

Shipping Agent and his assistant Liz were waiting for me at reception. Samme got right to the point. 'We have to hurry, the boat is leaving very soon'. Blurry-eyed and croaking (was I singing karaoke last night?), I jumped in the back of his car we raced towards the docks.

After some surprisingly speedy formalities, I was on board. Phew! The *Reykjafoss* was the biggest cargo ship I had been on so far and would be my home for the next week as we crossed the mighty Atlantic en route to Iceland.

The captain was Polish and the crew was a mix of Ukrainians, Russians and Filipinos. I had a nice clean cabin to myself and pretty much had the run of the ship, save from some restricted areas in which I liked to imagine we were transporting the Ark of the Covenant.

We left Halifax early that afternoon. My hangover coupled with my lack of seasickness pills (d'oh!) resulted in me spending most of the first evening on board with my head down the toilet.

The following evening we had a brief stop at the port of Argentia in Newfoundland. I set off to find a 24-hour pharmacy, although that was a long shot after the captain described the place as 'somewhere after a Nuclear Holocaust'.

Argentia was an important American Naval Base for many years, and once incorporated a sizable municipality with houses, shops, movie theatres and even a town hall. Then after the Americans left, the Canadian government were left with a bit of a problem. Pretty much everything in the town had to be (carefully) ripped down because some dickhead had made it all out of asbestos.

So I jumped in a taxi and headed to the town of Placentia, just a couple of kilometres down the road. When I got there the pharmacy was closed. I had to make do with these herbal capsules of nonsense from the all-night garage — basically powdered ginger.

"No drowsiness reported!" boasted the label. It should have also read "No alleviation of seasickness reported either!"

I headed to the pub.

Newfies are a funny bunch. Speaking to them you'd swear they were Irish, except for the fact they say "aboot" like Canadians. Newfies have this other-worldliness about them (I was asked, straight up, if I was from Iraq), but also a strong sense of identity and plenty of good cheer. It can't be an easy life living this far north, and I got the impression they take a healthy measure of pride in that.

The next morning one of the Canadian stevedores (dockers) came on board the ship with a surprise for the crew: moose meat. I was told that Newfies are only allowed to shoot one moose a year, so this was something of a special occasion. The ship's cook diced the meat and put together a stew, which tasted delicious. Sorry Bullwinkle.

That evening, a little later than scheduled, the ropes were loosed and the Americas slipped away into the night. After exactly 100 days on the road, Part One of *The Odyssey Expedition* was complete. It was now time to focus on Part Two: Europe.

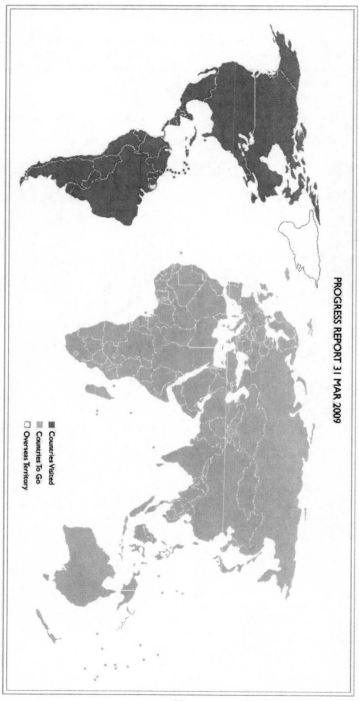

PROGRESS REPORT 31 MAR 2009

Countries Visited
Countries To Go
Overseas Territory

Chapter 8
The Five Nations Pub Crawl

I spent much of the journey aboard the *Reykjafoss* feeling somewhat nauseous, even though the sea was remarkably calm. Those pills I bought didn't even touch the sides. I would have been better off with a packet of McVitie's Ginger Nuts[13].

Even so, I found time to bond with the crew. Sunday April 12th was Easter Sunday and most of the guys had the day off. We had a celebration in the mess, beers and a delicious roast meal followed by karaoke. Since some of the crew couldn't drink as they would be on duty later that night, they plied me with alcohol instead. I didn't put up much of a fight.

The next day Andrey the Chief Engineer gave me a tour of the engine room. The engine was the size of a small house and had the power of 70,000 horses. We had to wear ear protection the damn thing was so loud. It was all very steampunk.

In a bit of a weird coincidence, the First Mate used to be part of the original crew on board the *Linge Trader* (the cargo ship that took me from the Dominican Republic to Mexico) when it was launched a few years back. He even had pictures of the old girl on his laptop.

On the Tuesday I was up on the bridge drinking coffee and chatting with the captain. He spoke about his life growing up behind the Iron Curtain in Poland in the 1960s and how he and his dad used to listen (illegally) to The Beatles on a homemade longwave radio.

I looked out to sea. 'What's it like for icebergs this time of year?'

The captain laughed. 'The worst!'

He then explained that it was iceberg season and showed me tracking charts throughout the year. There were very few in the autumn and winter, but in the spring the Arctic ice melts and heads south and things

---

[13] Editor's Note: British term for a ginger snap cookie.

go a little crazy.

'Don't worry — the big ones show up on the radar', he told me. It was the small ones, amusingly named "growlers", that we had to worry about. I noticed there was a small X right at the bottom of the current sailing chart, a hundred nautical miles south of our current marked position.

Next to the X was written *'SS Titanic, 14 April 1912'*.

I looked at my watch to double check the date.

It was April 14th 2009.

97 years to the day.

Yikes.

The ship's cook was a stocky guy from the Philippines who went by the name of Chivas Regal. Apparently when he was Christened 'it was either that or Johnnie Walker'. 'My dad was a big fan of whiskey', he beamed.

The previous year, Chivas was working on a cargo ship that departed the port of Mombasa in Kenya and was heading north towards Europe. Not far from the coast of Somalia the ship was captured by pirates and the crew was held hostage at gunpoint for an entire month.

Chivas was forced to cook not only for the terrified crew, but also for the pirates. They would sail from port to port to prevent other rival pirate gangs from taking the vessel. He said that as a Filipino (and the only cook) his treatment wasn't so bad (although they did apparently steal his underwear from his cabin), but the officers were not so lucky. They often founds their heads at the butt-end of a rifle for speaking out.

I asked him if he would sail that route again. To my surprise he said yes.

'The weather is better.'

Over dinner that evening, the captain informed us that he had heard on the radio that in the past week pirates had captured another three ships in the Indian Ocean. One of them would turn out to be *Maersk Alabama*, the ship made famous by the movie *Captain Phillips* starring Tom Hanks.

The captain mused that the shipping companies would have to run convoys like in the war, but whether the big shipping companies would be prepared to lose days (and therefore vast sums of money) waiting to put them together was another matter. In any case, all this did not bode well for *The Odyssey Expedition*. As I was later to find out, The Seychelles being situated slap bang in the middle of the "High Risk Area" for piracy made getting there without flying an almost insurmountable challenge.

We reached Reykjavik, the capital of **Iceland** (and where I would have to change ships), in the wee small hours of the morning of April 16th. I was on the bridge as the city lights came into view, but we were a few hours too late to make my connection with the *Bruarfoss,* another Eimskip container ship, which would be getting into the English city of Hull the following Sunday.

ICELAND	036/200

🏛 **REYKJAVIK**

👥 318,499

💬 Icelandic

💵 Icelandic Króna

💰 $40,263.39

Geologically speaking, Iceland is the youngest country in the world.

It was time for Plan B — the *Dettifoss*, which would be leaving at midday and arriving in Rotterdam (in the Netherlands) the following Monday. If I made all my connections, I could be home in Liverpool by 8:55pm that same day.

As luck would have it, the *Dettifoss* was conveniently moored right next to us in the Port of Reykjavik. After saying thank you and goodbye to the crew of the *Reykjafoss,* I transferred my gear onto the *Dettifoss* and introduced myself to the captain, an old salty seadog by the name of Mathias Mathiasson.

I had a couple of hours before departure, so I decided to check out Reykjavik itself, which is quite possibly most calm and orderly major capital city in the world. It was so quiet I was afraid to talk in anything louder than a whisper. I did manage to get my hands on some decent seasickness tablets though, thank God.

That afternoon the *Dettifoss* skirted the south coast of Iceland on our way to the port of Reydarfjordur to the east. I watched in a dreamlike trance, the ethereal sound of Iceland's Sigur Rós blasting in my ears, as great snow-capped mountains and volcanos, jagged cliffs, black sands and pebble shores passed by my porthole.

One question I sometimes get asked is why I skipped Greenland, and the reason is simple: it's not a country. It may be one day, but as it stands, it is part of Denmark. But I did end up visiting another Danish territory: The Faroe Islands. Not because I was making up for something, but because the *Dettifoss* had a scheduled stop there on the way to The Netherlands.

Remember how St Thomas in the US Virgin Islands came bottom of National Geographic's list of "The Most Appealing Islands in the World?" Well guess who came top? Yup, the **Faroe Islands**.

St Thomas and the Faroes were both ruled by the Danish for centuries, but St Thomas was sold to the USA in 1917.

Which explains a lot.

Unlike the Caribbean, the Faroes are refreshingly unspoilt by joyless concrete edifices, high-rises, shopping malls, jewellery shops, air conditioning units and all the rest of the unfortunate bilge that clutters up otherwise beautiful places.

FAROE ISLANDS (Denmark)

🏛 **TÓRSHAVN**

👥 **46,600**

❓ **Faroese**

💵 **Faroese Króna (Tied to Danish Krone)**

💰 **$44,317.31**

The Faroe Islands have only three sets of traffic lights.

The buildings of the capital Tórshavn are rather charming and many have grass growing on their sharply inclined roofs — I guess for insulation. It looks amazing. I wouldn't like to be the one who has to mow them in the summer though.

When we were crossing the Atlantic on the way to Iceland, I'd occasionally check the old radar on the bridge to see if there were any other vessels in the vicinity. But we would invariably be the only ship for a hundred miles in every direction. However, as we travelled south from the Faroes towards Rotterdam along Britain's east coast the radar screen went nuts: fishing boats, cargo ships, ferries, Spanish galleons, pangas, sailing boats, submarines, megayachts, pirogues, sloops, Chinese junks, dhows, oil rigs, feluccas, leviathans, giant squid, EVERYTHING.

It goes without saying that the entire crew needed to be on the ball and so for the last leg of the journey I was pretty much left to my own devices.

Happily, thanks to our proximity to the UK mainland I could finally get a decent phone signal. Lonely Planet had been in touch some news: they had come to an arrangement with the TV show budget. I would have to forgo most of my (already meagre) upfront fee and would get little in the way expenses, but I'd be on for a hefty percentage deal on the back end.

Or at least that's what I was led to believe.

In any case, the show was now officially greenlit. Eight episodes for the National Geographic Adventure channel. I could look forward to travelling with a separate camera op and would be finally getting some official support along the way.

Or at least that's what I was led to believe.

As soon as we hit **The Netherlands** I was chomping at the bit to get going. Compared with every other continent in the world, Europe is tiny. Some argue that it's not even a real continent; that it's merely a peninsula of Asia. But whatever it is, it's packed full of countries. 50 of 'em. I set myself two weeks to catch 'em all.

Rotterdam is the biggest port in Europe, which is probably why it took a while for me to be allowed the ship; as a consequence I missed the 8:50am train to Calais, which was part of my meticulously planned route back to Liverpool where my friends and family were waiting to welcome me home.

But Europe being Europe, things were nice and flexible. I took another train 20 minutes later, but it wasn't direct and would entail a mad dash to the cross-channel ferry.

I spent the entirety of my visit to **Belgium** on the train to Calais in **France**. Belgium's a funny old place, split linguistically between Germanic Dutch and Latin French. Over the years it has been the battleground for an obscene number of wars so the fact it was chosen to be the capital of the EU speaks volumes about how far the continent of Europe has come in the last 60 years.

The train arrived in Calais bang on time, but I missed my scheduled ferry over the English Channel by the skin of my teeth.

THE NETHERLANDS 037/200

🏛 **AMSTERDAM**

👥 16.53m

💬 Dutch

💰 Euro

💵 $51,906.46

Overall, the Dutch are the tallest people in the world.

BELGIUM 038/200

🏛 **BRUSSELS**

👥 10.8m

💬 Dutch, French, German

💰 Euro

💵 $44,996.45

According to The Hitch-Hikers Guide to the Galaxy, "Belgium" is the most offensive word in the entire universe.

As a consequence I had to wait an hour for the next one. I used the time to brush up on my French, a language that would prove essential for getting around West Africa later in my journey.

As I stepped off the ferry in **England**, beneath the white cliffs of Dover, I looked at my watch. I had travelled to more countries in five hours than I had in the previous five weeks. I took the train from Dover to London where I was met in Euston station by two of my old school friends, Michelle and Lindsey. They bought me carrot cake and coffee. It was good to be back.

Twenty minutes later I was on the train to my hometown of Liverpool. Two dozen of my friends turned up to greet me, plus my mum, dad and brother Alex, all cheering and waving flags for my arrival.

'Is he famous?', enquired a passing teenager.

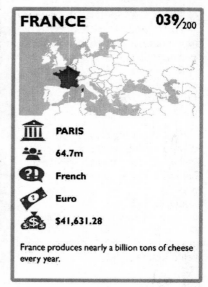

FRANCE 039/200

🏛 **PARIS**

👥 **64.7m**

💬 **French**

💵 **Euro**

💰 **$41,631.28**

France produces nearly a billion tons of cheese every year.

'Nah – more infamous', a friend replied.

ENGLAND 040/200

🏛 **LONDON**

👥 **52.6m**

💬 **English**

💵 **British Pound**

💰 **$37,075.53 (UK average)**

Technically speaking, all of England's swans belong to the Queen.

Before I knew it we were back in the old Heebie Jeebies, one of my favourite bars. I treated myself to a (much needed) shave and changed into fresh clean clothes that my mum had brought with her.

Those who had work in the morning left before midnight, whilst the more irresponsible amongst us headed to the Magnet on Hardman Street for more drinks and some good old fashioned rock n' roll.

We staggered back to my friend Scott's flat around 4am, hoping to get at least an hour's kip before we had to be at James Street Station for 6am. Why so early? Because me and my friends were about to embark on "The Five Nations Pub Crawl"; we had set ourselves 18 hours to get from England to Wales, Ireland, Northern Ireland, Scotland and back to England again.

Our motley crew was made up of myself and my always effervescent

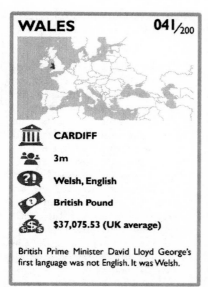

WALES

🏛 **CARDIFF**

👥 **3m**

💬 **Welsh, English**

💵 **British Pound**

💰 **$37,075.53 (UK average)**

British Prime Minister David Lloyd George's first language was not English. It was Welsh.

webmaster Leo; Scott, the designer of *The Odyssey* logo; fellow filmmakers Stuart and Laura (Laura filmed this portion of the journey for Lonely Planet); Matt the Mick, a university friend originally from Belfast; and my old school chum Hugh, who almost taught me how to sail back in Chapter 1.

The first leg of our journey took us to the city of Chester on the Welsh border. We grabbed breakfast with my friend Lucy, who was on her way to work. Then the magnificent seven of us bungled our way onto the train for the port of Holyhead in **Wales**.

Growing up in Liverpool, just a 30 minute drive from the Welsh border, meant I often took Wales for granted, but it is honestly one of my favourite places on Earth. Many of my best childhood memories involve holidays and long weekends spent in North Wales — camping, trekking, hiking, skiing, being all outdoorsy.

Technically speaking, I didn't need to include Wales in order to set the Guinness World Record (nor Scotland or Northern Ireland for that matter). But speaking as an Englishman with a Scottish first name, a Welsh surname and Irish ancestry, it was important to me to acknowledge that the United Kingdom is made up of four distinct nations, each with their own language, traditions and history. Plus my Welsh, Scottish and Northern Irish friends would probably kill me if I didn't.

A quick shot of whiskey at the ferry terminal in Holyhead and we were on the boat to Dun Laoghaire[14] in the **Republic of Ireland**.

Upon our arrival, we had just five minutes to get off the ferry and catch to the train for Dublin, or the whole plan would have gone out the window.

We ran like lunatics through the ferry terminal, slap bang into an Irish copper who wanted to know why we were filming ourselves running like lunatics through the ferry terminal. We spluttered out an excuse about being students or something, flashed our passports (thereby conclusively proving we weren't Al-Qaeda) and continued running for the train.

---

[14] Author's Note: Pronounced "dun leary".

On the platform we said goodbye to Stuart as he had work to do back in Liverpool and would be returning on the ferry while the rest of us headed north.

IRELAND 042⁄200

🏛 **DUBLIN**

👥 **4.535m**

💬 **Irish Gaelic, English**

💵 **Euro**

💰 **$51,493.52**

"Pogue Mahone", a popular name for Irish bars around the world, comes from *póg mo thóin*, meaning "kiss my arse".

NORTHERN IRELAND 043⁄200

🏛 **BELFAST**

👥 **1.8m**

💬 **English, Irish Gaelic**

💵 **British Pound**

💰 **$37,075.53 (UK average)**

Northern Ireland is often referred to as 'Ulster', but only 6 of Ulster's 9 counties are in Northern Ireland.

The Dirty Half Dozen continued on to Dublin railway station, where we each downed a pint of Guinness before jumping on another train to Belfast, the capital of **Northern Ireland**. Arriving around 4pm, we had a good 90 minutes before our ferry to Scotland. But, unbeknownst to us, a few months earlier Stena Lines had elected to move the ferry terminal from quite close to the railway station to somewhere to the left of the far side of the freakin' *moon*.

After walking for what seemed like days, we wound up at the ferry terminal with only ten minutes to spare before the damn thing left.

At this point, Leo said cheerio. He would be flying back to Liverpool because he knew that we wouldn't be returning until well after midnight and he had work in the morning.

So the Not-So-Famous Five boarded the ferry over to the port of Stranraer in Scotland. The sky was blue, the sea was calm and the bar was open. All was right in the world.

Once back on Terra Firma, we took the 7:40pm coach to Manchester in England and watched out the window the sun set over bonnie wee **Scotland**.

We pulled into Manchester coach station at 1:30am. Where can you get a world-class curry at that time on a Tuesday night? The Curry Mile in Rusholme, that's where. We piled into the Al-Nawaz restaurant where my friends Lovely Matt, Stan and Team Odyssey's Dino had been waiting patiently for us to arrive. Let the feasting commence!

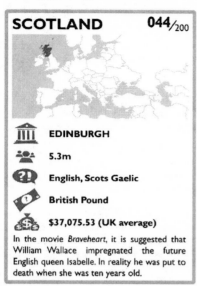

SCOTLAND 044/200

🏛 **EDINBURGH**

👥 **5.3m**

💬 **English, Scots Gaelic**

💷 **British Pound**

💰 **$37,075.53 (UK average)**

In the movie *Braveheart*, it is suggested that William Wallace impregnated the future English queen Isabelle. In reality he was put to death when she was ten years old.

What a day. Drinks in every country of the United Kingdom and Ireland followed by all the curry, rice, poppadoms and garlic naan we could eat.

We got back to Liverpool at around 5am. I said my goodbyes to my compadres and got a bit of a lump in my throat because I knew I wouldn't see them again for a year. It just goes to show that when you finally make it home, it's still there waiting for you like a pair of comfortable slippers. In many ways it was like I had never left.

I had just enough time to charge my laptop and have a conference call with Lonely Planet before sheer fatigue hit and I fell fast asleep, happy that another four countries had been ticked off the list.

I awoke in my old bedroom, the smell of home-cooking filling the room. My first thought was is that it? Is it all over? That was easy!

I rubbed my eyes and looked at the map on the wall, reminding myself that this was merely a pit stop. There were still 156 countries left to go.

I could hear downstairs that my brother Mike and my nephew Matthew had already arrived to see me, as well as my auntie Dorothy and my cousin Yvonne, so I dragged my carcass out of bed and got showered and dressed.

My mum made (a damn tasty) lamb roast for lunch and very soon it felt like a typical family meal at the Hughes household, just without the usual arguments (and the inevitable game of Trivial Pursuit). As I helped clear away the dishes, I realised that it was an hour later than I thought it was. As a consequence, I had just 45 minutes to stuff everything in my bag and get to Lime Street for my train back down to London.

I ran through all of the things that I thought I would need to keep me going for the next eight months of travel through Africa and Asia, but ten minutes isn't really enough time to make a decent checklist. It wouldn't be until I reached Denmark that I would come to realise I had only packed four pairs of underpants.

I said my hasty farewells to my family and my mum drove me to the train station, arriving with seconds to spare. Waiting for me on the train was Laura, who was there to film an interview with me for the TV show while we took the train down to London.

Once in London, I dragged Laura with me to Regent Street to buy an Interrail ticket which would allow me pretty much unlimited train travel around Europe for the following 21 days.

There was just time to meet my friend Lindsey again and eat an ice-cream on the steps of the British Museum before I had to say toodle-oo to my lovely lady friends and once again I was back on my own.

I took the 6:15pm train to Dover. It was packed full of commuters. I stuck out like a sore thumb with my scruffy bags, battered leather jacket and kangaroo skin hat. I could feel the commuters eyeballing me. *Look at this fella — he hasn't got a proper job has he?*

As I gazed out of the window, at the fields and villages whizzing by, it was like Monday evening — a mere 48 hours ago — was being rewound and put back on the shelf. Everything had gone swimmingly. I was happy to be back in Europe where travel is just — easy. But that's not to say things couldn't still go horribly wrong.

For example, the ferries from Dover stop taking foot passengers at 7pm. Did you know that?

I didn't.

Happily, the girl in the Eurolines coach office helped me out — she booked me on a bus and called the driver to make sure it would be okay to pick me up on the way to the ferry. He said yes so I was all set to travel on the 10:30pm coach to Brussels, arriving at dawn the next day.

I had a couple of hours to kill, so I headed over to a little nearby pub for my last proper "pint" for a while. I got chatting with the barman and a couple of regulars. One of them had served in the British Army and done a fair bit of travelling himself. Iraq, Sierra Leone, Kosovo etc.

As I was leaving, the army bloke shook my hand.

'Good luck scouse[15]', he said. 'When you travelling through Africa then?'

'Next month.'

'I have some advice for you: never pass up a toilet.'

The barman grinned.

'...and *never* trust a fart!'

---

[15] Editor's Note: Scouse is a meat stew that became so popular with people from Liverpool that it is synonymous for Liverpudlians and their accent.

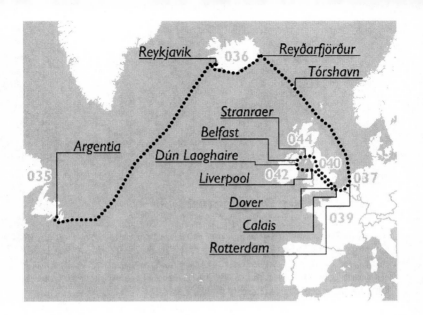

Chapter 9
Europe Is Our Playground

Thursday April 23rd 2009 was a day which, upon reflection, was about as perfect as an "Odyssey" day gets. I woke in Brussels in the wee small hours, just in time to catch the first train to Luxembourg. With a little help from the Deutsche Bahn website and seat61.com, it was time to kick *The Odyssey Expedition* into high gear.

I arrived in **Luxembourg** at dawn and hopped on the next available train to Hamburg. I'm sure Luxembourg is delightful, but at this point of my adventure, it wasn't even a pit-stop. This is what I always envisaged *The Odyssey Expedition* to be — a non-stop race around the world.

The Caribbean may have thrown a rather large spanner in those works, but if I couldn't get to every country in Europe in under three weeks, I was most certainly not the backpacker I believed myself to be.

The sky was blue and the train was fast and before I knew it I

LUXEMBOURG   045/200

🏛 **LUXEMBOURG**

👥 **497,783**

❓ **French, German, Luxembourgish**

💵 **Euro**

💰 **$100,729.28**

Luxembourg is the last surviving sovereign Grand Duchy in the world.

was in Hamburg, **Germany**, stuffing a hamburger into my face. I looked for something authentically Hamburgian, but in the end I settled for a Whopper from Burger King.

I had barely wiped the grease from my lips before I was on the train to Copenhagen, the gorgeous little capital of Denmark.

To get from Germany to Denmark the entire train rolls on board the *Vogelfluglinie*, a ferry from Puttgarden to Rødby. I don't think I've ever been on a train on a boat before. It's rather fun.

Later as we crossed the Storstrøm bridge from the island of Falster to the island of Zealand in **Denmark**, the train driver let me sit in the cab, surrounded by a proper sci-fi-looking control panel. I never wanted to be a train driver (I wanted to be an astronaut, *still do*) but there is something marvellously satisfying about the idea of pushing a lever and the train taking itself wherever the rails dictate. The tracks don't swerve in front of you, they don't pull out without looking, they don't sit behind you and flash their lights because you're not going fast enough, they just take you where you need to be.

GERMANY 046/200

<table>
<tr><td>🏛</td><td>BERLIN</td></tr>
<tr><td>👥</td><td>81.9m</td></tr>
<tr><td>❓</td><td>German</td></tr>
<tr><td>💵</td><td>Euro</td></tr>
<tr><td>💰</td><td>$41,668.79</td></tr>
</table>

The German word *donaudampfschifffahrts-gesellschaftskapitaenswitwe* means "widow of a Danube steamboat company captain".

Once in Copenhagen central station I met my cousin Christian, the chap largely responsible for getting my ginger ass across the Atlantic. He treated me to a beer (I should really have treated him, but he was quite insistent) and afterwards dropped me at his parents' house in the suburbs. My Auntie Christine married a Danish guy called Jens back in the 1970s and they're very much "whenever you're in Copenhagen...!" As a result, Denmark is probably the country outside of the UK I've visited the most number of times since I was a kid.

DENMARK 047/200

<table>
<tr><td>🏛</td><td>COPENHAGEN</td></tr>
<tr><td>👥</td><td>5.523m</td></tr>
<tr><td>❓</td><td>Danish</td></tr>
<tr><td>💵</td><td>Danish Krone</td></tr>
<tr><td>💰</td><td>$57,895.86</td></tr>
</table>

The Danish have a word for that nice cosy feeling of togetherness when you're relaxing with friends: "hygge".

By the time I had been fed, scrubbed myself clean and done my research into the next leg of the journey it was 2am. Just five hours later I was rubbing the sleep out of my eyes as my Uncle Jens ran me into town to catch the 8:23am express service to Oslo, via Gothenburg in **Sweden**.

Now I wouldn't be going all the way to Oslo. I only needed to *step foot* in each country, not sit for high tea with its head of state. My plan for

Norway was to get off the train at the first stop after the Norwegian border, then take the next train back to the Swedish city of Gothenburg.

The only problem was that my train was due in at 12:48pm. The train back to Gothenburg left at 12:50pm. A connection time of two minutes.

These are super-long-distance trains with journey times that exceed six hours. If I missed my connection, I'd also miss the ferry to Finland, which would put an extra day on my journey time. *Come on, famous Scandinavian efficiency, don't let me down!*

As the train approached the town of Halden, my watch read 12:47pm. I stood at the door raring to go. At precisely 12:48pm the doors opened. I bolted off the train and over the tracks to the opposite platform.

As things turned out, I could have sauntered. I could have bought a coffee and a Danish (ha!). I could have recited the "Winter of Discontent" speech from Richard III. There's a lot you can do in two minutes. The train was bang on time.

Soon enough I was back in Gothenburg. I had a couple of hours before my connection to Stockholm, so I checked out the vibrant old town, which I found surprisingly free of goths. Although I did spot the odd emo.

Sweden is known for being quite a pricey place to visit. Lucky for me I found a pub that had a free buffet for Gothenburg's overworked office workers looking to *tack Gud* it's Friday.

SWEDEN 048/200

🏛️ **STOCKHOLM**

👥 **9.299m**

❓ **Swedish**

💵 **Swedish Krona**

💰 **$46,206.94**

Young Swedish girls dress as witches and go out trick-or-treating for Easter, not Halloween.

NORWAY 049/200

🏛️ **OSLO**

👥 **4.829m**

❓ **Norwegian**

💵 **Norwegian Krone**

💰 **$78,457.38**

Together with Liverpool, Stavanger in Norway was the 2008 European Capital of Culture. While Liverpool has The Beatles, Stavanger has a museum dedicated to sardines.

Maybe I blended right in with the office workers or maybe everyone was too polite to say anything. Either way, I left with my face thoroughly stuffed full of BBQ chicken.

Then I hopped on the choo-choo to Stockholm, about three and a half hours east. Upon my arrival I found the nearest hostel and checked in for the night. I found myself sharing a dorm with a bunch of European backpackers getting dolled up for a night on the town. It was the birthday of one of their number and they were going out for drinkies. Somehow I got invited along.

We staggered back to the youth hostel at about 4am. I was a little miffed that I hadn't randomly ended up in a Swedish sauna, yet was acutely aware that the ferry to Finland would be leaving in just under three hours.

The ferry was insane. Talk about 24-hour party people! The Swedes and the Finns had transformed the ship into a floating house party. The aim? To get as drunk as humanly possible on duty-free booze. The cabin corridors looked like student digs and reeked of all the alcoholidays come at once. Pretty much everyone who attempted to speak to me fell over before they could finish their sentence. Most of them didn't even get off the boat when it arrived in Stockholm. They were just there to get wasted; a noble ambition, and one that I can happily report that they totally achieved.

Under normal circumstances, I would have wholeheartedly joined in with the festivities — dancing on the ceiling, popping balloons, showing complete strangers "my appendix scar" etc., but my lack of sleep finally caught up with me and I crashed out early in a particularly uncomfortable chair.

When I awoke I was quite possibly the only sober person on board, other than the Captain (I hope). We reached the port of Turku in **Finland** that evening and from there I took the 7:45pm train to Helsinki. It got in at 10pm, but in a bit of unfortunate timing, the last ferry boat to Estonia left at 10pm as well, so I'd have to stay the night in Helsinki and take the first ferry in the morning.

FINLAND 050/200

🏛 OSLO

👥 5.339m

❓ Finnish

💵 Euro

🏍 $47,104.32

The cost of traffic and speed violations in Finland are calculated as a percentage of the offending driver's income. Fines of over €200,000 have been handed out.

Even more unfortunate was that every hostel in Helsinki city centre was full. When I finally found somewhere to stay, I didn't have a clue where it was — the lady who ran the hostel said something about an island. Now, there was another backpackers on a "sort-of" island to the east of the city, so I assumed it would be close to there. So I walked. And walked. And walked.

The fine, clear spring day had given way to a frosty cold night and the chills were running down my legs. When I finally got to the backpackers listed in the Lonely Planet, I found out that no, the lady *had* meant an island, not a *"sort-of"* island but a proper one called Suommelinna — one that you could only reach by boat. By now it was past eleven. Luckily, the ferry ran once an hour until 2am, so I headed down to the harbour and waited.

It turned out that the island of Suommelinna was a UNESCO world heritage site, an old fort from back in the bad old days when Sweden and Russia liked nothing more than to knock seven shades of crap out of each other every few years. The youth hostel was rather spartan, but it beat sleeping in a bus shelter.

The ferry to Tallinn, the capital of **Estonia**, was quick and easy and I arrived around noon. What a beautiful town! Tallinn, you saucy little thing you! Where have you been hiding?! I took a taxi across the city and caught a bus to a place called Narva on the border with Russia.

Now I didn't have a Russian visa for a couple of reasons. One being that they cost £150. The other being that they cost £150. But I figured I could go over the border to talk to the border guards. Even if I get knocked back, then I've technically stepped foot in the country, yeah?

ESTONIA 051/200

🏛 **TALLINN**

👥 1.335m

Estonian

Euro

$14,717.42

Public transport around Tallinn is free.

However, the border post, and there was only one, was on the European side of the river. Fences, CCTV and border guards were everywhere. The Schengen free travel area this was not.

I had a look at a map and discovered that further down the river it runs either side of an abandoned industrial complex situated on the Russian side of the border. The water was pretty shallow. I thought I could wade over to this island and wade back without arousing suspicion.

I thought this because I'm an idiot.

I walked along the riverbank until I saw what I was after — a strip of concrete, possibly an old ford, half submerged in the flowing water, leading to this magical island. I could just amble across — as long as I didn't attempt to scale the small cliff on the far side of the river, I figured I'd be fine.

I was about halfway across when the flares started going off.

IDIOT!! WHAT WAS I THINKING? **Russia!** Putin! Gulags! The KGB!

I trotted back towards the safety of the European Union as nonchalantly as I could. *Just keep walking, Graham, you'll be fine, you're just a tourist who got a bit lost.*

I could hear sirens as I reached the river bank. Two police officers came running at me, hands on their holsters.

Before I knew it, I was whisked away to a tumble-down concrete estate on the outskirts of Narva. I just acted dumb (not too hard!) and explained that I read the map wrong and was trying to get to another island in the middle of the river — which was still in Estonia. That island was actually half a mile downstream from where I was trying to cross.

RUSSIA 052/200

🏛 **MOSCOW**

👥 141.9m

💬 Russian

💰 Russian Ruble

💵 $8,615.67

Every year on September 12, Russian workers are given the day off so they can stay home and have sex.

The good news was that these guys were Estonians, not the Russians. They told me that if I'd been caught by the Russians, I would have been held for three days because they would assume I was a British spy.

The border guys were really nice, they didn't shout and scream. They even gave me cake and orange juice until a lawyer got there.

When the lawyer arrived we had a quick chat. I think they were just concerned that I was exiting Russia illegally, but my pockets where stuffed full of evidence that I had arrived in Estonia that day. They photocopied all my stuff and made damn sure I was on the next bus back to Tallinn. Given that Estonia is now a frontier of the European Union, I guess they aren't too impressed with reckless ginger backpackers who don't seem to understand that some borders are a matter of life and death. For instance, if you have the misfortune of bordering Russia.

Once on the bus I checked my GPS log. I made it just about far enough across the river to say I had stepped foot in Russia.

Yes yes, it's perhaps a bit of a cheat. After all, Russia (all 11 time zones of it) *is* the biggest country on Earth. But my task was just to step foot in every country, and since nobody had done it before, *I got to make up the rules.*

I didn't want anybody trying to beat my record (if I was to set it) to feel obliged to stay the night in a warzone. Although if it makes you feel any better, this episode of brazen stupidity would eventually come back to well and truly bite me on the ass.

As soon as I got back to Tallinn I took the first international bus heading south.

Quick note to future surface-based globe trotters: before embarking on an overnight bus from Estonia to Lithuania via **Latvia**, stock up on water, as there will be no refreshment stops along the way. Don't make the same mistake I did! I almost died of thirst.

When I got off the bus in Vilnius, the capital of **Lithuania**, I was so thirsty I could have drunk a warm can of *Dr Pepper* and said 'thank you' afterwards.

After quenching my thirst courtesy of a wonderfully co-operative vending machine, I walked across the bus terminal and randomly ran into Lynn, the mum of my old school friend Michelle who had met me in London for coffee and carrot cake precisely one week earlier! She was on her way to the airport after a weekend away with one of her mates in Lithuania. It certainly is a small world.

I wished her a safe flight back to Liverpool, then set my sights on country number 55: Belarus!

Now Belarus is a tricky one. Europe's last outpost of old-school totalitarianism, the KGB is alive and well and living in Belarus. They want to be Russian even more than Russia does. With a dictator in charge since 1992 and political dissidents locked away without trial, the Belarusians like to party like it's 1959 — so they

LATVIA 053/200

🏛 **RIGA**

👥 **2.142m**

💬 **Latvian**

💵 **Euro**

💰 **$12,082.06**

Latvia has an entire museum dedicated to history's greatest teller of tall tales, Baron von Munchausen.

LITHUANIA 054/200

🏛 **VILNIUS**

👥 **3.163m**

💬 **Lithuanian**

💵 **Euro**

💰 **$11,713.90**

The Lithuanian language is the oldest of all living languages in Europe, predating Greek, Latin, German, Celtic and Slav.

presumably don't take kindly to amateur adventurer-types like myself thinking it a lark to waddle into their territory.

Thinking it best to avoid any more of the previous day's shenanigans, I took a taxi to the Belarusian embassy to get myself an official transit visa. But the embassy was closed until Wednesday.

What do I do? Sit on my hands in Vilnius for two days and then have to wait another 24 hours for the visa to come through?

I decided to go to the nearest border crossing and check whether it was as impenetrable as the one at Narva. I took a local bus which dropped me in the town of Medininkai, three kilometres from the border. I had to walk the last bit. Luckily I had some water with me this time.

I got to the European side of the border crossing. There was nobody there. I just kept walking until I passed the sign that said "Welcome To **Belarus**".

I thought I would see how far I could push it. I got to the Belarusian checkpoint and asked if, since the embassy was closed, I could buy a visa on the border. The officer asked to look at my passport and rather than just saying 'Nah, go away', he took me into a small room and began scanning my passport over and over again, while his colleagues made numerous phone calls and asked me a lot of questions.

BELARUS 055/200

🏛 **MINSK**

👥 9.507m

💬 Belarusian, Russian

💵 Belarusian Ruble

💰 $5,176.04

The highest point in Belarus is Mount Dzyarzhynskaya, which measures just 346 metres above sea level.

I did my best to keep calm. But then the officer, in the middle of a rather animated telephone conversation, wrote the word "NARVA" on a piece of paper... and I felt the floor drop away.

Oh.

Hang on.

It doesn't say NARVA — it's not even English, it's Cyrillic, plus you're reading it upside-down. You numpty.

The officer got off the phone and said in broken English, 'Yes the embassy is closed until Wednesday, you can get a visa then'.

As I was being escorted back across the border I asked if I could get a photo of me standing next to the "Welcome To Belarus" sign. The guard was having none of it.

But it was worth a try.

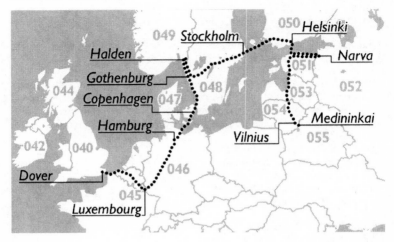

Chapter 10
Dude, Where's My Backpack?

I trotted back over to Lithuania and slogged the three kilometres to the bus stop. Returning to Vilnius in good time, I went for some good old-fashioned Eastern European meat n' potatoes in the old town, taking in the Gates of Dawn and the old city walls along the way.

Vilnius is pretty damn breathtaking for a place I had barely heard of before embarking on this ridiculous adventure.

That evening I took the overnight bus to Warsaw, the capital of **Poland**.

My coach arrived in the capital half an hour early, so it wasn't even a rush to the station for the first train to Bratislava. The train was proper old-school where you sit in wood-panelled compartments with six seats in each.

POLAND 056/200

🏛 **WARSAW**

👥 **38.15m**

💬 **Polish**

💵 **Polish Złoty**

💰 **$11,440.58**

No. 303 ("Kościuszko") Polish Fighter Squadron of the RAF was the highest-scoring squadron of the Battle of Britain.

I've been to The **Czech Republic** half a dozen times in my life. The first time it was still Czechoslovakia. The most recent time it had just become 'Czechia'. I wish they'd make up their minds.

But whatever they're calling themselves, Prague is one of the most magical cities in a continent packed full of magical cities. Plus the beer is incredibly cheap. What's not to love? This time, however, my experience would primarily consist of looking out of the train window at fields whizzing by en route to Bratislava, the capital of **Slovakia**.

Once I arrived in Bratislava I had a few hours to sit, drink a coffee and read up on where I was going to go next. Two of the most powerful resources at my disposal were my copy of Lonely Planet's *Europe on a Shoestring* and the Deutsche Bahn website, which may well be the most useful website of all time, ever. Well, if you're interrailing around Europe, that is. (It's not great for porn.)

You put in where you want to go (Edinburgh to Athens is perfectly acceptable) and then it will come up with every conceivable route, times, ticket prices, everything. When one is tearing across Europe like a man possessed, it's a lifesaver.

Next up: the 2:33pm to the capital of **Hungary**... Budapest!

I threw my bag into the luggage rack in my second-class compartment and paid the conductor a couple of extra euro to let me sit in first-class so I could make use of the electrical socket and provide some much-needed charge for my laptop and video camera.

A few hours later and the train rumbled into Budapest, or, to be more precise, Pest. The town of Buda lies on the opposite side of the river Danube.

As the train came to a halt I tried to get back to second-class, but my way was barred by the restaurant car, which was now

CZECH REPUBLIC 057/200

🏛 **PRAGUE**

👥 10.44m

❓ Czech

💵 Czech Koruna

💰 $19,698.49

The Czech Republic tops the charts for beer consumption per capita – it's over twice that of the UK.

SLOVAKIA 058/200

🏛 **BRATISLAVA**

👥 5.4m

❓ Slovak

💵 Euro

💰 $16.455.18

Slovakia has the highest number of castles per capita in the world.

closed. No big deal — I waited until we stopped, got off the train and then got back on again on the far side of the restaurant car.

Er, where's my bag?

Frantic, I searched up and down the coaches — nothing, nada, zip. It had GONE.

My clothes. My sleeping bag. My spare glasses. *The video tapes for the last few weeks!!!*

Everything.

Gone.

Vanished. Into the ether.

To make matters worse, my connecting train to Bucharest left in less than 20 minutes. And the next one was not for another two days.

I asked the Hungarians working on the train. They told me to go to the ticket booth. I went to the ticket booth. They told me to go to the station manager. I went to the station manager. The station manager told me to go to the police. I went to the police. They told me to go to information. I went to information. They told me to go to left luggage. I went to left luggage. They told me that they couldn't help. By now, it was just minutes until the train for Romania left from the very far platform of the station.

HUNGARY 059/200

🏛 **BUDAPEST**

👥 10.02m

💬 Hungarian

💵 Hungarian Forint

💰 $12,906.75

Hungarian sculptor and architect Erno Rubik's famous cube has 43,252,003,274,489,856,000 possible permutations – that's enough cubes to cover the Earth's surface... 275 times.

Up to this point, *The Odyssey* had been one difficult decision after another. Some had worked out (Norway) some hadn't (Cuba), but this was crunch time — I had only seconds to work out the permutations.

Okay, somebody wouldn't have stolen it. There were no valuables in there (it's got a toilet seat strapped to it, for heaven's sake!). So that left me with two options — somebody took it by mistake (it's got a toilet seat strapped to it, for heaven's sake!) or that the conductor of the train had picked it up.

Maybe everyone else in the compartment got off early and he saw a lonely bag sitting up in the luggage rack and thought somebody had left it behind.

Either way, I would have to stay in Budapest to get it back. And that would mean losing two days.

However, if it did show up — it had a stack of my business cards in it so I wouldn't be difficult to contact — I could always return to Budapest when I returned this way (kinda) to visit Austria.

Sod it.

I ran for the train.

Once on board, I found a compartment with an empty seat and took it, my face bright red, sweating like a pregnant nun, trying not to make eye-contact with the other passengers. My throat was dry and I was so hungry I would have eaten a cold Pot Noodle from the bin.

I barely had time to take my coat off when a conductor came and wanted to see my reservation, but with all the lost-bag shenanigans I hadn't had time to make one. To make matters worse I didn't have enough change to pay the conductor for the reservation — I only had a single hundred euro note, and Hungary doesn't even use the euro, it has its own currency, the forint.

Just as all seemed lost, a fellow passenger named Delia stepped in and paid my reservation fee. She also gave me a carton of juice and some chocolate eggs to eat.

What an angel.

It's times like this that I'm reminded just how bloody wonderful people can be.

Once I was settled I fired up my laptop. There was an e-mail waiting for me from a chap called Ors.

Subject: I have your luggage!

Thankfully, it wasn't a ransom demand. This guy had picked up my bag thinking it had been left on the train by accident, tried to give it to the police, the police refused to take it (seriously) so he had taken it home thinking that I could come meet him and pick it up.

Only I was now a good fifty miles away from Budapest heading into Romania.

I replied asking him to drop the backpack off at Keleti station's left-luggage office. I would return to Budapest that weekend to pick it up. But not before visiting Romania, Moldova, Ukraine, Bulgaria, Greece, Macedonia, Kosovo, Serbia, Montenegro, Albania, Croatia, Bosnia and Slovenia.

Christ my pants are going to smell.

The train pulled into Bucharest, the capital of **Romania** around lunchtime the next day. I headed to the coach station to catch a bus to the town of Galaţi, which is conveniently situated near the borders of both Moldova and Ukraine. If I timed it right, I could hop across both borders in about an hour, no visas required, and then be back in Bucharest in time for the 8:03pm train to Sofia in Bulgaria. Or at least that was the plan.

I arrived in Galați around 2pm. Getting out of Romania took half an hour, which was quite strange considering that (a) Romania is in the EU and (b) nobody else was attempting to cross the border at that time.

Eventually, through broken English and hand gestures I discovered what the holdup was. I couldn't cross the bridge into Moldova without being in a car, so the border guards were waiting for one to come along. When a car did ultimately turn up, the guards spoke to the driver and herded me into the back. Whether or not the driver wanted me in the car I will never know.

Once over the Prut river I had to get myself stamped into **Moldova**. It took about an hour. They scanned my passport with every instrument at their disposal, infrared, ultra violet, electron microscope. They seemed convinced it was a fake. Or maybe they wanted me to pay some "hurry up" tax. (That'll be the day!)

Once in Moldova there was a two kilometre walk before I hit the border with Ukraine. Looking around, I could have been anywhere in Europe. I was surrounded by fields; some in Romania, some in Moldova and some in Ukraine. I wondered just how much blood had been spilt in the drawing of these imaginary lines. I wondered if future generations will believe it was worth it.

ROMANIA 060/200

🏛 **BUCHAREST**

👥 20.37m

🗨 Romanian

💵 Romanian Leu

💰 $8,068.96

Vlad The Impaler's cruelty is renowned, with some reports that he killed 40,000 people in his lifetime. Nevertheless, he's seen as a bit of a hero in Romania.

MOLDOVA 061/200

🏛 **CHIȘINĂU**

👥 3.566m

🗨 Romanian

💵 Moldovan Leu

💰 $1,525.53

Moldova is the only country to have an extinct animal on their flag – it's an aurochs, a type of giant cow, the last of which died in 1627.

When I reached the border with **Ukraine**, I had another half-hour wait before the Moldovan border guards would stamp me out.

On the Ukrainian side of the checkpoint, I tried to get a stamp, just to make things extra official for the nice folks at Guinness World Records.

Instead, I got shouted at by a grumpy Ukrainian border guard for wasting his time. The fact that, once again, there was nobody else at the border didn't seem to faze him.

Oh well, no stamp, but at least I got my GPS reading and a photo. On the way back through Moldova my video camera battery died.

I had left the charger and spare batteries in my backpack which was now over 450 miles away.

By the time I had returned to Galați, it was dark. I had spent a whopping *four* hours getting over the borders. I had long missed the last train back to Bucharest, so I settled down for the night in a big old concrete hotel, built in the 1970s. I think I was the only guest.

The girl on reception was nice though. She made me sandwiches.

I was up an' at 'em for the 5am train to Bucharest. Arriving around 8am, I went on a quick mission to find a new charger for my camcorder. My taxi driver took me to past former dictator Nicolae Ceaușescu's palace (now called the Palace of the Parliament) — and I can report that it *is* ridiculously big.

UKRAINE 062/200

🏛 **KIEV**

👥 **46.05m**

💬 **Ukrainian**

💵 **Ukrainian Hryvnia**

💰 **$2,545.48**

Contrary to popular belief, Chicken Kiev did not originate in Ukraine, but from a 19th century French recipe.

BULGARIA 063/200

🏛 **SOFIA**

👥 **7.444m**

💬 **Bulgarian**

💵 **Bulgarian Lev**

💰 **$6,738.10**

The unique taste of Bulgarian yoghurt comes from the bacteria used to make it, *Lactobacillus bulgaricus*, which is only found naturally in Bulgarian air.

New battery charger in hand, I raced back to the railway station and bagged myself a one-way reservation for Thessaloniki in Greece, passing through **Bulgaria** along the way.

It was an overnight train with exceptionally comfortable bunk-bed compartments. Give me a night on a train over one on a plane any day.

One of the guys in my compartment was from Transylvania, and he had the pointiest canines I've ever seen. Best of all, he was called Vlad.

Unlike his namesake, this Vlad was a decent chap travelling down to Athens with his girlfriend. We shared a few beers and put the world to rights.

But still, I slept with a pillow around my neck, just in case.

The train rolled into Thessaloniki, **Greece** before dawn. It was raining hard. I guess I took too long getting off the train because it started moving again!

I ran down the corridor to find a conductor and he told me not to worry; they were just "parking" the train. I ended up having to walk half a kilometre back up the tracks to the train station from the shunting yard.

I had a few hours to mooch about the city, say hello to the Aegean Sea and drink an overpriced coffee before

GREECE 064/200

🏛 **ATHENS**

👥 **11.19m**

❓ **Greek**

💵 **Euro**

💰 **$29,483.73**

The very first Olympic champion was a cook named Coroebus who won the sprint race in 776 B.C.

returning to the station to take the train to Macedonia. It was lucky that I was taking an international train — all the domestic ones were not running that day. The drivers were on strike.

The journey to Skopje[16], the capital of Macedonia was only supposed to take a couple of hours. However, the Macedonian border guards had other ideas. At the frontier I found myself waiting on a freezing-cold platform for a doctor to show up and confirm that I didn't have swine flu.

I was joined in my misery by an American backpacker named McClane. He was also heading towards Kosovo.

Time and tide wait for no man, and so the train left for Skopje without us. The next one wasn't for another five hours. Eventually the doctor came and asked us if we were dying (funnily enough, no), and we were finally stamped into **Macedonia**, or to use its official title, the Former Yugoslavian Republic of Macedonia or FYROM.

The wonderfully silly acronym "FYROM" was dreamt up by the Greek government, who were concerned that people might confuse the *country* of Macedonia with the *Greek region* of Macedonia, like we often mix up the country of Mongolia with the Chinese region of

---

[16] Author's Note: Pronounced "skopia".

Mongolia, or the country of Colombia with the District of Columbia.

Don't dare tell them there are four separate countries with "Guinea" in their name — it'll blow their *minds*.

In any case, since the train was long gone we had to take the bus to the capital, wasting even more valuable time. Didn't these people realise I had another 135 countries to visit?!

But it wasn't all bad news. The bus to Pristina, the capital of **Kosovo**, was pretty much ready to go as soon as we got to Skopje bus station. I just had time to stuff a burger-and-fries-in-one-huge-bun into my mouth before I was off again.

This is the point at which pretty much every Serbian reader will put this book down. And then possibly burn it, or, if they're reading this on a Kindle or iPad, smash it and send me the bill.

Note to self: leave this bit out of the Cyrillic version.

But look, plucky little Kosovo has been recognised as an independent state, free from Serbian rule, by over 100 countries, including mine. So I had to visit. Hey, I don't make the rules. *Well, actually I do.* And if you go around "ethnically cleansing" areas of your country, you really can't complain when the people affected by the aforementioned "cleansing" decide they'd (on balance) be better off not being a part of your country anymore.

MACEDONIA 065/200

🏛 **SKOPJE**

👥 **2.101m**

❓ **Macedonian**

💵 **Macedonian Denar**

💰 **$4,433.86**

The Cyrillic alphabet, used in 12 countries across Eurasia, was developed in the 9th century by Macedonian brothers Saint Cyril and Saint Methodius.

KOSOVO 066/200

🏛 **PRISTINA**

👥 **1.761m**

❓ **Albanian, Serbian**

💵 **Euro**

💰 **$3,209.73**

In May 2009, Kosovo as a sovereign nation was just over one year old.

Upon my arrival in Pristina, I found myself in a bit of a quandary. I had bought a ticket for the bus into Serbia, but the driver wouldn't let me on board. Luckily, an American KFOR[17] guy was on hand to translate the situation.

Serbia may have normalised relations with Kosovo, but they still don't recognise Kosovo as an independent state. They see it as part of Serbia. Since I entered Kosovo (*i.e. Serbia*) from Macedonia, the guards on the Kosovo/Serbian border would want to know how on Earth I managed to enter "their" country without getting a passport stamp, and, of course, not let me travel any further.

This all meant I couldn't get on the bus to Serbia.

So I took the bus to **Montenegro** instead. You know what I like about Montenegro?

Montenegro don't give two hoots!

The bus dropped me off in a nowhere town in Montenegro called Rožaje in the middle of the night. I was assured that from there it would be possible to hail the late bus that ran from Podgorica to Belgrade in **Serbia**. I was the only one waiting. The constant drizzle had not abated since Thessaloniki. After a couple of hours a bus finally trundled towards me along the deserted road.

'Belgrade?', I asked the driver. He nodded. Thank goodness. I climbed on board.

MONTENEGRO 067/200

🏛 **PODGORICA**

👥 619,408

💬 Montenegrin

💵 Euro

💰 $6,713.08

Upon seeing Montenegro's shores, Lord Byron wrote: "At the birth of our planet the most beautiful encounter between land and sea must have been on the Montenegrin coast."

SERBIA 068/200

🏛 **BELGRADE**

👥 7.321m

💬 Serbian

💵 Serbian Dinar

💰 $5,821.31

Famed Serb inventor and/or wizard Nikola Tesla was born in the town of Smiljan, modern day Croatia.

I was stamped out of Montenegro no problem. The Serbian side, well, let's just say they were not impressed with my entry stamp for Kosovo.

---

[17] Editor's Note: The KFOR is the Kosovo Force, a NATO-led peacekeeping organization in Kosovo since 1999.

The border guard opened his drawer and took out a special stamp for me — the one that said "VOID" in Cyrillic. He inked the stamp and slammed it down into my passport.

I asked why he had just annulled one of my old entry stamps for Thailand.

He looked at my passport and smiled. I smiled. It was past midnight and I guess he was tired. Still, he found my Kosovo stamp and stamped over it anyway, just to be sure.

I got off at the first town over the border, Novi Padar, only to find they had not dropped me at the bus station. It was now 1am, not a soul around and I didn't really have a clue what to do. Luckily, a battered sign pointed the way to the bus station, so I started

ALBANIA   069/200

🏛 **TIRANA**

👥 **2.884m**

❓ **Albanian**

💰 **Albanian Lek**

💵 **$4,175.78**

Albanians shake their heads to say yes and nod to say no.

walking through the rain. It was a good kilometre away and when I got there, I was greeted by nought but a sleeping vagrant whose epic farts must have registered on the Richter scale.

Presently, a bus pulled in. I asked the driver if there were going to be any more buses back to Montenegro that night. He didn't speak much English, but I got the impression that there were no more stopping at the bus station that night, but if I went back to where the bus I was on had dropped me off, I could flag a one down from the road.

Urgh.

So I walked back along the deserted highway, pursued by stray dogs. I waited in the dark beside a huge puddle on the main road. Would I be waiting there all night? Would it ever stop raining?

After twenty long minutes, a bus came by. The illuminated sign in the front said "Podgorica". I practically threw myself in front of it just to make sure it stopped.

I got into Podgorica so early the next morning that my legs were shaking. I immediately hopped a taxi to the nearby border with **Albania**. My driver, Ratko, was a top bloke — he didn't speak much English, but he got the gist of what I was doing and was happy to take me into Albania for a couple of minutes to stomp around and get some footage and GPS readings to prove that I had actually been there.

I first came along this road a couple of years earlier on another adventure with my mate Stan. It was dark and we thought that we were in the middle of farmland or something because there wasn't a single light on in the distance. The road was so awful we were forced to turn back.

Well, I guess if we had waited until light, we might have discovered that the land surrounding the Montenegrin-Albanian border is a glorious national park filled with lakes and mountains. Also, I'm happy to report that the road has been fixed. Ratko and I spent a good twenty minutes enjoying the clear mountain air before returning to Montenegro.

Before long I was on the bus to Herceg Novi near the border with Croatia. I just had time to stuff some damn fine Montenegrin food into my face before tackling the (mercifully straight-forward) border crossing into **Croatia** at Dubrovnik.

Fans of *Game of Thrones* already know Dubrovnik reasonably well, since it doubles for King's Landing. It's a gorgeous walled city, a UNESCO World Heritage site and one of my favourite places in the world. But alas, I wasn't there to sightsee.

CROATIA 070/200

🏛 **ZAGREB**

👥 **4.429m**

❓ **Croatian**

💵 **Croatian Kuna**

💰 **$14,142.15**

Neckties originated in Croatia – hence the 'cravat'.

At this point I was a third of the way through the year, and a third of the way through the countries I needed to visit. That sounded great, but not everywhere in the world is as easy to get around as Europe. Consider this, in less than two weeks I had visited as many countries as I had in *three months* in The Americas. But I still had all the countries of Africa, Asia and The Pacific left to go. To be honest, the chances of me finishing the adventure in just one year were becoming increasingly slim.

Soon enough I was on a bus heading north along the coast from Dubrovnik to the city of Split. Happily, we would be passing through the town of Neum along the way. Why did that make me happy? Because it meant I could tick off country number 71: **Bosnia and Herzegovina**.

Something I brushed upon earlier is how countries can be damned by geography. And there is nothing more damning than being landlocked and surrounded by unfriendly neighbours.

Just ask Afghanistan.

Unfettered access to the sea is utterly essential for nations struggling to find their feet — or else trading with the rest of the world becomes an uphill struggle.

This isn't news; people have been aware of it for centuries, which is why the Nuem corridor dates back to 1699.

Nuem allows Bosnia and Herzegovina access to the Adriatic, but it also splits Croatia in two. Since Croatia is now part of the European Union, border controls on either side of the corridor have tightened and there's talk of the Croatians building a big horrible bridge to

BOSNIA & HERZEGOVINA 071/200

SARAJEVO

3.853m

Bosnian, Croatian, Serbian

Bosnia and Herzegovina Convertible Mark

$4,480.38

It was the assassination of Archduke Franz Ferdinand in Sarajevo that became the catalyst for the start of World War I.

bypass the town as well as the Bosnians building a big horrible container port in this otherwise picture-postcard seaside town. My hope is that Bosnia and Herzegovina join the EU sooner rather than later, negating the need for border controls, a bridge, or a container port.

The city of Split was as stunning as I had been led to believe, all stone passageways and old buildings. If Harry Potter was born in Yugoslavia, I'm guessing this is where he'd hang out. They even have a whopping great big statue of a wizard in the town centre.

There were no trains north until about 10pm, so I marched off to the local pub. Luckily, the owner of the pub was a fellow Evertonian[18], so, well, it was free drinks all round.

I staggered to the railway station just in time to get onto the night train to Zagreb. It would be getting in at silly o'clock in the morning and from there I could take an early train to Slovenia.

I know what you're thinking, haven't you already been to Slovenia?! Nope, that was *Slovakia*. **Slovenia** is a completely different country that just happens to sound almost the same and has pretty much the same flag (white-blue-red horizontal tricolour with a shield on the left).

Once again, if I had more time I would have visited the beautiful (yet unpronounceable) capital city Ljubljana and enjoyed a glass of sweet Slovene wine at the old Skeleton Bar on the Ljubljanica river. But on this occasion, I simply passed through on the Zagreb-Vienna train.

---

[18] Editor's Note: Everton is a football club based in Liverpool and their fans are called Evertonians.

Don't hate me!

All things being equal, I would have then travelled west through **Austria** off on the way to my 74th country — Liechtenstein. However, the necessity of retrieving my backpack meant that I was forced to instead head east through Vienna back to Budapest in Hungary. This added a whopping 750km onto my journey. But it would be worth it. I *really* needed to change my underwear.

Upon my arrival in the Hungarian capital I would only have just ten minutes to run off the train, grab my bag and board the train back to Vienna.

If I missed that particular train, I'd miss the connecting night train to Liechtenstein and end up waiting until the next day. Timing was critical.

As my train approached Budapest's Keleti station. I guessed which side the train platform would be on. I guessed wrong! The station was a sea of people. Left Luggage is on Platform 6. Not far. I ran. *Christ it's hot in here.* Through the barrier. The jacket wrapped around my waist dropped to the floor, tripping me, but my cat-like reflexes honed to perfection in a thousand mosh-pits prevented me from going arse-

SLOVENIA 072/200

🏛 LJUBLJANA

👥 2.04m

❓ Slovenian

💵 Euro

💰 $24,633.80

In some cities, Slovene embassy staff meet their Slovak counterparts at least once a month to exchange wrongly addressed mail.

AUSTRIA 073/200

🏛 VIENNA

👥 8.365m

❓ German

💵 Euro

💰 $47,526.27

At the end of *The Sound of Music*, the Van Trapp family "escape" the Nazis by crossing the border at Salzberg. That would actually take them into Germany.

over-tit. I grabbed the jacket off the floor. Hundreds of commuters coming the other way. I was fighting against the flow like a goddamn salmon swimming upstream. I zigged and I zagged, I looked at my watch — *six minutes.*

I reached Left Luggage...

Oh no.

Where's the guy I spoke to the other day?

He's not here!

Just a toothless old lady who doesn't speak a word of English. Panic panic panic. I tried to explain as best I could, gesticulating wildly. The seconds ticked away. Let me over there, I'll find it, it'll be there, I promise. *I know it's here.* She let me into the back room, dusty old shelves from before the war, shelves and shelves and bags and bags and nothing — no toilet seat, no *"please look after this ginger"* tag, no fresh clean underwear inside. *Two minutes.*

My shoulders slumped, the old lady was about to kick me out of the back room when an idea pops into her crusty old head. It might be in the office. I bounded over her in a single leap. I scanned the office. A desk, a lamp, dirty faded brown wallpaper. Nothing. My fists clenched. *One minute.* I turned around...

There!

There by the door. To the left of the door! BAM! My old grey *Lowe Alpine Pax 25*! The backpack that has accompanied me on every crazy adventure of the last eight years. *You can't be a backpacker if you ain't got a backpack.*

I looked at my watch.

Forty seconds.

The little old guardian of the bags wants me to write my details and sign a bit of paper. I have never written so fast or so illegibly in my life, not even in a school exam after we had been told to put our pens down.

Ten seconds.

I ran out of the office, bag in hand, sweat pouring down into my eyes making it difficult to see. What platform? If it was over the other side of the station, I was done for.

Platform 8. *Really close.* Run, Graham, run you crazy fool!

A whistle.

Zero seconds.

I flung myself into the rear carriage with reckless abandon. The automatic doors closed on my backpack.

I heaved with all my might — one last burst of energy.

My bag came free and the doors slammed shut.

Success!

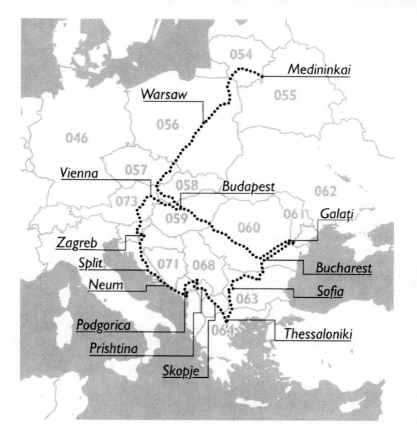

Medininkai

Warsaw

046 056

Vienna 057 058 Budapest 062

073 059 061 Galaţi

060

Zagreb

Split 071 068 Bucharest

Neum Sofia

063

Podgorica 064 Thessaloniki

Prishtina

Skopje

Chapter 11
Interdit!

Out of breath, face red, hair greasy I was transported into another world — a world of peaceful, relaxed, sedate commuters sitting in silence. My t-shirt (worn for six straight days) was stuck to me with sweat. I must have stunk to high heaven. All I needed was a can of Special Brew and a dog on a string for the vision to be complete.

I made a beeline for the toilet and washed myself with cold water and wet wipes. I brushed my teeth, changed my clothes and sprayed on a healthy portion of deodorant – or as I like to call it, shower in a can.

The train raced through the night, tearing back through Austria and entering the tiny country of **Liechtenstein** on the way to Switzerland. Liechtenstein is one of Europe's five micro-nations, the others being Monaco, Andorra, Vatican City and San Marino.

Although having a population of just 36,000 people, Liechtenstein (named after its ruling family) gets the same number of votes (one) in the UN as India. And India has a population of *1.2 billion*. Yay democracy!

I jumped off the train in the tiny town of Nandeln to stomp around for a moment and explain to my camera that I was in Liechtenstein. Then it was back on board and on to the country famed for its oddly-shaped chocolate bars as well as more familiar-shaped bars of Nazi gold: **Switzerland!**

LIECHTENSTEIN 074/200

🏛 **VERDUZ**

👥 **35,851**

❓ **German**

💵 **Swiss Franc**

💰 **$134,617.38**

There are more companies registered in Liechtenstein than there are people living in Liechtenstein.

I arrived in the town of Buchs before dawn. I had already stepped foot in both Liechtenstein and Switzerland and the day was yet to begin. By sunset I hoped to have also ticked off Italy as well as Italy's two micro-states: San Marino and Vatican City.

You know what would have been utterly hilarious? If I there were *two* places in Italy called 'San Marino' and I went to the wrong one!

Keep reading...

I took the next train back through Liechtenstein and down into **Italy**. Before long I was on the regional train that the Deutsche Bahn website claimed would take me to "S. Marino".

SWITZERLAND 075/200

🏛 **BERNE**

👥 **7.744m**

💬 **German, French, Italian, Romansh**

💵 **Swiss Franc**

💰 **$69,669.33**

Switzerland was the last nation that existed in 1945 to become a full member of the United Nations. It finally joined in 2002.

My suspicion that something was amiss was aroused by the fact that the train was going really slow. Intercity trains, in my experience, do not behave in this manner. I took out my laptop, inserted my Vodafone dongle, got online and pulled up Google Maps.

This is not the San Marino you're looking for.

One San Marino is a city state, an independent nation with a seat on the UN and its own Grand Prix; the other San Marino is a tiny village in the foothills of the Alps.

Something I didn't know: the nation of San Marino does not, in fact, have a train station. The tiny village of San Marino does. It appeared on the otherwise magnificent Deutsche Bahn website as "S. MARINO".

Oops!

ITALY 076/200

🏛 **ROME**

👥 **59.1m**

💬 **Italian**

💵 **Euro**

💰 **$36,992.88**

Of the four Renaissance artists who share their names with the Teenage Mutant Ninja Turtles, only Raphael was not born in Florence.

Panic stations. I tried to reschedule my route, but it was impossible. If I dilly-dallied about, I would miss a whole bunch of connections. There was nothing for it but to scratch this one down to experience and press on to Rome — I'd have to hit San Marino on the way back up through Italy, on the way to Monaco and the Iberian peninsula.

The train rumbled through "S. MARINO" and eventually arrived at Padua station, from where I could take the train to Rome. I needed to make a reservation (reservations are required on intercity or international trains even if you have a rail pass), but the queue for tickets was immense. There were only two ticket desks open (of ten). But that's okay, it wasn't like it was rush hour or anything.

Oh, hang on, *it totally was rush hour*.

With the train departing in three minutes and me still a good half-hour away from being served, I looked to see if I could make a reservation via a ticket machine. No such luck. Usually getting on a train without a reservation is no big deal, but there were so many people in the station I assumed the train would be packed. At which point not having a reservation *would* be a big deal and I could face a fine or even be ejected from the train.

So I bought a ticket from Padua to Rome at a cost of 60 goddamn euro — more money than I had spent all week.

However, I boarded the train to find it pretty much empty. I guess it was just one of those days.

I arrived in the capital at some ungodly hour, which felt strangely appropriate. I slung my bag into the Pop Inn Hostel (warmly recommended), and hit the streets with the intention of stepping foot in Vatican City.

Now Vatican City is tiny, ridiculous and not even a member of the United Nations, but it does have special observer status — you can't get your "every country" Guinness World Record without it.

It was past midnight when I finally reached Popesville. Unhelpfully enough, I found St Peter's Square cordoned off.

I found a member of the (fabulously dressed) Swiss Guard and asked if I could just step over the threshold, but he wasn't having any of it. No public access after 11pm.

Having never been to Rome before, I figured I might as well see if there was a back entrance.

What I didn't know was what a bleedin' fortress The Vatican is. A stone wall (40 feet high in places) bounds the area to the north, south and west of the city. A little insecure for somebody purportedly with God on their side, *quod non est*?

I would just have to return to St Peter's Square in the morning.

But as I had already started, I thought I might as well complete the circuit — my first (and quite possibly last) walking lap of an entire nation — a nation with its own flag, bank, leader and army (well, glorified security guards).

After seeing what I could see of the Holy See I trundled down to the Pantheon and the Colosseum. The night was fresh and the streets were empty — save for the rumble of the occasional car on the cobblestones. It's not just the buildings that are there that make the centre of Rome so beautiful, it's also the buildings that are not there — no multi-storey carparks, no concrete shopping malls, no high-rises, no office towers, no tacky gold-trimmed hotels. All the magnificence one might expect from a world-class city, but hardly any of the eyesores.

VATICAN CITY   **077**/200

🏛 VATICAN CITY

👥 451

💬 Italian, Latin, French, German

💵 Euro

💰 $21,198

Until 2013, the age of consent in Vatican City was 12.

I found myself lost amongst the glorious pillars of stone, finely carved wood and sun-baked bricks slowly eroding their way through history. It was 4am before I returned to the hostel. After a couple of hours of shut-eye I was back at The Vatican.

I asked my taxi driver to wait while I ran into the middle of St Peter's Square (which, FYI, is actually round) and yelled 'I'm in **Vatican City!** Woo!', down the barrel of my video camera before running straight back to the taxi. 'Termini station please!'

People often ask me how long I stayed in each country. As the journey ended up taking four years (spoilers!) I usually reply with "about a week, on average". But that's the thing with averages — they're simply a line down the middle of what can be some pretty epic outliers. While I ended up spending 36 weeks in Australia, I spent 36 *seconds* in Vatican City. Bite me.

Next up: Malta. To get there I'd have to take a ferry from Sicily. ALL ABOARD the 7:20am train to Catania. There I met with my filmmaker friend Laura, who had come with us on the Five Nation Pub Crawl a couple of weeks earlier. Lonely Planet were paying her to follow me around for a few days, filming for the TV show. I hoped for her sake things would be a little less manic than of late.

It was a great relief to see a familiar face (and a familiar video camera — my Sony Z1!) waiting for me at the train station. We hopped on the ferry and watched the sun set over the Mediterranean as we chugged onwards to country number 78: **Malta.**

MALTA 078/200

🏛 **VALLETTA**

👥 412,477

❓ Maltese, English

💵 Euro

💰 $19,636.01

The cross on the Maltese flag is not a Maltese Cross. It is the George Cross, awarded to the entire country for exceptional valour in WWII.

The capital Valletta was truly sublime — a fortress town, hilly, cobbled streets and sandstone walls. Our taxi driver was a splendidly garrulous and informed chap, who seemed able to compress the entire history of Malta into the space of the short ride from the port to our hostel.

That night, for the first time in weeks, I got to bed at a reasonable hour — we had to be up at 5am for the ferry back to Sicily.

The ferry took us to the tiny port town of Pozzallo, from where we took a gloriously rickety old train to Catania then a bus to Trapani on the other side of the island. From there we would be abandoning Europe for a few days. My sights were set on Tunisia, Libya and Algeria. The time had come to launch myself headfirst into the great continent of Africa.

Just because countries are situated next to each other doesn't mean that the border will be crossable. Just like Venezuela and Guyana, the border between Algeria and Morocco had been closed for years. This meant there was no sensible way of reaching Algeria from north-west Africa (short of travelling through Timbuktu — *literally*!). It would be best for me to go to the relatively small country of Tunisia and "border hop" into Algeria. While I was there I hoped to tick Libya off the list as well.

Then I would return to Italy and visit San Marino (fo' reals) and the other four countries I had left in Europe before heading to Morocco and down through West Africa. Cyprus, being closer to the Middle East than Europe, would just have to wait.

The ferry to Tunisia was supposed to leave at 8am, so Laura and I dragged our asses to the port for 7am. We were a few hours late setting sail. I'll admit to being spoiled by the clockwork-like timing of the European train network. Oh well, I thought, better start getting used to it!

In **Tunisia** there are mini-buses called "louages" that head towards a set destination when full, 24 hours a day. Laura and I took one to the town of Tabarka on the Algerian border. The driver drove through the night like a man possessed. How Laura and I managed to get any sleep is nothing short of a miracle.

If the Algerian border proved anything like the border into Panama, Ukraine or Belarus, it would be possible to get through the first set of border guards (the "home nation"), talk to the second set (the country to be entered), and by doing so step foot over the border, which invariably runs half-way between the two.

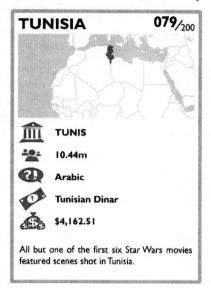

TUNISIA 079/₂₀₀

🏛 **TUNIS**

👥 10.44m

💬 Arabic

💵 Tunisian Dinar

💱 $4,162.51

All but one of the first six Star Wars movies featured scenes shot in Tunisia.

We arrived at the border just after dawn. Laura stayed in the cab while I spoke to the guard on the Tunisian side — would he let me pass to go and speak to the Algerian guards?

He would only say one word: *'interdit!'*

French for "not allowed".

No amount of pointing at my pocket and offering to pay a "fee" would sway his stance. If I wished to tick Algeria off the list I'd have to get myself a visa.

We arrived back in Tunis around midday. I headed straight for the Algerian Embassy. However, what we really needed was the Algerian *Consulate* (Embassy, Consulate, High Commission, whatevs). By the time we got to where I needed to be, the Consulate was closed. That's what happens on a Friday afternoon in a Muslim nation. I spoke to the guard and he assured me that I could get a visa for Algeria on Monday.

It was decision time — should I stay in Tunisia until Monday and try to get a visa then, or leave with Laura the next day on the ferry back to Sicily?

To add to the pressure, my parents would be arriving in Barcelona on Monday. The plan was for them to meet me there with all the extra kit I'd need for the Sub-Saharan leg of the journey.

But I figured that returning to Algeria via Tunisia *after* visiting all the other countries in Africa would put an extra week on my journey. Two more days in Tunisia didn't seem so bad in comparison.

In the meantime, I decided to attempt a border-hop into Libya, hoping against hope that the border controls would be a little more lax than they were with Algeria. I spent the rest of the day travelling south with Laura to the city of Ben Guerdane on the Libyan border.

We got in very late and stayed in some nasty border hotel. We would attack at dawn.

Well at least I would.

Laura's time was up and if she was going to make the ferry back to Sicily that day she'd have to return to Tunis as soon as possible. There wouldn't be time to accompany me to the border. We said our goodbyes and she got on a louage bound for Tunis.

At the time I didn't think anything of it; Tunisia is a country with a well-established tourism industry and, from what I had read, it was nowhere near as dodgy or as dangerous as, say, India or Egypt.

It wasn't until later that I would find out that the louage left with *just* Laura on board. She was then driven around the backstreets until she came to a small garage where three men started to argue with the driver in French. The row got heated. One of the men took Laura by the arm and pulled her out of the minibus. He dragged her bags out too and told her to go with him up the street. He eventually led her to a group of women who were waiting in a minibus and told her not to leave them.

The whole ordeal left Laura shaken and super pissed with me. Which was fair enough — it's all well and good being reckless when I'm the only one I have to worry about. I put my good friend in real danger just to get a stamp in my damn passport. It was a dick move and no mistake.

And I didn't even get the stamp. In a near carbon copy of what happened the day before, the Tunisian border guards turned me back.

Interdit!

I was told I could get a visa from Sfax, a city halfway between Ben Guerdane and Tunis, and that the embassy was open, even though it was a Saturday. I raced to Sfax, passing up my chance to go and visit nearby Tatouine (oh yes it exists!) and the *Star Wars* film sets.

Upon arrival in Sfax, I headed to the Libyan embassy, but there was no chance. In 2000, the Libyan leader Colonel Gaddafi decided that any western tourists would require a chaperone (because we might steal antiquities), so they wouldn't let me in without an invite.

So I hit the streets of Sfax to shake things up and see if I could make something work. I still had 40 hours before the Algerian embassy opened on Monday. Maybe I could convince somebody to take me over the Libyan border in a Jeep. It's all desert, right? It's not like there's a wall.

I got chatting with a few guys who spoke English — Semi, Anis, Wahleed and their friends. At first they were full of ideas, but then after making a few phone calls, they came to the conclusion that it was "impossible". I then started walking back to the hotel where I had left my bags, which is when I ran into a guy called Raouf — who introduced himself as a poet. He said he could get me a journalist visa, and, out of any better options, I thought I'd give it a punt.

So I decided to stay in Sfax for the night, and try again for the border with Raouf in the morning. Raouf and I went out for a meal and a few drinks. My Spidey-sense started tingling when I wound up paying the entire bill. Those tingles intensified when, on the way back to my hotel, Raouf started asking for an insane amount of money for the visa. I told him to leave it and I'd see him in the morning.

As promised, I met Raouf that morning and we went for something to eat. There he pulled out a letter, written in Arabic. The only words I could read were "visa" and "BBC" in Roman lettering. It had a stamp at the bottom and all looked quite official.

But when Raouf wouldn't let me film it, that ol' Spidey-sense turned into full on alarm bells. Something wasn't right. We walked around the town to where the *louages* leave for the border. There Roauf asked me for £250 for the visa. I asked him what he was going to do with it, and he said he was going to take it to the guy who had sorted it for me. I had to wait there and he'd be back in half an hour. I asked to come with him, but he said it was 'too dangerous'.

Alarm bells? Full on KLAXONS!! Aroooooooga! Aroooooga! *Get your arse out of there, Graham!*

'I'm out. No Deal.'

I was on the next train to Tunis, ready to hit the Algerian consulate in the morning. Libya would have to wait until after the rest of Africa.

That night I stayed at the gorgeous Tunis Youth Hostel (heartily recommended) in the heart of the sprawling labyrinth of the medina. The hostel was a grand old Tunisian villa and included not only breakfast, but also dinner — and the dinner was superb. Oh well, at least *something* was going right.

I got to the Algerian consulate at 8am, waited for it to open, waited to be let inside and then waited to find out if I could get a visa. By 10am, I had my answer.

Interdit.

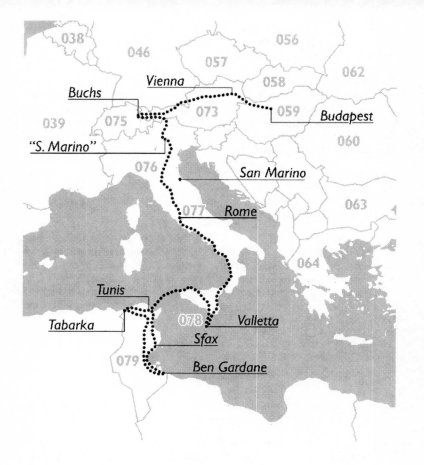

Buchs

Vienna

"S. Marino"

San Marino

Budapest

Rome

Tunis

Tabarka

Valletta

Sfax

Ben Gardane

Chapter 12
A Funny Thing Happened on the Way To The Frontier

It turns out that you can't get a visa for Algeria unless you apply for it in your home nation. My first foray into Africa had been a disaster. That's okay, I only had 52 countries of the continent left to visit.

Groan.

If I had known I couldn't get a visa, I would have returned to Tunis with Laura on Saturday, she would have been spared all that bullshit in Ben Guerdane, I wouldn't have wasted €70 on a return cabin that I didn't use and I'd be in Barcelona by now, where my mum and dad were waiting.

Since the next ferry to Italy didn't leave until the following day I was going to be three days late getting to Barcelona. My parents had to extend their stay and re-arrange their flight home. The pressure from the journey to keep moving is bad enough; it is worse when I know that people are waiting for me. I felt acutely aware that I had seriously let my friends and family down.

The next day I said my goodbyes to the chaps in the hostel and headed to the port to take the ferry back to Italy. I stopped at a bank on the way. 'Can I change this wad of dinars to euros please?'

Interdit.

Oh don't start that again!

Yep, it's against the law. You can only rid yourself of your dinars in the airport.

'What about the seaport?'

The cashier merely shrugged.

Tunisia, I love you but you're really testing my patience here.

I arrived at the port and asked at the information desk if I could change my money. They said I could but I'd have to wait for the bureau de change to re-open.

There was only one ferry leaving that day, with hundreds of people on board. It left at 1pm. And the only bureau de change was closed for lunch.

'So, will I be able to change my money before getting on the ferry?'

'Er, probably not, no, they'll be closed for a couple of hours.'

Not for the first time, I felt like Steve Martin in *Planes, Trains and Automobiles*. Only without the planes.

'You'll have to go to the bank, it's downstairs.'

"Downstairs" meant "down the ramp, then walk around the entire dock for half an hour in the baking heat with all your bags until the sweat is pouring from your brow".

By the time my dinars were changed and I had got back to the terminal, the customs guy shouted at me for being late. I explained about the bureau du change being closed.

SAN MARINO 080/200

🏛 **SAN MARINO**

👥 30,698

❓ Italian

💵 Euro

💰 $62,188.93

Established in 301 AD, San Marino claims to be not just the oldest extant sovereign state, but also the world's oldest constitutional republic.

'Il est pas mon problème.'

I ran on board.

And with that, the ferry didn't leave for another two hours.

Not being able to afford a cabin, I made do with sleeping on a cushioned bench seat. The ferry had just three toilets between every male on board, which were pretty much trashed within minutes of leaving Tunis, water and piss all over the floor.

Not for the last time, I skipped dinner to avoid having to use the karzi[19].

As soon as we hit the port of Civitavaggio on the west coast of Italy the following afternoon, I jumped on the first train back through Rome and up to Rimini — the closest train station to San Marino.

I arrived in Rimini around 11pm and took a taxi from the station to the tiny republic of **San Marino**, ticked it off the list and got some exciting

---

[19] Editor's Note: While apparent from context – this actually *is* British slang for a toilet.

footage of a roundabout. Then it was straight back to the station. The trip cost €50.

I then sat around waiting for the train to the south coast of France. It wasn't due until 3am.

I knew I'd be whizzing through Monte Carlo on the train, but I didn't realise it would be an underground station. As a consequence I got to see less than bugger-all of **Monaco**, which was a shame, as I had not been there since the mid-80s and my recollection of that trip was a bit sketchy, given that I was six. But whatever, I raced onto the southern French town of Foix, a couple of hours from Andorra.

On arrival in that cute little mountain town I missed the last bus to Andorra and the backpackers was full, so I had to make do with a hotel. In general I try to avoid hotels; aside from the fact that they're too expensive, they're also rather lonesome. In any case, all I need is a couch and a bucket of water, I don't need a TV and complementary soap.

By 8am the next day I was already in **Andorra**. I could tick the last of Europe's five micro-states off of my list. It is slap-bang on the border between France and Spain, and until recently it was jointly ruled by the President of France (as proxy for the king) and a Spanish bishop. But being a crazy little nation of two princes was a bit too interesting for the people of Andorra, and so in 1993 they got their own parliament.

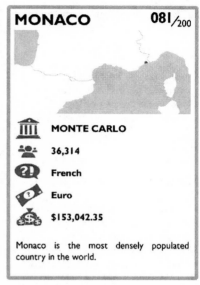

MONACO 081/200

🏛 MONTE CARLO

👥 36,314

💬 French

💵 Euro

💰 $153,042.35

Monaco is the most densely populated country in the world.

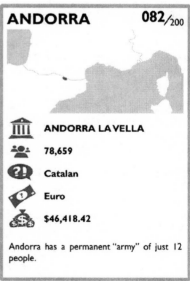

ANDORRA 082/200

🏛 ANDORRA LA VELLA

👥 78,659

💬 Catalan

💵 Euro

💰 $46,418.42

Andorra has a permanent "army" of just 12 people.

If you're into slapping two boards to your feet and hurtling down a hill before falling over and breaking something, Andorra is *the* skiing destination of the Pyrenees; but it doesn't seem to do an awful lot else. It's rather pretty, though.

A coffee and a croissant (or two) and then I was on the 10am bus to Barcelona. You know what that means don't you?

ESPAÑA![20]

I was met at the bus station by my mum and dad as well as Matt Bourke, the series editor of my TV show. Matt had flown over from Australia to travel with me down into Africa as far as Senegal, filming along the way.

SPAIN   083/200

🏛 **MADRID**

👥 **46.75m**

❓ **Spanish**

💵 **Euro**

💲 **$32,331.52**

The national anthem of Spain — the Marcha Real — has no lyrics, saving footballers the embarrassment of having to pretend to sing along.

We went for lunch on the top floor of the Corte Ingles Department store (great view). After Matt left, my parents and I headed to the apartment where they were staying. My dad faffed about for half an hour trying to find the damn place. I just had time to chuck my backpack into the room before I had to high-tail it to the doctor's in time to make my appointment.

Yeah, even though I'm a double-hard bastard and have no need for your human "medicine"(!), I needed a check-up in order to keep Lonely Planet's insurance company happy before I headed down into Africa (proper).

I was asked how tall I was and whether I had anything obviously wrong with me. Five minutes later I was handed a bill for €150. And that, ladies and gentlemen, is why so few British backpackers dare bitch about the NHS once they return home.

After the doctor, I took a trip to the dentist to get my tooth filled in. Remember the big chunk of my mouth that fell out just before I left the UK? I certainly did! Then it was back to my parents' apartment for a cup of tea and to go through the stuff that my mum had brought me, which included my second passport, loaded with visas for Africa.

We met up again with Matt and headed over to La Fonda — a restaurant you simply have to visit when in Barcelona. We had to queue up to get in, which got my dad all agitated. He then started going on and on about the fact I was wearing a hat (which is what I do) before going completely

---

[20] Editor's Note: **Spain.**

bananas, not allowing us to order our own food, instead writing our orders down on a scrap of paper, *in English*, for the Chinese Waitress (in Catalonia) to decipher.

Looking back now, it may have been the beginning of his now-diagnosed struggle with dementia, but at the time it was just embarrassing as hell.

After a particularly strained dinner, my parents and I retired to the apartment. All I wanted to do was pack my things properly (the last time in England was a bit of a rush-job) and get a good night's sleep.

Possible?

Nah. My dad started losing the plot about my visa for Angola. He wanted to know what date to put down on the application form. I had told him over and over again to put "June 15th", but he wasn't having it for some reason. He then started kicking off again because I wore a hat to dinner (even though I had acquiesced to his complaints and stuffed it in my bag).

After all the shit that had gone wrong over the past couple of weeks, this was the last thing I needed. To make things worse, Matt was supposed to be dropping around to give me some more blank video tapes for my camera. I didn't want Matt seeing my dad throwing a tantrum (not great material for the TV show), so I waited downstairs for him. He arrived just after midnight.

I went back up to the apartment, but I could hear my dad still ranting and raving at my mum. I decided to go for a walk.

I didn't get very far before I realised that I had left my wallet in the apartment. Returning to the main entrance I further realised I didn't have a key to get back in. What's more, I had no idea what number the apartment was. I tried calling my mum on my phone, but there was no answer. I ended up sitting outside on the doorstep for two hours, staring across the road and looking forward to travelling on my own again.

By the time I got back inside my dad had mercifully fallen asleep. I got just four hours of shuteye before getting up and stuffing what I could into my bag to meet Matt for the 7am train to Madrid. I said a teary goodbye to my lovely mum. For all she knew it might have been for the last time.

I met Matt at Barcelona Sants and very soon we were on our way to Portugal, via Madrid and Seville.

Madrid's train station is stunning — old-school Golden-Age-Of-Steam architecture with a lush tropical garden in the middle of the concourse. I could have stayed all day, but we only had time for a coffee before hopping on another superfast train to Seville.

Now Matt was a top bloke (for an Aussie!), but Lonely Planet really did throw him in at the deep-end. He hadn't done much of the world-traveller stuff (just a trip to New York) and in a few days we would be ankle-deep in West Africa — one of the poorest regions of planet Earth. He spoke no French or Spanish whatsoever. I was acutely aware of the culture shock this was going to be for him, so I drew up some rules to help him get by.

Graham's 20 Rules of Travel:

1. Walk with determination, even if you're completely lost.
2. Travel LIGHT — Don't take anything you can't afford to lose.
3. No matter what, keep a cheery disposition — don't let them see you bleed.
4. Don't drink the water or eat salad.
5. No drugs. Ever. Have you seen Bangkok Hilton?
6. Never take a towel with you travelling, unless you plan to camp. It's a heavy wet smelly mess you can do without.
7. Trust your gut.
8. No, it's not your first day here.
9. Whatever price they ask, halve it.
10. If something sounds too good to be true, it invariably is.
11. Always have a Plan B. And C. And D.
12. McDonalds will always have clean Western toilets.
13. NEVER use traveller's cheques.
14. Have at least two cash cards, preferably five.
15. Always keep a $100 bill somewhere safe.
16. Deodorant is your one true friend.
17. Never let your bag out of your sight (ha!).
18. Wet-wipes.
19. Biscuits.
20. If someone asks you if you're a god, you say YES.

We pulled into Seville early that afternoon and took the first train west, arriving at the Spanish town of Huelva at around siesta-o'clock. The place was like a ghost-town. Then it was a fun local bus ride to the border town of Ayamonte — the southern-most point of the border between Spain and **Portugal**. There we jumped in a taxi for my final border-hop of Europe.

Our driver took us over the bridge that separated the two old rivals — a bridge that spanned hundreds of years of conquest and bickering. But look at this border today: no checkpoints, no visas, no entry stamps, no questions, no rummaging through your baggage. The EU is an amazing thing.

I savoured the moment. I knew there would not be too many more of them on this adventure.

After stomping around on Portuguese soil for a few minutes, we returned to Spain. Our driver took us up to see the panoramic view of the Guadiana River (which separates the two nations) before dropping us back at the bus station.

That night Matt and I checked into a backpackers in Seville. He told the receptionist that he was "basically my boss", which, I have to admit, put my nose out of joint. If he decided to quit, they would simply find another series editor. If I decided to quit, there'd be no show. Nighty night.

The plan was to take the 7:30am bus to the coast. We took a taxi to the southern bus station (a good bet as we were heading due south!), but the driver of the bus to Algeciras wouldn't let us on, and then drove off 15 minutes early while we were trying to buy tickets. The rotter!

It wasn't until the information post opened at 8am that we discovered that the bus left from the *Eastern* bus station (obviously!), and that's why the Algeciras bus driver didn't allow us on board. Even though it was just there!

PORTUGAL   084/200

🏛 **LISBON**

👥 10.57m

❓ Portuguese

💶 Euro

🪙 $23,062.58

Only four members of Magellan's original crew made it all the way around the world. That number did not include Magellan himself – he was killed in The Philippines.

The next bus for the coast wasn't until 10am — man, I could have done with those extra few hours of sleep. Oh well. Matt and I sat drinking coffee until finally the bus departed with us on board. We thundered down towards the Mediterranean coast. From there we hopped on a ferry and before I knew it we had arrived in Ceuta, a Spanish enclave in Morocco, which makes up the African side of the "Pillars of Hercules".

Since it's technically part of the EU, getting into Ceuta was a piece of cake. However, getting into **Morocco** entailed fences and barbed wire and a metric ton of bureaucratic bullshit. The open borders of Latin America and Europe were now a thing of the past. Africa's frontiers, drawn (mostly) by a gang of white guys in a conference room in Paris in the 1880s, would come to dominate my life for the next year. I had better start getting used to them.

After faffing about on the border for an inordinate amount of time, we took a taxi to the nearby town of Tetouan and from there took the bus to Casablanca.

I had come this way before, seven years earlier with a friend of mine. We saw in the new year of 2002 singing Auld Lang Syne in Rick's Café, Casablanca. We awoke the next morning to find ourselves not just in the wrong hotel room, *but in the wrong hotel.* That was a good night.

On the bus I got chatting to Fatima, a Moroccan girl who dreamt of travelling the world. When somebody with a North American, Australian, New Zealand or European passport says 'I wish I could travel like you', it tends to get my back up, because the fact is, generally speaking, they can.

The same can't be said for people like Fatima, born in a developing nation. They can't travel as freely as my fellow countrymen and women, nor can they travel to as many countries as us, no matter how much they might want to.

That night in Casablanca Matt and I said *ta ta for now* — he had to organise a visa for Senegal (no such necessity for Mr. EU citizen here) and would fly to Dakar and meet me there, once I had overlanded it through Western Sahara and Mauritania.

On the bus from the Moroccan city of Agadir to Dakhla in **Western Sahara**, I found myself sitting next to Abdullah — a young, well-spoken Western Saharan who was happy that I was counting his nation on my expedition. (My reasoning being that, unlike Morocco, Western Sahara is a member of the African Union.)

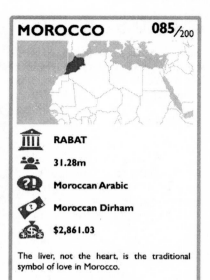

MOROCCO 085/200

🏛 **RABAT**

👥 **31.28m**

💬 **Moroccan Arabic**

💵 **Moroccan Dirham**

💰 **$2,861.03**

The liver, not the heart, is the traditional symbol of love in Morocco.

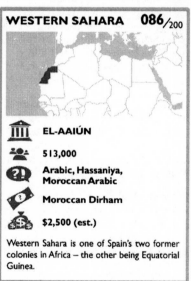

WESTERN SAHARA 086/200

🏛 **EL-AAIÚN**

👥 **513,000**

💬 **Arabic, Hassaniya, Moroccan Arabic**

💵 **Moroccan Dirham**

💰 **$2,500 (est.)**

Western Sahara is one of Spain's two former colonies in Africa — the other being Equatorial Guinea.

When the Spanish pulled out of what is now known as Western Sahara in the mid-70s, the territory was quickly annexed by Morocco. Border skirmishes with neighbouring Algeria and Mauritania, together with a nascent resistance movement, led to the UN getting involved in the 1980s — ostensibly to set things up for a referendum to decide the future for the citizens of this forgotten land, only 0.02% of which is arable.

That referendum has yet to take place.

From Abdullah's point of view, Western Saharans are treated like second-class citizens in their own country. There are no universities, very little industry, few jobs and an overabundance of police checkpoints — which makes travel difficult for local people. There's a refugee camp in Tindouf, Algeria, where displaced people of Western Sahara have lived for the last thirty years — Abdullah has relatives there who he has never met.

At 5am the next day I arrived in Dakhla, the most southerly settlement of Western Sahara. The 200 miles from there to the border with Mauritania is nothing but sand. As there were no buses I had to take a bush taxi.

Shared long-distance taxis can be found in other places around the world, but throughout West Africa it's often the only option.

The deal is straight-forward: I go to the taxi "station" and wait for the taxi to fill with passengers. We all get crammed into the taxi like sardines and it speeds off. It's not unusual for a car designed for five people to cram in ten uncomfortable and overheated souls — often the front passenger seat will be shared with another person. Filling the taxi might take five minutes, it might take five hours. But as soon as it's full it's all *QUICK QUICK LET'S GO LET'S GO-GO-GO!!*

Seatbelts are rarely an option.

I was told by a local policeman that it could take up to three days to fill a taxi for the four-hour journey to the border, so I bought all the spare seats in the first taxi that came along.

I arrived at the frontier in good time and was stamped out by the Moroccan guards. So far, so good. Next there was the small matter of navigating the couple of miles of dunes and abandoned vehicles that make up the No-Man's Land between Mauritania and Western Sahara.

Did I mention that this No-Man's Land is heavily mined?

You can't walk across the area (for obvious reasons, many of which go *boom*), so I hitched a ride on an oil truck driven by a cheerful Moroccan guy called Adam "Not Saddam" Hussein. We hit a top speed of 3mph along the sandy track, littered with burnt-out shells of cars and trucks that seemed to have crawled out into the desert to die.

After a rather tense but otherwise jovial half hour we reached Mauritanian passport control. There I tried to buy a visa, something that my Lonely Planet guidebook said I could do on the border.

The Mauritanian border guard begged to differ.

'No visa here.'

He obviously hadn't read his Lonely Planet.

'Can I get a visa in Dakhla?', I asked in broken French.

The border guard chuckled. 'No. Only Rabat.'

I'll save you the hassle of consulting a map — Rabat is *2,000 kilometres* north of the Mauritanian border. *Back through the Sahara Desert.*

Bribery wasn't possible. I headed back over No-Man's-Land. With the Morocco-Algeria border being closed, this was the only viable overland route into Sub-Saharan Africa. I didn't have a choice. I would have to travel to Rabat and get that bloody visa.

Having blown my budget for the week on the taxi here, the taxi back to Dakhla only took about 30 minutes to fill. The policeman in Dakhla must have meant three hours, not three days.

I shared the single front passenger seat with a rather jovial guy called Ahmed. Under normal circumstances, we might have had a good laugh, but that afternoon I was not in the best of moods and he really did my head in. When we arrived back in Dahkla (not a moment too soon) a chunk of one of my teeth fell out. It was the filling I got in Barcelona.

Okay, I thought, I'm having a bad day. But when the going gets tough, the tough go for kebabs.

After a tasty shawarma and Coke my hit-points were restored. I wrote in my blog "Is this the best Africa can throw at me? Ha! BRING IT!!!" and jumped the bus north.

As I was soon to learn, Africa hadn't even *gotten started* "bringing it".

I arrived in Rabat two days later and headed straight to the Mauritanian embassy. Visa application submitted, come back tomorrow.

The rest of the day I spent mooching about the rather wonderful city of Rabat, enjoying the hustle and bustle at the medina, eating some great food and drinking copious amounts of coffee. I even got my hair cut. That night I joined some locals (over)crowding a café to watch the footy on the TV. Casablanca were playing Tunis in the Arab Champions League Final — it was 1-0 to Casablanca until the last minute when Tunisian team pulled one back and won on aggregate. Gah!!

The next day I picked up my visa for Mauritania and headed back down south.

That night the bus stopped at a roadside food court that I can only describe as Morrissey's worst nightmare. I had to go to a counter and stand between two hanging lamb carcasses, dripping with blood and covered in flies, to place my order. A butcher carved me some meat which I then took to a nearby barbecue where a nice man with no teeth cooked it up with some spice. I then got myself a piece of French bread from another counter and gave it to the barbecue man. He cut it open, threw the meat inside, a bit of salt and pepper on top — et voilà!

Surprisingly delicious.

I was hoping to get to the border before it closed at 6pm the next day, but it was 8pm before I even reached Dahkla. After spending the night at the Auberge Du Sahara camp-ground, I reached the border around noon the next day. There I met Michel, a French guy heading to Senegal in his camper van. He agreed to take me over No-Man's Land.

As we bumped our merry way over the (possibly explosive laden) sand-dunes, I asked Michel if he had a visa. He told me he didn't need one. 'No really — I was here last week and they wouldn't let me in', I protested.

'Ah — they change the rules all the time', said Michel with a wink.

He was right, they had changed the rules. Mauritanian visas were once again available on the border. What's more, they were $5 cheaper than the one I went all the way to Rabat for; *4,000km back and forth across the Sahara Desert.*

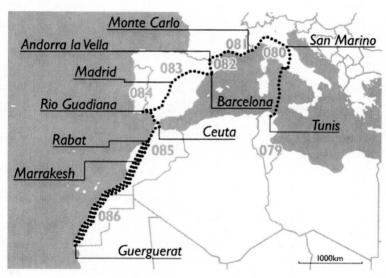

Chapter 13
Voyage Of The Damned

You think a pointless 4,000km round trip through the Sahara desert and back again to get a completely unnecessary sticker in my passport is bad? Oh my friends, Africa was just getting started...

It was another 500km to Nouakchott, the capital of **Mauritania**. In a stroke of surprisingly good fortune, my shared taxi arrived at the level crossing of the famous Iron Ore railway just as the once-a-day train was approaching.

At 1.6 miles in length it's the longest train in the world, and as each of the 200 cars carry up to 84 tons of iron ore, it's also the

MAURITANIA 087/200

🏛 **NOUAKCHOTT**

👥 **3.51m**

💬 **Arabic**

💵 **Mauritanian Ouguiya**

💰 **$860.91**

Under intense international pressure, Mauritania finally banned slavery in 2007.

heaviest. It took a good twenty minutes to pass by. I stood there watching it with a big goofy train-spotter grin on my face — my travel hero, Michael Palin, had ridden the passenger car at the back of the train. I was almost tempted to see if I could clamber on board, but it wasn't going my way.

That night I arrived in Nouakchott and stayed in a cute little guest house. The next day I took the first *sept-place* south. A *sept-place* is an old Peugeot 504 designed to take seven passengers, as the name implies. This one took fourteen.

After several uncomfortable hours, exacerbated by the fact that we stopped every few miles to pay "road tax", we hit the town of Rosso on the Senegal river. At the border post I approached a guy in army fatigues. He spoke pretty good English.

'The border's closed until 3pm.'

I looked at my watch. 12:15pm.

A calculation in my head — if I wait until 3, I'll get into Dakar about 11 at night. Dakar, first time, by myself, at 11pm. Hmm...

'Okay, how much will it be to go through now?', I asked, bracing for a hit.

'Twenty dollars.'

Is my ass worth 20 bucks? Of course it is. With the money wedged into my passport, I was quickly and painlessly stamped out.

Next up, I had to pay a guy to row me over the river into **Senegal**. It's not that big a river, just five minutes to get across. But you wouldn't want to swim it. My ferryman wasn't happy with the €5 I offered him (which I thought we had agreed on in advance) so he followed me around for the next half-hour complaining in some language that I (thankfully) didn't understand.

SENEGAL 088/200

🏛 **DAKAR**

👥 12.59m

French

💵 **West African CFA Franc**

🏍 $1,017.97

The name "Senegal" is believed to have come from the Wolof "sun gal" meaning "our boat".

I went to talk to the border guard, who had better things to do (like watch the telly).

You want to come in? Wait until 3pm.

C'mon man!

'You have money?'

'I've got a twenty'.

The guy shook his head. I was soon to learn that US dollars in West Africa were about as welcome as a dose of the clap.

'Forty?'

He went back to watching the telly.

'Okay. Sixty.'

He turned, smiled, took my passport and my money and stamped me in.

149

I squeezed into another *sept-place*. It made its way over the pot-holes and through the police "check-points" (or should I say "bribery-points").

By the time I arrived in Dakar, my arse was numb, my back was killing me and my balls felt like they had been sitting in a hot vice for several hours.

To cap it all, Matt was no longer in Dakar. He had waited for me for a few days, contracted anaemic dysentery and (sensibly) returned to Australia.

Up to this point, all of the logistics had been up to me, with some help from my friends and family, Team Odyssey. But the next country I needed to get to was Cape Verde, a small chain of islands 650km west of Dakar. The production team at Lonely Planet said they'd "sort it".

This was the first and last time I let Lonely Planet help me out with my logistics.

Apparently, sorting my passage to Cape Verde involved paying for a local "fixer" called Mentor to find me a way of getting there.

Okay, I thought, it's a good name to have for an expedition dubbed "*The Odyssey*".

So I gave this Mentor fella a call. He asked if I wanted to stay at his place while he worked on getting me to Cape Verde. I said yes and thanked him for his generosity. It wasn't until I got there that I found out it would be €30 a night for a thin sponge bed and a cold shower. Left to my own devices I would have gone CouchSurfing.

The next day, Mentor and I hit the streets. We went down to the beach where the fishermen sell their catch. Mentor made some phone calls, talked to some people. By 2pm, it was clear that I would not be leaving that day. I decided to head over to The Gambia for a quick border-hop, get it out of the way.

The Gambia is the smallest country in Africa — a thin sliver of land completely encompassed by Senegal. It was supposed to take 5 hours in a *sept-place* to get there, but the reality of life in a country where the roads have more holes than the plot of *Star Wars Episode I*, was that this wasn't the case. It was easier to drive on the dust at the side of the road than on the road itself.

We got to the border around 10pm. I got my passport stamped into The Gambia, did a piece to camera, and then headed back to the *sept-place* garage on the Senegalese side, sparking a near-riot amongst the motorcycle taxi guys on the border along the way.

I had to wait for two hours for the *sept-place* to fill. By the time I got back to Dakar it was morning. I didn't sleep. I couldn't even if I'd wanted to. The taxi was so old and beaten up, I was surprised the driver could see given all the cracks in the windscreen. Every time the car reached a certain point in third gear, it lost all power and all of us on board would be rudely jerked forwards. I spent the night running through almost every song on my iPod.

As a consequence, I got back to Dakar in a rotten mood. A mood that was not lightened when I checked my GPS log. Turns out both border posts are in Senegal. After a 15-hour round trip along a muddy undulating track the majority of which I was squished into a shared taxi with no third gear... I hadn't actually crossed the border.

But that was the least of my worries.

After four more days in Dakar, all of the stuff that was supposed to happen, all of the stuff that Mentor "had a good feeling about" had come to nought. Lonely Planet was paying him by the day, so I guess that there was no big rush. For him, anyways.

Mentor told me that there were no yachts for hire, no fishing boats, no cargo boats I could hitch a ride on, nothing. I began to get despondent. And I started to really dislike Dakar.

Why is everything here so expensive? Why is nothing here nice? Why are the roads so unfeasibly bad? Why are there no traffic lights? Why does every single piece of pavement have to have stacked up breezeblocks, piles of rubble and piles of sand (from long-abandoned building projects) blocking the way? Why does every single cab have to have a cracked windscreen? Does a pixie go round with a little hammer at night doing them in?

I had to get out of there. I had to move on. In my desperation I agreed to take a wooden fishing boat over to Cape Verde with Mentor's cousin. He told me the trip would take four days and cost an eye-watering €3,500, most of which would go on fuel.

Yes, that's right, more than a fortnight's cruise in the Caribbean. More than a sailboat for the same number of days. A lot more. It was a "pirogue" — little more than a long wooden canoe. I would be sleeping on the deck under a tatty piece of canvas. We would be going over there with just an outboard motor, the captain and nine deck-hands. Quite why we needed as many deck-hands as a 1,200ft container ship I had no idea.

The captain spoke no English or Portuguese, and had no navigational charts. I printed some maps off Google for him.

Mentor told me that this would be the only way.

Well, at least Lonely Planet would be picking up the tab, right?

Wrong!

Apparently, when I was told that the production company was going to "sort out" my trip to Cape Verde, they didn't mean they'd actually, you know, pay for it.

I didn't even get a life-jacket. I had to buy my own. But then again, with no radio, no distress beacon or flares all it would do is keep me alive a little longer before the sharks got me. Earlier in the year I rented an emergency sat-phone, a large personal expense that I thought the production company might pick up once I signed up for the TV show, at the very least to keep their investment (me) safe. They refused, so I returned it to the company I hired it from.

If anything went wrong, I'd be utterly fubar'd.

The next day I found myself standing on a beach surrounded by rubbish, dead fish, squid ink and effluent. I signed a contract with the fishermen to take me to Cape Verde and back. Mentor had driven me to several different cash machines so I could withdraw the maximum amount from my bank account each time. I paid half up-front and would pay the other half upon my return. All in all, it was a full third my budget for the entire year.

> *Blog entry, 31 May 2009:*
>
> *This will be my last blog entry for a little while. I leave on HMS Deathtrap tonight. I better leave you some particulars.*
>
> *The name of the boat is the Mustafa Sy and the captain's name is Mbaye Séne Faye. He was born on 08 Nov 1975 in Dieleumbane. I should be getting into Praia, the capital of Cape Verde, on Tuesday or Wednesday. The boat I'm on doesn't have a radio and the guys on-board don't speak Portuguese. Can somebody ensure that the port authorities in Praia are informed of when we are coming in? Otherwise they might turn us back.*
>
> *It's rather important. Thanks.*
>
> *You have no idea how much I don't want to do this.*

It was the last day of May — a frustrating, infuriating and eye-wateringly expensive month of travel. The last words I wrote on my blog were '*June will be better, I'm sure of it.*'

How wrong I was.

I boarded the *Mustafa Sy* just after midnight. A 40-foot wooden pirogue. We were on the beach and the boat was a good 10 metres or so in the water. In an effort to keep me and my things dry, I was scooped up onto the shoulders of one of the fishermen and he waded out to the boat.

Plonked on board, I took a seasickness pill and used the torch on my mobile phone to have a look around.

The pirogue had no steering wheel (just a rudder) and nowhere to sleep that didn't involve being squished in between several other fishermen. There was no chance of keeping myself or any of my things dry. If there was a big storm, we hit something at full speed or we were clobbered by a freak wave, I'd be dead. No two ways about it.

The outboard motor was fired up and we set off into the inky blackness of the night.

I tried to sleep under the canvas sheet but around 3:30am, I couldn't take the rocking, the stuffiness or the smell of fish and feet anymore, so I hung my head over the side and proceeded to recall in high-resolution 3D with surround sound what I had eaten for dinner that night.

I needed to feel the wind on my face, so I re-organised myself on deck between the wooden fish bins. I spent the rest of the night getting splashed by the relentless waves until my clothes and sleeping bag were as wet as physics would allow.

I awoke at dawn. It was then that the true horror of my situation began to sink in. I was miles away from any land, on a wooden boat with ten other people who didn't speak a word of English and I had no way of communicating with the outside world. Furthermore, I had left with no confirmation that the message to the authorities in Cape Verde had got through.

The first day passed slowly — I spent my time reading and getting sunburnt out on deck. The relentless swaying of the boat met with no more resistance from my guts — thank God.

I had to piss into a bucket, as pissing off the side would result in me falling overboard. Luckily for me, my ninja training (and extensive experience of European music festival toilets) allows me to go for a surprisingly long time without having to take a dump.

Lunch consisted of a damp baguette. Dinner was a huge bowl of rice and fish that had been cooked on deck on an open fire. Everyone dived in with their right hands — not their left, obviously. That would be unhygienic.

Happily we met with no inclement weather or freak waves. I saw a good number of dolphin fins distributed between the hordes of flying fish. (I hoped they weren't sharks.)

I'd say it was plain sailing. If we had a sail.

I learnt the names of the fishermen — Captain Mbeye, First Mate Modou, Saliou, Ablaye, Adama, Aleen, Aleen, Mahmoud, Doudou and Elage. They were a good bunch and did their best to put me at ease.

That night, I slept once again between the wooden bins. Every hour or so, a large wave would wake me in the manner of a cold bucket of water to the face.

The highlight of the next day was seeing a small bale of loggerhead turtles swim by. We circled round to get me better look, but then I was gripped by the fairly reasonable fear that a fisherman would pick one up out of the sea and cook him up for din-dins. I'm happy to report they didn't, as loggerheads are an endangered species and it would have been a tricky one to explain to the folks back home.

That night the sea picked up and those buckets of water to the face became so ubiquitous that I was forced under the canvas. Squished in with all the fishermen, I didn't get much sleep, but I was happy in the knowledge that we'd hit Cape Verde in the morning.

That was the hard bit over.

Or so I thought.

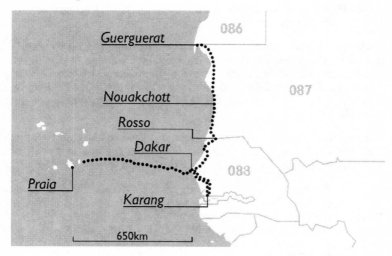

PROGRESS REPORT 31 MAY 2009

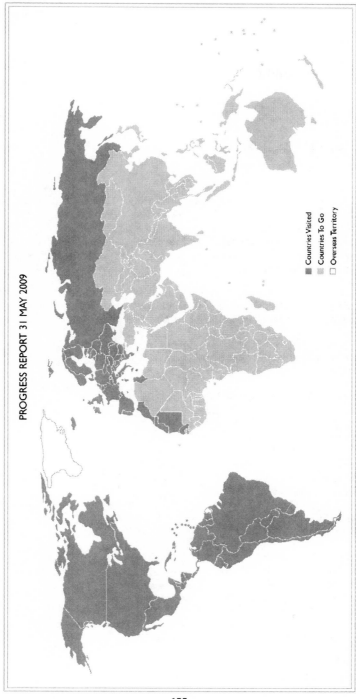

Countries Visited
Countries To Go
Overseas Territory

155

Chapter 14
Do Not Pass Go

It was the early hours of Wednesday morning, still dark, but I could see light coming from a nearby island – the Cape Verdean island of Maio. After four days at sea aboard the *Mustafa Sy,* to call it a welcome sight would be an understatement. Captain Mbeye suggested we go straight there; we could pull up on a beach, tick Cape Verde off the list, turn around and go back to Africa.

But I was afraid of the authorities thinking of me as some kind of people smuggler. I suggested we ignore the lights and press on — on to the main island of Santiago and the capital city of this chain of islands, Praia.

This would turn out to be a terrible mistake.

Somehow I fell back asleep. I re-awoke around 9am. It was muggy and overcast. I climbed on top of one of the wooden fish bins and stood tall. On the horizon there was the unmistakeable shape of an island in the distance. We had made it. 650km in a wooden canoe. Country number 89. **Cape Verde**.

Just like when famous yachtsmen and women arrive back home, we had a welcoming committee. A fishing boat, a *proper* fishing boat, came alongside, helpfully guiding us to the Port of Praia. I waved and smiled. This was all rather unexpected — and exciting.

CAPE VERDE 089/200

🏛 **PRAIA**

👥 **485,714**

❓ **Portuguese**

💵 **Cape Verdean Escudo**

💰 **$3,524.33**

There is one goat for every two people in Cape Verde.

That boat was joined by a few others, and before long there was a small flotilla of boats guiding us to our safe harbour. When we pulled into the ramshackle old city docks, it was as though half the city had come out to see us — hundreds of people lining the quayside, fighting for a glimpse. There was even a local news crew.

My phone now had signal, so I sent a tweet:

Graham Hughes
@theodysseyexp 3 Jun 2009

I have made it! I am alive in Cape Verde, going back to Senegal! If not updated in 3 days, search for me.

But very quickly my joy turned to apprehension. A police boat blocked our entry. There were two police officers on board, and an army guy clutching an AK-47, all staring menacingly at our little pirogue and the eleven souls she had somehow carried safely over from Dakar. What if they wouldn't let us dock? What if they sent us back without allowing me to step foot on dry land?

Some words were shouted in Portuguese. On the quayside, a container was lowered into place to block our potential "escape" should we reach land and make a run for it.

At this moment, my apprehension turned to dread.

More words. More angry faces. The police boat moved and allowed us to pull into an empty mooring. A cop motioned for us to stay in the boat. The container was lifted to allow two white minibuses to approach. They came to a halt, metres from the pirogue.

A dozen police officers and a TV crew jumped out of the minibuses. The officers came on board. My camera was confiscated. Everything was a whirl. I remember thinking that it would just be a simple misunderstanding and we'd all be back on the pirogue within a few hours. I even left my green leather jacket on board the boat.

We clambered off the pirogue and onto the concrete quay and were all shepherded into the minibuses. In the back seat I was interviewed by the TV crew, as were a few of the fishermen. I kept asking what was going on. *Where were we going?*

Soon we were out of the port and driving alongside the litter-strewn beach, past a collection of charmless pastel-coloured concrete buildings, up to the police station at the top of the hill.

Before the Portuguese arrived (looking for a convenient stopover for the slave ships heading west from Africa to the New World) nobody lived on the Cape Verde islands. It isn't hard to see why. They are ten rather barren islands in the middle of nowhere. It has the feeling of an old penal colony and a general tone of melancholia. It's not quite African, not quite Caribbean, locked forever in between — gazing out to sea.

As mentioned in the last chapter, I had asked on my website for somebody to let the authorities know we were coming. I kinda expected it to come from the Cape Verde representative in the UK (who at the time lived in Liverpool) or else the TV production company, something on letterhead paper, explaining in detail — and in Portuguese — the nature of my adventure.

Instead, all the Cape Verdean authorities got was a fax off my mum with the following, written in English:

To Whom It May Concern

Graham Hughes will be arriving by boat in Praia on the morning of Wednesday 3rd June 2009.

And that's it. Now I'm not a police officer, but I can see why somebody *might* just read that as a tip-off that a major criminal/drug dealer/terrorist/people smuggler was coming to town.

Which was exactly how they read it.

Although, at that point in time, I knew nothing of this fax. I was totally bewildered by this turn of events. Even when I was bundled into the police station I was still thinking that one call to the British embassy and they would have me out in a jiffy. After all, I hadn't broken any laws. Seaports are international zones, and I didn't leave the seaport of my own free will.

But I didn't get to call the embassy. I didn't get to call anybody.

Instead I was relieved of my bags, belt and shoelaces, and I had my fingerprints taken.

Now I had never been properly arrested before, but I had watched enough episodes of American cop shows to be pretty sure that they have to tell you what they think you've done wrong before they can throw you in a cell.

Not, it seems, in Cape Verde.

We were forced downstairs into a lock-up, a narrow concrete bunker beneath the cop shop. There was a caged metal staircase in the middle of the room and along one side there were three cells, each perhaps ten foot by ten foot, each with a fetid squat toilet in the corner.

The cage door slammed shut behind us.

We sat on the dusty cement floor and waited.

We would be left down there all day. My requests for habeas corpus, a statement of arrest, a phone call, a lawyer or even my malaria medication fell on deaf ears.

Meanwhile, on the other side of the lock-up, two teenage boys and one young girl, alleged to have been caught stealing, were made to hold out their hands, and had them soundly whacked with a metal rod. The girl fell on the floor in pain. The policeman tried helping her back onto her feet by beating her some more with the rod. Instead, she curled up into a ball crying for somebody to help her.

The fishermen held me back. What the hell had I got myself into?

By evening I was beginning to panic. What if I get deported — by plane? What if I never get out of here? The last tweet I sent said we were heading back to Senegal, which was obviously not the case. Nobody knew where I was.

At 8pm the police officers instructed all eleven of us to get into one of the tiny 10-foot by 10-foot cells. A cell that was designed for one occupant. They slammed the door shut and locked it. Lights out.

There was me, sitting in the dark with ten rather bemused (but thankfully not angry) fishermen. The cell had no bed. I used my jumper as a pillow and fell asleep on the cement floor, trying not to breathe through my nose. None of us had washed in four days.

The next day I began (very vocally) protesting against my treatment. At the very least, I should be allowed to call my family. Most of the day we were kept in the cell. We were only allowed out into the larger lock-up for a few hours, as if for exercise. I spent my time constructively demanding a phone call off anyone who had the misfortune of walking past the lock-up. My pleas fell on deaf ears.

I was surprised that none of them gave me my phone call just to shut me the hell up.

The crew of the *Mustafa Sy* took it all in their stride. They whiled away the hours playing cards or playing football with an empty plastic bottle. When it was time to pray (Senegal being a predominantly Muslim country) my compass watch came in handy for pointing to Mecca.

On the third day I was beginning to suspect I was a victim of one of Stanley Milgram's psychological experiments. I had been given no change of clothes, there was no shower and by now it was either crap or risk bowel cancer. It was now Friday and I hadn't gone since the previous Sunday. Luckily, I had befriended one of the cops, a guy called George. He went out and bought me a toilet roll (I have no intention of ever using the old wet-left-hand trick). You know you're in trouble when the most exciting event of your day is going for a shit.

I tried to keep a brave face, but was all rather miserable. Although they did feed us well (we had two decent meals a day, usually rice and meat in gravy), bottled water was a little difficult to come by, so I had to make do with tap water. Actually, the fact that I still hadn't suffered the squits the entire journey, despite me having to brave some pretty damn insanitary conditions along the way, only goes to prove that my DNA should be extracted and cloned in order to create the race of ginger super-soldiers that will one day RULE THE WORLD. Yeah!

That night, after banging on my cell door for a good hour, a cop came down, opened the door and told me to shut the hell up. He looked like a Portuguese Will Smith. I didn't like him. But seizing my opportunity for a bit of amateur dramatics, I put on the waterworks, got down on my knees and explained that my mother will think I'm dead. I may have even dribbled a bit. It was a jolly good show.

But the copper wasn't impressed. He just threw me back in the cell and went upstairs.

By the fourth day of my incarceration I had been held beyond the 24-hour limit of habeas corpus, and even beyond the 48-hour limit of extenuating circumstances, so unless I was suspected of being a terrorist, I was now arguably more sinned against than sinning.

The police told me that the British consulate had been informed; they told me they had spoken to my family; they told me a lawyer was on the way. None of these things would turn out to be true.

I surveyed the possibilities of escape. I timed the appearance of cops (totally random), attempted to scrape away at the walls Shawshank-style with a spoon that I had pilfered at dinnertime (not much use against reinforced concrete). I even had a go at the metal window bars with a large bit of scaffolding that the cops had left in the lock-up (dramatic, but futile). It was no use.

I decided the only way out was to injure myself sufficiently in order to be taken to hospital, then to seduce a nurse to get her on-side and pull a fast one dressed as a doctor before heading under cover of darkness to the relative safety of the US embassy.

They say when you travel you find out things about yourself you never knew before. I discovered that I'm bloody difficult to knock out (even more reason to create an army of super-soldier clones from my DNA). Or maybe I'm just a wuss. Either way, after banging my noggin on the cell door far too many times, I had to pretend to be knocked unconscious. (More superb acting — where's my Oscar, eh?)

I lay on the floor for over an hour, not moving. Nobody gave a crap. In any case I was getting pins and needles so I got up and dusted myself down. All I had achieved was giving myself a splitting headache.

Not long after, one of the policemen who had taken pity on me rather unexpectedly handed me his mobile phone.

'Para sua família', he whispered. He told me I had five minutes, and left me to it.

This was my ticket out of this nightmare. Unfortunately, I was not familiar with Sony phones and wasted most of the five given minutes attempting to unlock the damn thing. When it did finally open I had to navigate not just an unfamiliar phone but an unfamiliar phone that was set to Portuguese.

I dialled my parents. The call connected, but all I could hear was my own voice repeated back at me so I hung up. As the seconds ticked away, I made my way to the text message interface and, hands shaking with adrenaline, I typed the following message:

**Graham.here.been.arrested.in.praia.cape.
verde.4.days.no.lawyer.no.phone.help.**

(I couldn't find the space key.)

Now all I needed to do was type in a number and hit send.

Oh hang on —

Think of all the mobile phone numbers you actually remember (and your own can't be one of them). If you know more than two you really need to get out more. At that moment, I could recall precisely none. And the police officer was coming back down the stairs to collect his phone.

Think think think think think!!!

Okay – my brother Mike had not changed his mobile number in years. Although I probably hadn't had to manually punched it into a phone for a good decade and I didn't remember the number, I reckoned I could remember the pattern. I closed my eyes and typed a number through the power of muscle memory. I opened my eyes. It looked about right. I hit send just as the policeman held out his hand to take the phone back. I thanked the policeman profusely, yet I had no way of knowing if the message had gone to the right place.

An hour passed.

And then another hour.

Night fell.

Nothing.

You know, until 1980, Cape Verde was a part of Guinea-Bissau on the African mainland. Had that still been the case, my life would have been a whole lot easier.

My fifth day of incarceration began with a wonderful surprise. And by "wonderful" I mean "horrible". Shouts, screams, and laughter drew my curiosity from out of my cell and into the lock-up area. Some of the other prisoners were already up and had gathered around what I can only describe as the most drunken mess of a human I have ever seen; a guy who was so wasted that he had defecated all over himself, rolled in it, puked up, pissed himself and then passed out in his own faecal matter.

There was shit everywhere! All over his bare feet, in his hair, all over the floor. The other prisoners were trying to hose him down when I got summoned upstairs — the first time I had been allowed to leave the lock-up in over 120 hours.

There was a phone call for me.

The text message had got through.

I picked up the phone. It was a lady called Isabelle, the assistant to the British Consulate. She told me that they were doing everything they could to get me out. Once I had answered one call, they couldn't really stop me — I spent the best part of the day upstairs taking calls from my Mum and Dad, Mandy, my brothers Alex and Mike. I even did an interview for a British news network.

When I returned to the cells several hours later, the cack monster was curled up Gollum-like in the corner of the lock-up, beside a bike with a broken chain. He had managed to defecate himself even more and now the whole jail now resembled the aftermath of a German scat orgy.

The fishermen were pressed against the back wall, praying for the wind to change and deliver them from the stench.

I felt awful that the fishermen didn't have the opportunity to go and use the phone. I felt awful for putting them in this situation in the first place. If the police had let me make a phone call on the Wednesday, we would have been out on Thursday at the latest, and yet here we were; five days later and the police were STILL not telling us what was going on.

That evening the cack monster returned from whence he came, unlike his cack, which was left all over the floor and up the walls.

At least I knew this would be our last night in this damn jail.

Well, that's what I hoped.

On Monday morning, Captain Mbeye and I were taken away with four other members of the crew. It'll come as no great surprise that we weren't told where they were taking us, but it turned out to be the courthouse, the Palácio Da Justiça. There I met Maria, the wonderful lawyer that my parents and the British Consulate had organised for me. She assured me we'd be out before we knew it — the police had no case and no right to hold us for so long. It was a clear breach of habeas corpus.

However, they didn't have a translator for the fishermen, so we had to go back to the cells. The fishermen and I ate lunch together, and just after 2pm we left that infernal lock-up for what we hoped would be the last time.

At the courthouse, I met a dapper Englishman by the name of Piran. He was from Sheffield and had taken the day off work to help out a fellow Brit in need. He translated for me as Maria explained the whole sorry affair to the judge.

While we waited for each of the fishermen, one by one, to be interviewed by the judge, I chatted to local reporters outside the courtroom. Around 6pm we were all called back into the courtroom to hear the case for the prosecution and the case for the defence.

The prosecutor said it was his considered opinion that the whole thing was a big mistake and that we should all be set free. Keep in mind, this was the *prosecution!*

That made Maria's job a little easier — she simply stood up and said she agreed with the prosecution. The judge took a few seconds to deliberate and then delivered his verdict.

He set us all free.

The police chief stormed out in a fury at this travesty of justice — he obviously thought he had caught the "Carlos the Jackal" of people smuggling.

So there we were, free men. Well, not quite. We had to wait for another hour for our court papers to be written up.

My mind raced through all I had gone through in Africa so far; my failure to visit either Libya or Algeria; the slog back and forth through the Sahara desert to acquire a visa I didn't even need; my trip to Gambia where I heroically failed to cross the border; the stress and mindboggling expense of Dakar; the 650km journey across open ocean on an open wooden boat, arriving wet and sunburnt in Cape Verde only to be arrested; the week spent sleeping on the floor of a tiny concrete jail cell; the big bruise on my head; the cack monster...

Then came what I regard as the definitive example of the expression "adding insult to injury".

When they finally arrived, my court papers were printed in Comic Sans.

Comic f---ing Sans.

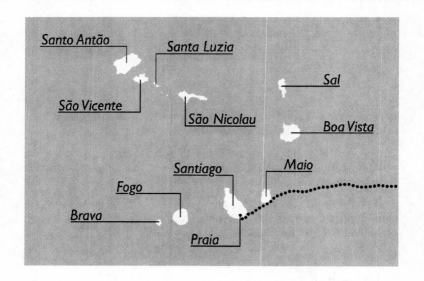

Chapter 15
Santiago's Revenge

The *Mustafa Sy* had been impounded by the police and had been declared un-seaworthy (to be fair, it probably was). The fishermen would be flown back to Dakar the next day. Thankfully, I was permitted to stay in Cape Verde and find an alternative way back to mainland Africa.

Maria contacted the minister responsible for the police and he ensured that all of my Senegalese chums had somewhere to stay for the night. Piran gave us all a lift in his 4×4 monster truck to their hotel, and I said my goodbyes to Captain Mbeye, Modou, Saliou, Ablaye, Adama, Aleen, Aleen, Mahmoud, Doudou and Elage. I told them if I manage to get any compensation out of this traumatic and frustrating experience, I'll be sure to pass it on to them. Heaven knows they deserve it.

Piran offered to put me up for the night and I wasn't going to say no. After a much-needed shower, I headed out for a "pizza of liberation", washed down by copious amounts of alcohol. We met up with some other British ex-pats and drank the night away.

I woke up at Piran's place with a bit of a hangover. He loaned me a T-shirt so at least I looked somewhat presentable. The police still had all my stuff, including my backpack and video camera.

At Piran's office in town he introduced me to a local guy who worked for him called Mito. Mito took me to the police to try and get my stuff back. They referred us to border control at the docks, who then referred us to customs, who then refused us point blank.

The Cape Verdean authorities seemed intent on making it as difficult as humanly possible for me to get my stuff back. And that was just the start of it, if I wished to ship the fisherman's boat back to Dakar or leave Cape Verde any time soon it would be an uphill struggle.

They would not let me have my passport back until I had booked passage out of the country. However, I was on the island of Santiago and the main sailboat marina was on another island, São Vicente. I couldn't leave the island of Santiago, even to go to another island in the Cape Verde chain, without my passport. This massively reduced my chances of finding a yacht.

Not only that, but the police had thrown away my awesome green leather jacket. The bastards!

So we asked around the shipping agencies for a cargo ship heading to Africa. The only boat that seemed to offer any hope was called the *Micau*. It would be arriving in Praia from Sal, another island in the Cape Verde chain, the next day. It would be going to Dakar, then Guinea Bissau. There was nothing else for the next 10 days.

I met the owner and he agreed to allow me passage and to take the pirogue back to the fishermen — for a price.

Later on that day, I was interviewed for the local paper with Mito acting as translator. I had a few choice words to say about the police and my treatment since my arrival.

I soon learnt it would have been better if I had kept my gob shut.

That night I had a very long Skype call with Mandy on Piran's computer (I had left my laptop with Mentor in Senegal). She had been beside herself the whole time I had been in jail and implored me to quit while I was ahead. But there was too much at stake. And the TV show added a lot of pressure for me to get this thing finished.

Although my relationship with Lonely Planet was at an all-time low (I pretty much blamed them for everything that had happened since I arrived in Dakar), I didn't want to get sued by the world's biggest travel book company for breach of contract, even if they were paying me less than minimum wage to single-handedly film a TV show in some of the most dangerous countries in the world.

The next day I got my backpack and video camera back, which was good news. The bad news was that the *Micau* had been delayed and wouldn't be getting in for "a couple of days".

That night, Mito and I grabbed some barbecued chicken and went to a basketball game. Afterwards, we got rotten drunk and I staggered back to my hotel at about 3am.

A week later and I was still waiting for the *Micau* to arrive.

I felt like I had left one jail only to be released... into a bigger jail.

On June 16th I got the call I'd been waiting for. The *Micau* would be arriving in Praia the next day.

The cost of transporting me and the fishermen's boat? €5,000. Seriously. Mito managed to get them down to €3,500, but still, I never for a moment believed Africa would be so expensive.

Nevertheless, I woke the next day excited and invigorated. *The Odyssey Expedition* was back on the road! All I had to do was pay the shipping agency and get my passport back.

I grabbed a bite to eat at Café Sophia and headed over to the office to meet Mito. Then we went to the shipping agency. I got a letter off them saying they wished to take the pirogue and were giving me passage. Then I went to see Maria the lawyer, got a letter requesting that the authorities let me take the boat, went to the port office, got told to come back with a copy of the boat's ownership documents, went back to Mito's office, got in touch with the fishermen and got them to fax the ownership documents over to Maria, made a number of calls to my bank who decided to pick that day of all days to lock my telephone banking service, got Mandy to transfer the money instead (we had a joint account and she was able to make the transfer just in time before the banking day was over), went back to see Maria, picked up the fax from the fishermen, headed back to the port office, got all the papers stamped and signed and then...

And then...

And then...

Mito had a conversation in Portuguese with the Captain of the Port of Praia. He turned to me, looking despondent, 'The Captain of the Port on Sal[21] has decided not to allow the *Micau* to leave until Friday.'

He didn't know why.

Another two days.

'Are you still here?', asked a kid the following morning as I walked down for breakfast at Café Sophia. I told him I'd be leaving tomorrow. 'That's what you said last week', he said with a cheeky grin.

I shrugged.

When Friday finally rolled around, I was all packed and ready to go and standing at the port when I got the news. The *Micau* wouldn't be leaving Sal until Monday.

To give this a sense of scale, in less time than I had been stuck on Cape Verde, I managed to visit every single country in Europe. When I arrived in Cape Verde, the police took everything from me — my camera, my GPS, my passport, my wallet.

It was now clear that they also took any chance I had of completing *The Odyssey Expedition* within a year.

And there was another problem. Remember I mentioned a passport full of visas for Africa that I picked up in Barcelona? Those visas had

---

[21] Author's Note: Another island in the Cape Verde chain

exceptionally limited "use by" dates. They were beginning to expire one by one. The longer I was in Cape Verde, the longer I'd be in Africa waiting for new visas.

The timing couldn't be worse. West Africa was now well into the rainy season, when the rivers are flooded, roads impassable and malaria runs rampant.

Futhermore, the *Micau* did not leave the following Monday.

A couple of days earlier I had met a captain of another ship, the *Manx Lion*, which was heading to Banjul in Gambia. He said he'd take me but I believed the *Micau* would actually be leaving. If I had jumped on board the Manx Lion I could be halfway back to Africa by now.

I had Mentor phoning me every day. The fishermen, whose livelihood depended on getting their fishing boat back were going (understandably) ape-shit. I'd speak to Mandy, but that didn't help lift my spirits. She cried and that made me cry. I could only talk to her for short time because it cost her so much to call me — with my laptop in Dakar, Skype was not an option.

To pile on my misery, I was informed that my TV show would be called *"Graham's World"*. For a white British middle-class bloke to go around the developing nations of the world declaring them "his" is about as culturally insensitive as it gets. I implored them to change the name, writing a 1,700 word essay and coming up with a list of 74 alternative titles that would be somewhat more sensitive than bringing out an Anne Frank-branded drumkit. But my pleas fell on deaf ears.

Signing up to make the TV show also meant that I was forced to take all of the weekly blog videos that I had made down, even though they were getting tens of thousands of views. My plan had been to donate my YouTube partnership money to WaterAid — as things stood I'd have made more money for WaterAid climbing into a bath of baked beans. I wasn't even allowed to capitalise on all the media coverage I received after being arrested.

I had never, ever, in all my life been this miserable, frustrated, hopeless, lonely and lost.

The pressure to give up and go home was becoming intolerable.

The *Micau* finally came into port of Praia on June 25th. I frantically tried to find Mito to help me organise transporting the pirogue to the docks, but without success. In the end, a local guy named Val said that he'd help me out, but he seemed dodgy as hell, and I had been warned to keep away from him.

But as things turned out, the *Micau* wasn't going anywhere.

The next day I met with a local woman called Ines, who had offered to help me with my boat situation, but all I learned was: (a) that Michael Jackson had died and (b) that if I knew what was good for me, I should be getting the hell out of Cape Verde *as soon as the next flight would allow*. Ines was in tears as she told me this, which prompted my (already heightened) fears for my safety.

In short, I really shouldn't have done that newspaper interview.

For the first time on *The Odyssey Expedition* I was justifiably scared for my life. From that point on I never walked anywhere alone in case somebody who is handy with a knife came looking to avenge the slight I had spat on the otherwise good name of Cape Verde.

My only respite from this horrible situation was playing chess with my new friend Yuri, the security guy from Café Sophia. Yuri wasn't like anyone else I met from Cape Verde (he was born in Angola) — he was friendly, cheerful and had a wonderfully positive outlook on life. In return I helped him compose sweet text messages to his girlfriend in Switzerland, like a latter day Cyrano de Bergerac.

As far as my own love life was concerned, things weren't great. It had been six months since I last saw Mandy. It would be at least another six months until I saw her again, maybe more. Things were becoming increasingly strained.

Café Sophia was a great place for meeting people. Possibly because there was nowhere else in Praia where you could sit under a parasol, drink a beer and watch the world go by. On a typical day I would sit and chat with Maggie from Zimbabwe and Debbie from Connecticut and their mate Tomek from Poland who was studying Cape Verdean anthropology.

They would be relieved by Colin, an English guy who was working for a GPS company setting up relay stations. Then we'd be joined by Margarita; a remarkable lady born in Britain, raised in Africa, a citizen of Spain now living on the island of Maio. She was in her 60s, but still working as a builder.

Then I'd meet a girl from Sierra Leone called Nazia and her friend, before settling down to a good ol' game of chess against Yuri.

Everyone I spoke to seemed to be waiting for something. I was waiting for the goddamn *Micau*, Maggie was waiting for her passport to return from Copenhagen, Colin was waiting for his GPS equipment to arrive, Margarita was waiting for her niece to arrive from the Canary Islands (the Cape Verdean airline wouldn't let her on the plane for some daft bureaucratic reason) and Yuri was waiting for his girlfriend from Switzerland to arrive — she was stuck in Portugal.

All of us had in some way been slowed down, hindered, disrupted or inconvenienced by the powers that be of Cape Verde.

By the time June became July I stopped believing that the *Micau* was ever going to leave, so I started looking for serious alternatives. I went with Margarita to talk to the other shipping companies in Praia, but none of them went to Dakar. The closest was the *Manx Lion* (the captain of which I spoke to the other week), which would be returning from Banjul in Gambia at the end of the month.

I met a nice bloke from Maersk, the biggest shipping company in the world, but the only way to Dakar would be a trip of a few thousand miles north to Spain, change there and head back down to Dakar, crossing the Sahara for a fourth time. It didn't seem like much of an option.

Meanwhile, the crane guys turned up to take the *Mustafa Sy* from outside the port authority offices half a mile down the road to the port, but Cape Verde being Cape Verde, there was another form they required in order to take the pirogue away. Val, the rather disreputable character who — through a lack of other options — had been "helping" me, demanded €100 "to pay for their time" — even though they didn't actually do anything. Whether he actually gave it to the crane guys is another matter.

I then went to speak to the *capitão do porto* to find out more about the situation with the *Micau*. Turns out it had been refused permission to leave the port. He presented me with a checklist of TWENTY things that need to be repaired on the *Micau* before they'd declare it seaworthy and allow its departure.

A couple of weeks earlier, I had met an American girl named Callie who was ex-peace corps. After running into her again (and after the predictable 'are you *still* here?!'), she put me in touch — through her mate Rachelle — with a German guy named Milan who was on Maio, the island a few miles east of Santiago that I passed on the way to Praia. Milan had a sailboat. He had been on my website and had learnt of my predicament. I called him up and almost immediately he said the words I had been waiting over a month to hear.

'Yes. It's possible.'

'What? You'll bring your yacht here to pick me up and take me to Dakar?'

'Yes,' said Milan, my new favourite person in all the world. 'Why not?'

The boat required a few minor repairs before it left, but Milan assured me we would be on our way by the end of the week. I felt something I hadn't felt in a long time — hope.

Freed from the shackles of being told that the *Micau* was "definitely" going to leave the next day, I took Colin — the GPS guy — up on his offer to visit a place up the coast called Cidade Velha, a UNESCO World Heritage site and the location of the very first European colony in the tropics. It happened to be Cape Verde's Independence Day, so there was a big crowd down there and some singers and a few television cameras. I even saw the chief from the police station that I was held in. I gave him a smile and a wave. I'm not one to hold grudges.

A couple of days later I travelled to the town of Tarrafel on the far north of the island (Praia is on the south coast) with an American called Gary. Gary had lived for over thirty years in West Africa, specifically Liberia and Sierra Leone. He was there during the wars, working for the UN and development agencies. He was a very interesting guy.

We passed through Santiago's central mountains along the way. In between the desolate brown, barren wastes, there were snippets of green — microclimates caused by valleys in the hills. Otherwise, it was like driving on the surface of Mars. It hardly ever rains on the island of Santiago.

The road up the middle of the island alternated between dreadful and not-so dreadful. We stopped at a few villages along the way; I had a good giggle at the one called "Assomada" which I imagined was Portuguese for "Mad Asshole". Sadly nobody else was in the slightest bit amused. Turns out it's not just the citizens of the capital city who are damn hard to make smile — it's everyone.

There's a thing the Portuguese call "saudade" — a deep emotional state of nostalgic or profound melancholic longing for an absent something or someone. It clings to the island of Santiago like a heavy fog.

Tarrafel has the only decent beach on the island. Brightly coloured fishing boats give the place a splash of character. However, the town, such that it is, looks like a building site. A rather silly government rule allowed residents not to pay tax on an unfinished property, meaning that hundreds of buildings were exactly that — unfinished. There were rows and rows of empty, half-built breeze-block constructions set out in a grid pattern. I dubbed it "Unpleasantville".

We drove back along the east coast, down a well-kept cobbled road with delightful views of the sea. We stopped and grabbed a drink in the village of Calheta de São Miguel, looking out over one of the many black beaches on the island. Black volcanic sand. Like sunbathing in a coal scuttle.

When we got back to Praia I had to duck into Café Sophia in order to avoid Val. He was now demanding that I pay him €600 for his "services". These "services" included not getting me my passport back, not getting the pirogue to the dock and not finding me a yacht to come and pick me up. He just flapped around for a few days, spent a lot of my money on phone calls, took a lot of taxis (which I paid for) and generally swanned about doing nothing constructive or even mildly helpful. It could have been a metaphor for the entire island.

I wasn't really concerned though. Val was wanted by the police. He ripped off a fellow Brit to the tune of €1,500 and the guy wanted his money back. I knew if I hung around in a public area, Val would be reluctant to make a scene. But still, I had to watch my back.

On the morning of July 10th 2009 I checked out of the Hotel Atlantico, the place where I'd been hanging my hat for the past month. The first person that I ran into was Val, who was demanding money or else he would burn the papers that would otherwise allow me to get my passport back. I'm a pretty good liar when I want to be; unfortunately for Val, he is not. I knew damn well that I didn't need any papers to get my passport back, I just needed the captain of a boat — and Milan had texted me an hour earlier, he was on his way.

I pushed Val aside. I had things to be getting on with.

Milan arrived that afternoon with his friend Sebastian, a Frenchie and fellow ginger who would be sailing with us. We had to hurry to get everything sorted before everything shut for the weekend.

First, we went to the immigration office and they made the necessary phone call to release my passport. The guy who made the call — Mr Samedo — had been a right pain in the arse for the duration of my confinement on that bloody island, so it was with great delight that I waved him goodbye, a face I hoped to never see again.

Then it was down to the port to sign out and retrieve my dear old passport. The port official opened the metal cabinet. My eyes lit up as I spied the familiar burgundy booklet, the golden lion and unicorn adorning the cover.

"Without let or hindrance" indeed.

However, it was not all plain sailing. The authorities denied our request to take the fishermen's engine, handheld GPS and fuel back with us. They'd have to return on the *Micau*. The shipping agency still had my money and said it would all be sorted when the boat was ready to depart, whenever that should be.

I headed over to Café Sophia and grabbed a quick drink with Tomek the Polish Guy, Debbie from Connecticut, and Maggie from Zimbabwe, while Milan and Sebastian stocked up on supplies. When Milan and Sebastian returned, we loaded up the boot of a taxi and were ready to head to the port.

Saying goodbye to Yuri was surprisingly emotional. We had formed a real bond over the weeks and his cheerful, happy-go-lucky attitude had rubbed off on me in a positive way — it had helped to keep me going. He asked who was going to help him with his text messages to his girlfriend once I had gone. I told him to just be himself and he'd be fine.

Down to the port, into an inflatable dingy and over to Milan's boat — the *Fleumel*. After six weeks stuck in country 89, it was time to get the goddamn show back on the goddamn road.

It was time to feel the rain again.

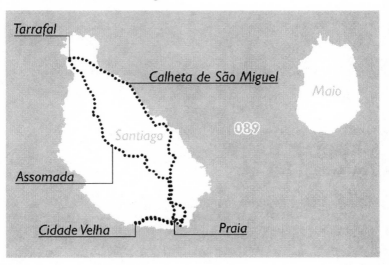

Chapter 16
The Great Escape

Milan had been living on the Cape Verdean island of Maio for the previous few years. He was outwardly warm and cheerful, but his story was not a happy one.

He was the owner of a large real estate company in Germany, with a nice car and a nice house and all the trimmings. Then, one day, he left for work, kissed his wife goodbye and never saw her again. She was killed a few hours later in a car accident. Milan decided to make a clean break of it after that. He sold everything: his business, his house, his car and set out to sail the world. He somehow wound up on Maio, liked the place, and stayed.

Sebastian grew up not in France, but in Côte d'Ivoire. He lived there for almost two decades. His reasons for staying in Cape Verde were that he came, liked what he saw and stayed. He wasn't a sailor — in fact this was his first proper jaunt. But he was a great cook — he refused any help in the kitchen and took great delight in ribbing me about English cuisine. He once went to Bristol to see AC/DC live and stayed with an English family. They fed him — get this — boiled beef and jellied mint.

Way not to impress a Frenchman, England!

Or, for that matter, anyone born with taste buds.

For Milan and Sebastian to take all this time, leave their friends on Maio and rescue me is the stuff of legend. A 1,322km round trip to help a ginger in need who strayed too far from the beaten path. My experience in Cape Verde may have shaken my faith in humanity, but thanks to Milan and Sebastian it was now stronger than ever.

However, our great escape didn't go *exactly* to plan.

We were supposed to leave on the night of the 10th, but upon waking, I discovered that we were still in the port — we hadn't moved an inch. The electrics were down on the boat after Milan accidentally crashed it on some rocks the previous month. This meant no engine and no radio. We would be completely reliant on the wind, and — worst of all — there would be no cold beer.

It was noon before the breeze picked up and we could set off. But we didn't get very far — by nightfall the island of Santiago was still in view.

It was shaping up to be a long goodbye.

There was painfully little wind on the second day as well. We bobbed along at a sedate two-and-a-half knots.

The third day was even slower. There was not one iota of a smidgin of a skerrick of a sub-atomic particle of a whisper of wind. The sea was as flat as it could be — more like a boating lake than the second biggest ocean in the world.

It occurred to me that the sea is not that different from the desert: nothing to drink but what you bring with you, the sun bearing down, no shade, no trees, no escape. A vast undulating landscape that stretches as far as the eye can see. Food can be found, but you need some decent hunter/gatherer skills to obtain it. None of which I possess.

A more attractive aspect that the sea shares with the desert is the wealth and clarity of stars that pepper the night sky. From this latitude (about 15 degrees north of the equator), I could see both the North Star and the Southern Cross. Orion was keeping a low profile so it was up to Scorpius to be the most startling constellation in the heavens. If we kept that wee stingin' beastie to the right side of the boat we'd eventually hit Africa.

We plodded along on the fourth day, picking up a bit of speed around noon which ebbed away as the afternoon wore on. We had hoped to be in Dakar that night. We were still 300 miles away.

Just as the sun was setting behind us, we spotted not one, not two, but *five* sperm whales coming to have a mosey at our boat.

Sebastian and I, being non-seafarers, were delighted to see our cetacean friends take an interest — people pay hundreds of dollars to see stuff like this. But Captain Milan was a lot less starry-eyed. He jumped up on deck and started banging a stick on a metal rail as hard as he could.

BANG BANG BANG!!!

'What are you doing?', I asked him.

'We don't want them to mate with us!', he yelled, flummoxed that I hadn't considered that a possibility.

He had a point though, it would be like Jabba The Hutt trying to mate with a hamster — the little *Fleumel* wouldn't stand a chance.

Thankfully, the whales harmlessly passed by, fellow wayfarers on the same wibbly-wobbly road of improbable blue.

On our fifth day at sea, the wind really picked up and by midday we were flying over the waves. At one point, a school of over 50 dolphins came to play with us. They lined up perpendicular to the *Fleumel*'s bow and put on a display of synchronised swimming that wouldn't have looked out of place at the Olympics.

I slipped off my shoes and dangled my legs off the prow of the boat as dozens of the playful tykes danced about in the water below. Great fun.

On Friday we were still at sea. That night would make it a whole week on the *Fleumel* for the three of us. There was no sign of Dakar, although the GPS insisted it was less than 100 miles away.

I was particularly worried that Mandy and her over-active imagination would be concerned that I had been attacked by a giant squid, swallowed by a white whale, consumed by the ghastly kraken or stuck frantically lopping the heads off a hydra only for more to grow in their place.

No such excitement I'm afraid, but that night there was an epic thunderstorm over yonder, flashes in the distant clouds every couple of seconds. I hoped Senegal hadn't descended into war, but with no radio and no contact with civilisation for a week, who's to say what was going on in the real world?

The storm encouraged the wind to buck its act up, and we had a night of good sailing. Milan stayed up all night battling to keep us going in the right direction (no electrics = no autohelm). The wind, being fickle, started blowing from the south, usurping my usual sleeping position on deck. With the *Fleumel* now tilted over to the left (sorry, port), any attempt to sleep on the right (sorry, starboard) of the boat would almost certainly end in some sort of crashing-to-the-floor based injury.

I had no choice but to head below deck and attempt to sleep on the spare bed at the very front of the boat – where the constant rising-and-falling motion is at its greatest.

That, along with the lack of fresh air, the whiff of the chemical toilet and the unpleasant sound of the bilge water glooping around under the floor was enough to turn me Hulk green. After just a few minutes I was back on deck chucking my guts up over the side.

Mercifully, Sebastian said I could sleep in his bed near the back of the boat and he'd take the nightmare that was the forward berth. I still have no idea why anyone would do this kind of thing for fun.

Early the next morning, I could just make out two vast grey forms on the horizon — a pair of hills, one with a massive half-built statue sticking out of the top like a great big nipple. Dakar. We were nearly there. Within a few hours, we had phone contact, but British SIM cards don't work in Senegal. Sebastian came to my rescue and gave me his phone so I could text Mandy and let her know that her favourite travelling monkey was still alive.

The approach to Dakar seemed to take an eternity. Milan was shattered, and so finally allowed me to take the helm for the first time all week. We sailed past the half-built statue, past sunken ships and an old lighthouse.

Eventually, Milan steered us into the marina using just the wind, which really is a skill and a half. We were greeted by two guys in a shuttle boat eager to take us ashore. I jumped in with them and they took me over to the broken-down wooden jetty. I clambered onto the rotting wood, stood tall and punched the air with my fist.

I had made it.

Back on dry land. Back, back, back to Africa.

I had been told that there was no marina in Senegal. In the marina bar I met a French family who were heading out the next day on their sailboat. Their destination? Cape Verde.

I laughed. We clinked beers. 'You don't want to come with us, do you? We could do with a deckhand.'

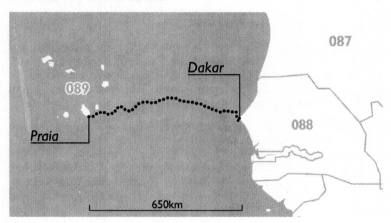

Chapter 17
Guinea Foul

That night I took Milan and Sebastian out for a well-deserved slap-up meal. Later, we were joined by an American guy named Jared, my CouchSurf contact for the night.

After dinner, Milan and Sebastian retired to the *Fleumel* and I headed out with Jared to meet with Mentor and Captain Mbeye to discuss how the hell we were going to get his damn boat back.

Predictably, the *Micau* still hadn't left Praia.

Mentor brought my things he'd been keeping for me: my clothes, my chargers, my laptop. I have to admit that I was still pissed with him for putting me on that damn boat. Although it was good to see Mbeye. He asked if he would ever see me again — I said I'll be back one day. I would like to keep that promise. I owe him a slap-up meal too.

Late as it was, it was great of Jared to come with me. Jared was a peace corps volunteer of rural Californian stock. He was living with a Senegalese family in Dakar. Their home was pretty basic — I had to stand in the squat toilet in my bare feet to use the cold shower with just my mobile phone for a light. But it was heaven compared to bobbing up and down all night and day on the *Fleumel* — I hadn't showered in over a week.

At this point it had been eight weeks since I arrived in Senegal from Mauritania. The following morning it was time to hit the road.

Said road was quite good until the town of Kaolack. Then it became the nightmare I knew it would be, having experienced the damn thing twice on my previous attempt to enter The Gambia.

I wondered why on Earth the Senegalese government allowed the North Koreans to waste millions building a big pointless statue in Dakar when the main transport artery for tens of thousands of Senegalese people was little more than a cattle track.

When I got to the border I wasn't taking *any* chances — this time I'd be passing through the entire nation of **The Gambia** and out the other side.

My biggest worry was that the Senegalese border guys would spot the Cape Verde exit stamp in my passport. Naughtily I didn't get a Senegal exit stamp when I left on the pirogue and didn't report in when I arrived on the *Fleumel*. I hoped my original Senegal stamp (the one that cost me sixty dollars all those weeks ago) would still be valid. As a precaution, I altered the Cape Verde stamp so it read 10.07.08. Unfortunately, that passport was issued on 08.10.08, so there was a slight continuity error, but I figured I'd pass it off as a glitch in The Matrix.

THE GAMBIA 090/200

🏛 **BANJUL**

👥 **1.68m**

💬 **English**

💵 **Gambian Dalasi**

🛵 **$488.57**

In 2009, the President of Gambia's official title was: *His Excellency Sheikh Professor Alhaji Dr. Yahya Abdul-Aziz Awal Jemus Junkung Jammeh Naasiru Deen Babili Mansa.*

After crossing the border and being warmly welcomed into the country (makes a change!), I decided to celebrate 200 days on the road without getting the squits by treating myself to a prawn salad cooked in a shack by the side of the road. It was delicious.

After checking my vision and my pulse, I jumped into a bush taxi and headed to Barra, from where I could take a ferry over the great river Gambia to the capital, Banjul.

On the ferry over the water, I met a fellow scouser called Richie and a wry Cumbrian named Tony. They wanted me to come with them for what they told me was the best pizza in the world in the town of Kololi near the sea.

I was planning to stay in Banjul, get up early the next day and get myself a visa for the next country on my list, Guinea-Bissau.

Kololi was on the way south, towards The Gambia's southern border with Senegal. I could probably get a visa from the city of Ziguinchor in the Casamance province of Senegal, but I didn't know how long it would take to get there, nor how long it took to issue a visa (maybe up to two days) and the Casamance region hasn't exactly got the best reputation.

Ah, to hell with it, I thought; who cares about personal safety when there is delicious pizza to be had?

I'm happy to report that the pizza was, indeed, delicious. I stayed up late drinking and playing pool with my new buddies Richie and Tony.

The next day was a perfect slice of Odyssey Pie. It began (after about 2 hours sleep) with a crankin' hangover in The Gambia. So far, so good. I then took a shared taxi down to the southern border, which brought me into the Casamance province of Senegal. A beautiful place — green and lush, hot and steamy. From there, I headed to Ziguinchor, or Zig, and made plans to stay for the night while I waited for my Guinea-Bissau visa. But good news — the Guinea-Bissau embassy in Zig gave me the visa right there and then.

And so I headed down into **Guinea-Bissau** — the first of the four Guineas I had to visit on this journey (the others being Guinea-Conakry, Equatorial Guinea and Papua New Guinea). I crossed the border and got as far as the town of São Domingos, a ramshackle town on a tributary of the Rio Cacheu.

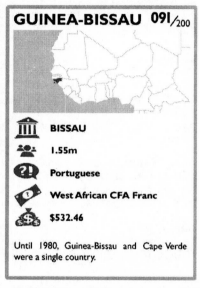

GUINEA-BISSAU 091/200

🏛 **BISSAU**

👥 **1.55m**

💬 **Portuguese**

💵 **West African CFA Franc**

💰 **$532.46**

Until 1980, Guinea-Bissau and Cape Verde were a single country.

At the time, Guinea-Bissau was on the UK's Foreign and Commonwealth Office's danger list — the President had been assassinated a few months earlier and the leading opposition candidate and his wife were murdered the previous month. I didn't fancy having to travel through.

So I threw a couple of stones into the river and returned to Senegal. By the time I got back to Zig, West Africa remembered that it was supposed to be rainy season and it began to chuck it down.

By now I was in desperate need of new MiniDV tapes for my camera if I was to continue filming for the TV show. Near the *sept-place* station/parking lot I found a little shack, filled to the brim with electronic bric-a-brac from China — and lo and behold, they had the exact tapes I needed. Nice one West Africa!

Then it was a short wait while my *sept-place* filled (and for once, it took just *seven* people). We headed east towards my next country: Mali.

I had been expressly told not to travel at night, especially through Casamance. But I figured I'd be out of the region before it got dark.

I figured wrong.

The road was good — all sealed and new tarmac, but the bush taxi only took us as far as the town of Kolda, 150km away. From there I was on my own. The next taxi which was vaguely going my way didn't leave for an age and when it did it was dark. We arrived in Tambacounda, 200km to the north-east, just before midnight. Tambacounda is the crossroads of Senegal, and from there it was fairly simple to find yet another bush taxi that would take me to the border with Mali, 175km further east.

We drove through the night and as a spectacular dawn broke ahead of us, myself and two guys from my shared taxi crossed the bridge over the Falémé River into **Mali**. It was awesomely cinematic.

In less than 24 hours I got from The Gambia to Mali via Guinea-Bissau and Senegal.

Four countries in one day. In West Africa. Amazing.

The bus to Bamako (the capital of Mali) was waiting when I arrived. I was raring to go. Sadly, the bus was not. Isaac, one of the guys who had shared the taxi with me from Tambacounda, told me that many of the people already waiting had been there since yesterday. This did not bode well for our chances of reaching Bamako at a reasonable time.

MALI   092/200

🏛 **BAMAKO**

👥 13.56m

💬 French

💵 West African CFA Franc

💰 $661.13

At one point, Mali was called Ghana. Later it was called Sudan. It didn't become "Mali" until 1960.

When the bus did get going a few hours later, it had a blow-out just a few kilometres down the road. But did that stop the bus driver? Nope. He just kept going and hoped for the best. Unfortunately for Isaac and myself, we were sitting over the wheel arch as the shredded tyre went *fwap fwap fwap* like an irate washing machine. The banging was not too bad at the front of the bus, but where we were sitting, it was unbearable.

It also kicked up all the dust from the road, which entered the chassis through the many rusty holes it had to choose from.

Eventually they pulled over and tried to "fix" the tyre. This involved cutting the shredded tyre off the wheel. At first they tried this with a blunt axe.

Now you have to understand — these are BIG tyres — somewhat larger than the ones you have on your pushbike. They are a metal mesh covered in double-hard rubber. You need a pneumatic drill to make a dent. A rusty old axe ain't going to cut the mustard. Eventually somebody got hold of a machete but it was just as useless.

I suggested they make a hole in the rubber, feed through a length of rope and drive forward, twisting the rope (and the unruly rubber) around the wheel. They did this and it was good for the next few kilometres, but then the rope broke and old fwappy started singing his super annoying song again.

My hair, clothes and bags got covered in dust, but we limped on ever so slowly to Kayes, the first major town after the border. All things being equal it should have taken just over an hour to get there. It took seven.

On the way I got chatting with a couple of guys — brothers — from The Gambia. They asked me a ton of questions about Morocco. They were going to attempt to get into Europe across the Sahara.

I tried to put them off as best I could, by simply telling the truth — there are a ton of checkpoints in Western Sahara and Morocco — they'd never make it. I was also concerned that even if they didn't get caught or end up dying in the desert, they'd drown attempting to cross the Mediterranean. But given the level of poverty I had already experienced in West Africa, I could understand why they'd be willing to risk everything for the chance of what they believed to be a better life.

In Kayes, we crossed the River Senegal. The new bridge was down so we had to cross the 'ford'. Imagine driving along an invisible road, covered by over a foot of fast-moving water, in a bus with a missing tyre and no tread on the ones that remain. The river was about 400 metres across and fast flowing — I was convinced we were going to slide off into the brown raging torrent that teased inches from our left-hand side.

My butt cheeks were clenched tight enough to crack a walnut, but we made it. Once we got to the coach station, Isaac and I decided to stage a mutiny. We headed to the rival GANA bus station around the corner. I bought new tickets for Bamako on what we were both hoping would be a much better bus.

We returned to old fwappy-fwap-fwap to get ourselves a refund for the rest of the journey, but was told there was no refund on the tickets.

'Keep it', I said, 'put it towards a new tyre.'

The bus guys seemed genuinely upset that we were abandoning them, and made a big show that they were going now and that they'd be in Bamako very, very soon.

But we jumped ship and never looked back. The GANA bus had air-conditioning, television, space to spread out and all tyres necessary to complete the journey. We passed old fwappy before the first police checkpoint.

The first checkpoint of many.

Isaac experienced what I considered a surprising amount of prejudice — he alone got tapped for a bribe at pretty much every stop along the way. He told me it was because he was from Ghana. Even though he spoke fluent French, Ghana is an English speaking country and old rivalries die hard.

Isaac and I got to Bamako in the wee small hours, greatly relieved to have made the decision to change buses.

From Bamako I took a shared taxi the 120km to the border with Guinea.

Dear Christ, **Guinea**.

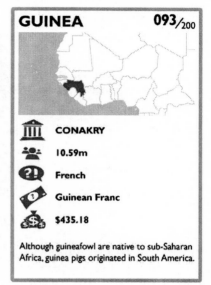

GUINEA   093/₂₀₀

🏛 **CONAKRY**

👥 10.59m

❓ French

💵 Guinean Franc

💰 $435.18

Although guineafowl are native to sub-Saharan Africa, guinea pigs originated in South America.

I arrived at the Guinea border just after sunrise. I cheerfully went through all the usual formalities before marching towards the *sept-place* taxi rank.

It was a beautiful day and I was in a surprisingly good mood.

Once I was a good few hundred metres from the border, I whipped out my camera and explained where I was and all the usual palaver I mention upon entering somewhere new. It was then that a mean-faced old man sitting at the side of the road started going ape-shit at me for filming him.

I tried to explain that I was filming myself, but before I could show this guy the footage, a border policeman had turned up on his motorbike and ordered me to climb aboard. He was armed so I didn't say no. He took me back to the border post, accused me of filming the border and demanded $200 and the camcorder as payment for the fine.

I made him watch back the footage, which featured absolutely no shots of the border, the buildings of the border, the guards of the border or in fact anything other than my fat head and the sky behind it. He didn't care. He wanted his money. He then claimed that my visa had run out (actually, it had, but I had expertly skilfully altered the expiry date with a ball-point pen). He shouted and bawled and banged his fists and behaved quite like a child throwing a tantrum. The mean-faced man from the side of the road showed up, whining that he wanted his soul back or some such nonsense.

They weren't keeping my camera and I most certainly wasn't going to pay this ridiculous $200 fine for doing nothing less than bugger all. There is actually a government decree stating that tourists *are* allowed to use cameras, for this very reason.

Then a guy from Cape Verde came in with his passport to get it stamped in.

Seriously.

He recognised me straight away (perfect timing or what?) and spoke to the guys in French, telling them about me and what I was doing. We all know that my French could do with a little improvement, but I don't think he mentioned me getting arrested, held in jail or any of the rest of all that nonsense.

Or at least I hoped he didn't.

In any case, they still wanted me to pay the fine. So I stonewalled. They wanted to keep me there all day? Fine. I had nothing better to do. Just then one of other border guards walked into the office.

He was wearing a Chelsea top, so I moved the topic of conversation around to the international language of football. Specifically, the FA Cup final that year in which Chelsea beat my team, Everton. After a bit of banter, he asked the chief what the problem was. He reviewed my footage and told the chief I had done nothing wrong.

The chief stuck out his bottom lip and gave a classic Gallic shrug. 'Tu peux partir.'[22]

And that was that.

Thinking my troubles were now behind me, I walked over to the bush taxi 'station'. There wasn't a taxi leaving until 6pm. It was 12 noon, and I didn't really want to be hanging around all day and travelling at night. I tried to get a shared taxi to the nearest big town, Siguiri, but the taxi drivers didn't want me to do that, because they would lose a customer for the much longer journey to Conakry.

So I left the taxi area and attempted to get a private vehicle to take me, just to get out of this aggressive bear-pit. The taxi drivers did not like me doing this. They did not like it one bit.

One of the taxi drivers broke rank and agreed to take me to Siguiri, but I didn't get into the car in time. Another driver dragged him out of the car and they started fighting. Like, really fighting. I sat down and drank a Coke while the other drivers held them back from each other, shouting Christ-knows-what in the local dialect.

Eventually, the taxi drivers reached a compromise — one of them would take me to Siguiri so long as I also paid for another passenger — a soldier who needed to get to the hospital there to see his son.

So I arrived in Siguiri a few Guinea francs lighter than expected. Once there, I was exceptionally lucky (or at least I thought I was) — there was

22 Editor's Note: 'You can leave.'

one space left in a *sept-place* taxi going direct to Conakry. Once I was on board it would leave right away. Groovy.

Only this battered old Peugeot 504 was more of a *douze-place*. I had to share the front passenger seat with another guy whose arse pretty much took up the whole bloody seat. I spent most of the journey sitting on the handbrake.

The road was *terrible* — the worst yet. Riddled with potholes; it hadn't been re-surfaced in years. Our driver did his best and was remarkably careful compared with your typical gung-ho bush taxi driver, but the car was just not up to it.

I could tell by the way he had to pump the brakes to get us to slow down that we had a problem, and by nightfall we had only made it 100km south to the town of Kankan. We pulled over, the steering wheel was taken off and mysterious things were done in the name of car maintenance.

After a while we hit the road again. But only for five minutes. We then turned back and more tyre changing and brake pumping followed. We waited a good two hours.

After the driver was happy we set off again. For a few hours. And then we stopped.

I wasn't supposed to be travelling these parts after dark. And here I was — in the dead of night, with a laptop, a camcorder and a stack of cash — trying to get to sleep with a handbrake poking into my arse at the side of the road in the middle of the *Parc National du Haut Niger*.

The morning dragged by as the driver and latest mechanic (who had been summoned from the nearby village of Sanguiana) took the front left tyre off (again), replaced the bearings and then stuffed everything back into place. If it didn't fit, they would bang it until it did. The tyre was plonked back on and the brakes were tested — nope, still not working properly, but it'd do. I hoped we wouldn't need to make an emergency stop at any point.

We set off again around midday. Given the state of the brakes (and the fact that the car was held together with bubblegum) our driver took it easy. But that meant that the journey took all day. And then some.

Something I hadn't really prepared myself for was the sheer number of police/army checkpoints in West Africa. There was one every few miles. They all want to see your "papers" and, if possible, net themselves a bribe. You think speed cameras are an affront to your human rights? At least they only make you pay when you've done something wrong.

I've met some rather wide-eyed backpackers who tell me that the bribes are fair since the police often don't get paid. Damn right they don't get paid! Why should they get paid? They don't do anything. It's not like they're out solving murders or working deep undercover with the mob. They sit at the side of the road manning a "barrier" (sometimes a couple of tin cans hanging from a string) demanding money at gunpoint.

That's not a job. That's highway robbery. Literally! Some countries are better than others, but Guinea was quite honestly a nightmare.

What's particularly sad is that the people I met along the way (excluding taxi-touts and police) were really good-natured types with time for a chat and a smile. It's therefore a shame that Guinea is now in the rather exclusive club of countries that I would be loath to return to.

The journey was supposed to take 12 hours. After 36 hours, we had arrived on the outskirts of Conakry. I had been tremendously uncomfortable since the start of the journey and I'd had precious little sleep over the previous week, never mind the last couple of days. It was coming up to 4am. At what was to be the final checkpoint, we were told to get out of the car, which we did, all twelve of us plus our driver.

We were then taken into a concrete building at the side of the road, where they checked our "papers". They explained that there was a fine to pay. 200,000 Guinea francs. For allowing two people to share the front seat.

I thought they had to be kidding.

But they weren't.

I told them that 200,000GF was *all* the Guinea francs I had.

We don't care.

We just want the money.

I said it was the middle of the night and I couldn't pay for a hotel without the francs — I would have to wander the (rather dangerous) streets until dawn.

We don't care.

We just want the money.

I explained that if they took all of my money, I would leave immediately for Sierra Leone and tell everyone who'd listen what happened to me – and to *never* to visit Guinea.

We don't care.

We just want the money.

I really didn't want to cave, but there were two young mothers with babies. I offered to wait there until morning and pay them then — if they would just let the others go. They refused my offer and threatened to arrest our driver. They started taking his belt and his shoelaces, ready to throw him in the cell.

Reluctantly, I coughed up the cash.[23]

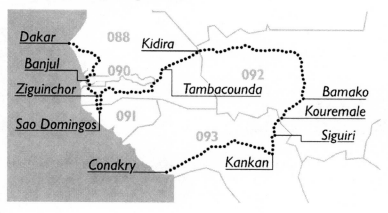

---

[23] Editor's Note: In 2009, 200,000GF was around $28 US.

Chapter 18
Drunk And Laughing

I stormed off into the night, disgusted by all things Guinea, but was caught by the taxi driver who told me it wasn't safe.

'Bandits!'

He begged me to let him drive me to the city centre. The guy that I was sharing my seat with even gave it up and squished himself in the back of the car to say "thank you" for paying off the cops.

We reached Conakry city centre around 5am.

The driver let me snooze for a couple of hours in the back of the taxi. While I slept it started raining. There was an inch gap at the top of the car door; as a consequence I awoke with a rather wet arm.

I grabbed my bags and jumped *a petit taxi* to the main bush taxi area. The driver tried to brazenly rip me off — he drove me just around the corner and then demanded ten euro. Silly man, incurring my wrath in the mood I was in.

Anyway, without having to wait too long, a taxi driver offered to take me all the way to Freetown, the capital of Sierra Leone. He had some people to pick up on the way, but I could have the whole front seat to myself. Sounded good to me.

We drove around Conakry for a bit (it's remarkably unappealing), and picked up a lovely chap from North London and his family who were from Sierra Leone. He had been visiting friends in Conakry. I told him what a rough time I had getting down from the border with Mali. He assured me that once I got to Sierra Leone, I would be welcomed with open arms.

'Why would that be?', I asked.

'Because you're British of course', he answered, with a little incredulity that I wasn't already aware that this would be the case.

I'm happy to report that he was absolutely correct. The first official I met from **Sierra Leone** heartily shook my hand and welcomed me into his country. As did the next guy; and the next.

This outpouring of affection might seem a little incongruous, especially given Britain's appalling historical record of enslavement in this region, not to mention the age of colonisation which came after.

But Sierra Leone has a slightly different story to the rest.

During the American War of Independence, the British army offered any slave who fought on

🏛 **FREETOWN**

👥 **5.64m**

❓ **English, Bengali**

💵 **Sierra Leonean Leone**

💰 **$435.01**

Almost all Sierra Leoneans are bi-lingual.

their side their freedom as payment for their services. America sadly won the war (with the help of the French) and demanded the British hand over all land and property to the fledgling American government. That "property" included the slaves that the British had promised to liberate.

But the British dug their heels in and refused to "hand over" these now ex-slaves. George Washington, that great defender of the slave trade, is said to have stormed out of the negotiations. But the British got their way.

Some of the ex-slaves were re-located to London, and others to Nova Scotia (Halifax, in fact). However, they faced immense hardship and prejudice in their new homes. So British MP William Wilberforce and his mates bought a bit of land in West Africa from a local chief and established *The Province of Freedom* — which would eventually become Freetown, the capital of Sierra Leone.

The liberated slaves from London and Nova Scotia were relocated to this West African settlement where they could live as free and equal men (and women, I guess). Then, once Britain outlawed slavery in 1807, any American, French, Portuguese or Spanish slave ships that they intercepted crossing the Atlantic would have their "recaptured slaves" set free in The Province of Freedom. This practice continued for fifty years until the American Civil War put an end to this grossly immoral business once and for all. Well, kind of (See: Mauritania, Country #87).

Anyway, that's how Sierra Leone got started, and so *for once* the British got off on the right foot. Some Leoneans even protested *against* independence in 1961.

But then the war came.

In March 1991 a conflict in neighbouring Liberia spilled over into Sierra Leone. A group of rebels from Liberia calling themselves the RUF set about raping and murdering with impunity, propped up by profits made from conflict or "blood" diamonds.

The Leonean government did not have the military capability to take on the RUF, and the rebels managed to push all the way to the outskirts of the capital, Freetown. Thousands died, and many more were maimed and injured. Disgracefully, both sides used child soldiers to fight for them. These poor kids were usually forced to inject heroin and made to commit unspeakable acts; a dark episode in the history of West Africa.

With Freetown poised to fall into rebel hands, the British government sent in a team of soldiers to evacuate the city's foreign nationals. Tony Blair, in one of his more lucid moments as British Prime Minister, allowed the troops to stay and help the Sierra Leone army fight back.

From what people told me, the mere sight of a properly uniformed and fully equipped British squaddie made the rebels (a lot of whom were just kids) piss their pants and run away.

While Nigeria and the UN were involved in restoring peace to the beleaguered nation, it was the British that the people of Sierra Leone seem to remember with most fondness — as I learned from just about everyone that I spoke to.

We reached the capital just before nightfall. Freetown was amazing — like no capital city I've ever seen — all set out on the hillsides, which run down to the sea. The roads are predictably shambolic and hilarious, and getting across town is a mission in itself.

But before long, I was enjoying the hospitality of Paul and Helga, friends of Mandy's sister's husband's mate Matt. Six degrees of separation? You betcha.

After the backache, buttache, walletache and heartache of the last five days, Helga made something for which there were just no words to express my appreciation: roast chicken, spuds, and gravy. Just like my mum makes. Yum.

Helga was from the south of England and worked for the UN on youth development, and Paul was a Sydneysider who was working in the security sector, but was about to give it up for the much less stressful job of cocoa quality control. In other words, he was giving up a job as an international super-spy so he could work in Willy Wonka's Chocolate Factory instead.

At least that's how I chose to interpret it.

I didn't need a visa to get into Sierra Leone, but I did need one to get into neighbouring Liberia. However, the Liberian embassy was closed until Monday so I was stuck in Sierra Leone for the weekend. But on balance, not a bad place to be stuck. Not bad at all.

On Saturday afternoon I went to the pub down by the beach to watch the rugby with Helga and Paul. I met their friends, and proceeded to get utterly, utterly legless. Drinks kept magically appearing in front of me, and I, being a meek and mortal man, had no choice but to ride with the devil all the way to glorious oblivion.

That night I headed off to a house party with Helga, at which I ate lasagne (I think) but I missed out on the chocolate cake (I think). Then I staggered to a nightclub called Aces, at which more of this magic beer appeared. I didn't put up much of a fight.

I chatted with a lovely girl (everyone is lovely when I'm drunk) who worked with chimps. I remember telling her that chimps and humans are the only mammals that can't make their own vitamin C, which she found really interesting.

Well, I think she found it interesting. To be honest with you, I can't remember if she was a girl or a boy. She could have been a pot plant. All of a sudden it was Sunday morning.

I had a bloody superb Sunday. Slept in, uploaded some videos, wrote some blog entries, chatted to Mandy and (best of all) had a bath. My kind of Sunday.

Helga rustled up some scouse (Liverpool stew) for me to eat and it was *proper boss la*.[24] Belly full, it was early to bed – like a normal Sunday for normal people leading a normal life. Believe me, you miss it after a while.

It was an early start as I left the comfort of Paul and Helga's place for the Liberian embassy, which turned out to be the ambassador's family home on the edge of town. When I arrived it wasn't quite open, and I accidently managed to wake everyone up. I filled out my entry form on the kitchen table while the ambassador's kids ate breakfast.

In the Lonely Planet guidebook, it indicated that it would take fifteen minutes to get my visa, but they asked me to come back at 2pm. I explained that I was in a bit of a rush and asked if they could ring me when it was ready. 'Of course! No problem.'

While they were processing my passport, I headed into the city centre to see if I could get a visa for Ghana (my next destination after Liberia and Côte d'Ivoire) while I was there.

The taxi system in Freetown takes a delightful form of ordered chaos. Shared taxis ply set routes like buses. However, there are no timetables and no way for an outsider to know what direction any given taxi is

[24] Editor's Note: Apparently in Liverpool this means really good.

going in just by looking at it.

I was very much up for a game of taxi roulette, but all the cabs going past the embassy were full. Luckily for me, a guy in a 4×4 offered me a ride. He explained that he hated driving somewhere with an empty car. His name was Mohammed.

Mohammed was born in Sierra Leone and he had lived in America for many years as a technical consultant earning a six figure salary. He had returned home after the war — and in doing so taken a 90% pay cut — because he wanted to help the rebuilding process. As I was to learn, not everyone in West Africa is desperate to leave.

Mohammed dropped me at the Ghanaian Embassy. There I discovered it would take three days to get a visa — three days! And here's me getting pissy about having to wait three hours! I resolved to press on and see if the process was any quicker in Liberia. After lunch, I picked my Liberian visa and hit the road east, towards the town of Bo.

It was dark when I arrived in Bo. I checked into a little hotel, ready to cross over the border into Liberia in the morning.

I sprang out of bed at the unholy hour of 4am, because that's when I was told that the bus left for Monrovia, the capital of Liberia. When I got to the 'bus station', there was no bus. To be fair, there was no station either. So I paid for a spot in a bush taxi for the border. Since I was the only one there I called shotgun, thinking I'd have the front seat all to myself.

Ha!

I had to share the front seat with an American girl called Sharanya. Then there was the driver, who was *also* sharing his seat with another bloke. He had to reach over said bloke in order to change gear. Then there were four people crammed into the middle row and another four crammed into the back row. Then there were two guys in the boot of the car (it was a hatchback) and — get this — a further two people *sitting on the roof.*

Sixteen people. In a clapped out old Peugeot designed to carry eight.

On top of all that, it was a right-hand drive car; in a country that drives on the right.

We had barely got out of town before we were stopped by a traffic cop in the brightest, whitest, most impeccably tidy uniform I've ever seen outside of a military parade. He was not in the slightest bit concerned about the clearly overloaded vehicle, but our car registration papers were missing a stamp. Heaven forfend! A quick "fine" later and we were on our way.

We had been driving for a couple of hours when we passed an accident on the road. A bush taxi had hit a motorbike, leaving the bush taxi smashed up in a ditch and the poor motorcyclist sitting at the side of the road covered in blood.

Our driver didn't want to stop, but Sharanya screamed at him to pull over. Medically, there wasn't a lot we could do for the motorcyclist. He had fair amount of broken bone sticking out of his wrist and, at the time, I didn't even have a first aid kit. But I could use my mobile phone to get in touch with Médecins Sans Frontières (MSF)[25].

Once we were assured that an ambulance was on the way, we jumped back into the taxi and continued to the border. About five minutes later, a MSF ambulance thundered past us going the other way, so with any luck the motorcyclist would get to keep his hand.

We soon reached a river, which — like in Guyana — we crossed via a wooden raft attached to a chain that was pulled over the water by hand. All of us passengers pitched in. We finally got to the border at about 5:30pm, after having spent nine hours picking our way through the jungle in a bush taxi with 16 people crammed in (and on) it. But I can't say it wasn't fun.

As we left Sierra Leone, Sharanya and I were told to go and see the health inspector. He called us into his office and asked to see our passports. When he saw mine his eyes lit up. 'You're British?!'

He shook my hand and said, 'The British came in my darkest days. They saved my life, they saved my wife's life and my children's lives. When you go back home tell them. Tell them "thank you".'

Liberia was one of America's few colonies around the world, and the only one in Africa. It was founded as a safe place for black Americans who wished to "return" to Africa and escape the restrictions and prejudices of the antebellum United States.

Sharanya and I took a shared taxi bound for Monrovia. The driver seemed to be getting his practice in for next year's Nascar championship. Knuckles whitened and hair sufficiently risen, we arrived in the capital.

Mandy — being a total legend — had managed to find me somewhere to stay via the CouchSurfing network. Good job too — Monrovia is bafflingly expensive.

I met my host, Shadi, in the Boulevard Café in the Sinkor area of town — where all the embassies are. Shadi was a journalist, originally from Jordan, who was working for UN radio in Liberia. Before he landed this gig, he covered stuff in Lebanon and Iraq. At one point he was kidnapped by Hezbollah. He had to talk them out of killing him.

---

[25] Editor's Note: Also known as Doctors Without Borders.

And I thought The Odyssey Expedition was risky.

We ate dinner in the café before heading over to Shadi's place. *Blood Diamond* was on TV. I found myself muttering, 'that looks nothing like Sierra Leone!'

I later found out that *Blood Diamond* was filmed in Mozambique.

The next morning I was up at 7am. My first stop was at the bank to grab some cash, but the ATM was not playing ball. I ended up having to convert my emergency West African CFA[26] (the currency used in most countries around these parts) into Liberian dollars.

🏛 **MONROVIA**

👥 **3.82m**

❓ **English**

💵 **Liberian Dollar**

💰 **$302.28**

2,500 container ships are registered in Liberia – 10% of the world's entire shipborne carrying capacity.

I proceeded to waste a couple of hours searching for the Cote d'Ivoire embassy. Turns out it had recently moved.

Monrovia, like Freetown, is devastatingly impoverished. Everything was in a state of half-repair — the cars, the roads, the buildings. Most of the small businesses in the embassy area are shacks at the side of the road. People stand about watching the ubiquitous white UN rhino trucks drive by.

After picking up my Cote D'Ivoire visa in next to no time, I headed over to the Ghana embassy, but again I was told that it would take three days to process the visa.

Luckily for me, my dad, through one of his friends, managed to put me in contact with a guy in the Ghanaian government called Tanko Hamza. Tanko told him that if I had any problems getting my Ghanaian visa I should give him a call. Which is exactly what I did.

Within the hour I had my visa.

It's not what you know...

I took a "mini" taxi to where the long distance taxis congregate, and (as is the practice around here) it picked up other passengers along the way. One of them was Dr. Eddie — a medical doctor who trained and lived in America, but like Mohammed in Sierra Leone, had come home after the war. He presented a radio show on Thursday mornings, dispensing free medical advice over the airwaves. The world needs more people like Dr.

---

[26] Author's Note: Pronounced "say-fa".

Eddie.

Soon I was sitting in a bush taxi in the Red Light area of town (really, that's its name, "Red Light"). Just before we set off, I received a call from Shadi — I had accidently left some of my stuff at his place.

Thank goodness I was in Africa.

The driver drove me (and all the other passengers) back to Shadi's flat in the Sinkor area of town. Imagine trying to get a Greyhound driver to do that!

Ha! Never.

I picked up my gear and we sped off into the night towards the town of Ganta, near the border with Cote D'Ivoire.

My driver was called Bobby. The nice lady seated behind me said a prayer behalf of us all before we left. Being a heathen, I put on my safety belt. This turned out to be a good call. Bobby drove like a goddamn maniac.

We thundered along the road, night-time, no streetlights, no cat's eyes, massive potholes, blinding headlights. Every so often there'd be a truck ahead of us with no rear lights. Bobby would see it at the last possible second and swerve accordingly. We got a puncture after hitting a pothole too fast. But did that slow him down? No. He changed the tyre and hammered the accelerator even harder than before. And — predictably — hit another pothole and gave himself another puncture.

As a result, despite Bobby's mapcap driving it was 3am before we reached Ganta.

I tried to check into a hotel for a few hours, but the cheapest place wanted €25 for a grotty little room that I wouldn't pay a fiver to stay in even if it came with a fizzy lollypop.

I couldn't things could be so expensive in a country where so many people are forced to survive on less than a dollar a day.

Liberia is one of the poorest countries on Earth. In the mid-90s its GDP per capita was $65. That's $65 per person per year, less than 18 cents *a day*.

When I visited in 2009, Liberia's GDP had improved a little, but it still worked out to less than a dollar per person per day.

Coupled with a low life expectancy and low levels of education, it can be difficult to see any way out of the morass.

While I was travelling across West Africa, I read a book by an American guy who worked for the Peace Corps in Zambia.

He reckoned you could always tell where Peace Corps volunteers had been by how they behaved when they returned home. If they came back all politicised and radical, they had been to South America. If they came back all holistic and spiritually aware, they had been to Asia. If they had been to Africa, they returned drunk and laughing.

It's the only way to get your head around it all.

So I returned to the shared taxi area, jumped in a cab and asked the driver to wake me when it was full.

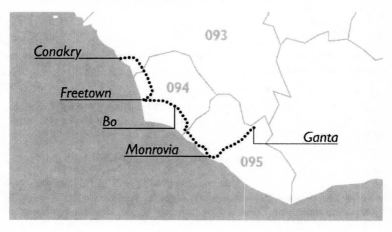

Chapter 19
The Land Of Upright Men

At the time, **Côte d'Ivoire** was split in two and had been for a number of years. The north was run by the "rebels" and the south by the "government", but the reality was that they were two sides of a religious divide.

Côte d'Ivoire's borders, like nearly all borders of modern Africa, were a European invention, and, like Nigeria and Sudan, purposefully drawn to pit a Muslim north against a Christian south. Divide and conquer.

Luckily for Côte d'Ivoire, these are two religions of peace, which explains why they're so often at war.

The only border crossing that was practical for me to use was in the northern ('rebel') half of the country.

I got tapped by the guy on the border for 5000CFA (about €7) but I managed to get away with just giving him 1000. The bloody visa cost me US$75 so I wasn't in the mood for being generous.

I wanted to press on towards the main city of Abidjan, but there was hardly anybody at the border. Eventually — after a bit

CÔTE D'IVOIRE 096/200

🏛 **YAMOUSSOUKRO**

👥 18.6m

💬 French

💵 West African CFA Franc

💰 $1,305.15

Côte d'Ivoire is the world's biggest producer of Cocoa, the essential ingredient of chocolate.

of haggling — I got the solitary motorbike taxi to take me to the nearest town, Danané.

Holy crap — I thought the road was bad on the Liberian side. It was less a highway linking two nations and more an obstacle course for dirt bikes.

We made it through the first few rebel checkpoints (one every kilometre) without incident, but then about halfway to Danané the police pointed out that the back tyre was a bit flat would have to be fixed.

Another motorbike taxi came by and the police suggested that I get on the back of it. The only problem was that the other bike already had a passenger riding pillion — and she wasn't exactly petite.

After a quick argument between my original driver and this new guy, I found myself sitting behind both the driver and his lady passenger on the metal luggage rack, my backpack on my back and my laptop and camera bags on my knee. They felt as heavy as hell.

My backside had been hurting pretty badly before I got on the damn bike. It did not improve matters. Every time we went over a pothole, I winced. And there were a *lot* of potholes.

I got to Danané around 3pm and was keen to press on to Abidjan. I was told that there was a bus "leaving at six" and got mighty excited. Then I found out that it was leaving at *six in the morning*.

It wasn't until later, after checking into a local guesthouse for the night, that I discovered (via the bathroom mirror) why my backside hurt so much. I had two huge bites on my arse of the spider, snake, something nasty variety.

I sprayed some liquid Germolene on my *oh-my-god-the-skin-has-gone-black* bum bites.

Holy shit it stung.

By way of contrast, on the bus the next morning we drove along some of the best roads I'd experienced since Morocco. Dual carriageways! Armco barriers! Road signs that tell you where you're going! My word. They weren't joking when they told me that Côte d'Ivoire was once one of the richest countries in the whole of Africa.

By the time I got to Abidjan that evening, Mandy had already woven her magic on CouchSurfing and had found an amazing place me to stay with a local girl called Aya.

Aya lived in a penthouse apartment in the Riviera district of the city amongst some of West Africa's tallest buildings. I was given her spare room all to myself — en suite[27], king-sized bed, spectacular view. CouchSurfing is an amazing thing.

That night Aya treated me to dinner at a fancy restaurant downtown. The meal was fabulous. The French may have left a long time ago, but

[27] Editor's Note: Meaning the toilet and bathroom are directly adjoining the room and not shared with others.

their cuisine lingers in the popular imagination.

Aya was well educated, fiercely independent and eminently capable. I asked her why she chose to stay in West Africa. Her answer was like a breath of fresh air.

'Why would I leave my family and friends and work every hour that God sends to live surrounded by strangers in a cold flat in a cold city when I can work fewer hours and have a much higher standard of living by staying in Côte d'Ivoire? This is my home.'

She made a good point. I mean, London is cool to visit, but I wouldn't want to live there. Ditto New York. Aya had a great job with one of Africa's biggest mobile phone companies and an amazing apartment overlooking the ocean. What more do you need?

The following morning I thanked Aya profusely for her incredible hospitality before continuing on to my 97th nation: **Ghana**.

During *The Odyssey Expedition*, I wasn't just travelling and blogging, I was filming the adventure, pretty much every waking hour. In the first year I amassed over 135 hours of footage. By the end of the entire journey I had shot, catalogued and backed-up almost 400 60-minute MiniDV tapes.

So when the production company told me they were sending a cameraman to travel with me for a few weeks, my initial reaction was *thank God for that*.

I had just one caveat: they weren't allowed to slow me down!

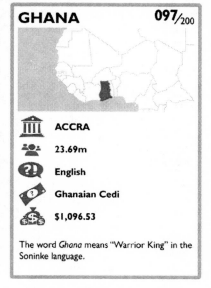

GHANA   **097**/200

🏛 **ACCRA**

👥 **23.69m**

💬 **English**

💵 **Ghanaian Cedi**

💰 **$1,096.53**

The word *Ghana* means "Warrior King" in the Soninke language.

I need not have worried — the guy they sent, Rocco Fasano, was an experienced world traveller and took everything that West Africa had to throw at us in his stride. We met in Ghana's capital, Accra. I was more than happy to abuse his hotel room's hot shower — unlike me, Rocco had an expense account. Afterwards we headed out into the night to find the wonderful Tanko Hamza, the total legend who had expedited my Ghanaian visa a few days earlier.

Not only that, but Tanko had brought my second passport with him from the UK loaded with the most important thing I needed to get down to South Africa without a hitch — my visa for Angola, something you can't buy on the road.

Tanko invited Rocco and I out for some pukka Ghanaian scran. We went to a restaurant and sat outside in the warm night air. I was given a ton of meat for starters and some kind of special chilli concoction on rice for mains. It was my favourite meal in Africa thus far. If the way to a man's heart is through his belly, Ghana was doing a bang-up job. Yay Ghana!

In the morning, Tanko's nephew took us out for a quick jaunt around Accra. We headed to the Memorial Park only to find out it cost €75 to film in there, so we went to the castle instead — only to discover that filming there is banned outright. So we went to the Ghanaian version of McDonalds and settled for stuffing our faces with hamburgers and chips for breakfast.

Back at the hotel, Tanko dropped by to say his farewells. He had just come straight from a wedding (don't worry — it wasn't his and yes I made that joke) and was dressed in traditional Islamic attire. We had a chat about the road ahead — turned out he had a friend in Kuwait who he thought might be able to get me into Iraq when the time came.

Hearty handshakes and thanks all around, then it was a quick stroll over to the minibus depot and before too long, we were on a bus hoping to go to **Togo**. Togo-a-go-go!

Unlike Guinea, Liberia, Côte d'Ivoire and Ghana, Togo issues visas on the border, so after filling out some forms we quickly found ourselves in the capital, Lomé.

While we waited for the taxi to the border with our next country

TOGO 098/200

🏛 **LOMÉ**

👥 6.14m

💬 French

💵 West African CFA Franc

💰 $514.77

The Togolese are really into their 'fetishes'. No, not the type you're thinking of, but objects that are considered holy or are believed to have some special power.

(Benin) to fill, I got chatting to a Togolese guy who told us the fantastical story that German Togoland (as it was then) was only *leased* to the French when they took it over in 1914. What's more, by 2014 the lease would be up.

He genuinely wanted the Germans to come and reclaim "their" country so that Togo could have "somebody sensible" in charge "for a change".

So if any Germans are reading this and are still longing for a bit of *lebensraum*, I've found a place where at least one guy will welcome you with open arms.

Like Togo, we could buy our visas to enter **Benin** on the border itself. This made life so much easier and before long we were in the major Beninese city of Cotonou.

🏛 **PORTO NOVO**

👥 **9.24m**

⁉ **French**

💵 **West African CFA Franc**

💰 **$712.55**

Benin is widely regarded as the home of Voodoo.

The next day was August 3ʳᵈ. It began with a trip to the embassy of Niger. However, August 3ʳᵈ is Niger's Independence Day and of course the embassy was closed. Great timing eh?

So instead we went to the Benin Immigration office and tried to get hold of a five-country "Ecowas visa" that is alluded to in the Lonely Planet. Funnily enough, there were a few other backpackers who were trying to get their hands on exactly the same thing — Ahmed from Germany, Eve from The Netherlands and Ben from America. Hell yes I met a guy called Ben in Benin.

Sadly, this mythical visa turned out to be just that: a myth.

With all that faffing about, it wasn't until 5pm that Rocco and I began our journey in a bush taxi north. I was hoping to get as close as possible to the border with our next country (Burkina Faso), but a cop at one of the ubiquitous check posts along the way told the driver it was too dangerous to drive at night, so he pulled over and everyone had to sleep in the car until daybreak.

Unfortunately for us passengers, the driver opted to park next to an open drain which stunk to high heaven, causing Rocco to chuck his guts up at the side of the road.

Recommencing the journey in the morning twilight, we reached the far northern town of Tanguieta before noon. There were no buses to the border, so we hopped on motorbike taxis to the imaginary line that separates Benin from Burkina Faso.

Country number 100. It was the beginning of August and I was halfway to the magic 200.

However, by this stage I had given up all hope of completing the journey in twelve months, so Mandy and I had begun to discuss the possibility of meeting up at the end of the year — wherever I might be.

So then, Burkina Faso. In a stroke of marketing genius, the late Thomas Sankara (Tom Sank to his friends), President of Upper Volta in the

1980s, changed the name of his country to **Burkina Faso**. Why? Well, because it means 'The Land of Upright[28] Men.'

As any educational psychologist will tell you, if you say to someone they are bad, they will eventually think, 'Oh well, if everyone says I'm bad, I must be a bad person, so it's my nature to do bad things.' Then they'll go off and set fire to a cat, invade Poland or make the Star Wars prequels.

The converse is also true. Tom Sank cleverly changing the name of his country meant that being corrupt made a person not just a petty criminal, but also a *traitor*. And everybody hates traitors, even bona fide criminals hate traitors.

BURKINA FASO 100/200

🏛 **OUAGADOUGOU**

👥 **15.09m**

⁉️ **French**

💵 **West African CFA Franc**

💰 **$553.04**

From 1932 to 1947, the country of Upper Volta (as Burkina Faso was once known) did not exist.

I don't know if it really worked, but I do know that for my entire time in Burkina Faso I wasn't tapped for a single bribe.

Rocco had left his passport in Cotonou processing his visa for Cameroon, which meant he couldn't cross the border with me. So our plan was thus: while he stayed in Benin, I would cross through Burkina Faso into Niger, get my photo at the "Welcome To Niger" sign, turn around and then come back through Burkina Faso to Benin.

I was making good time until I reached the junction town of Fada N'Gourma.

Because of recent bandit attacks (seems like *somebody* didn't get the message about being honest), the road east was closed except at certain times of the day, when cars and buses were escorted by the police in convoy. I ended up waiting until 4pm. The plan of returning to Benin before nightfall went straight out the window.

When I finally got to the border I ran into another problem. In addition to having had an inconveniently-timed (for me) independence day 24 hours earlier, now they were having an election. Which meant the border was closed, *to everyone*, until the next day. I wondered if somebody had tipped Niger off to the fact I was coming and Niger was purposely taking the piss.

I had a chat with the border guards on the Burkina side and explained

---

[28] Author's Note: Or "honest".

what I was doing. They said I was free to go over to the border and step back if I wanted to, but that the Niger border guards were not nearly as much fun and may well shoot me.

I thought it best to wait till the next day.

So I found a grotty little *auberge,* run by a great guy named Frederick, and crashed for the night.

Early next morning, Frederick offered me a lift over the border on his bike. Before I knew it we were hurtling towards Niger at a great rate of knots.

I found there was a good 20km of dusty wasteland between the border posts, so there was no bureaucratic tomfoolery to cause me problems on this little border hop. Once past the sign welcoming me into **Niger**, we rode for another couple of kilometres into the country, just in case they had put the sign in the wrong place or something.

Thanks Frederick!

Afterwards, I took the bus back to Fada N'Gourma and sat with a couple of hearing impaired guys from Liberia. They were heading to Burkina Faso's capital Ouagadougou[29] (the best name for a city ever) to teach American Sign Language. In just a couple of hours, I learned the signs for British, Australian, Film, Travel, Love, Beer, Whiskey (amongst others) and the entire alphabet. We all agreed that ASL was much easier to learn than French.

NIGER 101/200

🏛	NIAMEY
👥	15.3m
❓	French
💵	West African CFA Franc
💰	$352.69

In Tuareg culture, it is the men who veil their faces, not the women.

Later, I found a minibus that was going to Porga (the village in Benin where I had stranded poor Rocco). While I was getting stamped out of Burkina Faso the bloody minibus upped and left. It was a good few kilometres to the Benin border post.

So I had to wait for another minibus, which got about halfway to Porga before breaking down. The driver was adamant he'd have the problem fixed in a jiffy, but they *always* say that. I got out, and flagged down a motorbike taxi to take me the rest of the way.

---

[29] Author's Note: Pronounced "wagga-doo-goo".

Once reunited with Rocco, I stuffed my face with some grilled mystery meat cooked at the side of the road before paying double to get the front seat in the shared taxi back to Cotonou all to myself.

By the time we got to Cotonou it was 5am. I was beyond tired. All I wanted to do was grab a couple of hours sleep before taking on Nigeria. We jumped on the back of a couple of motorbike taxis.

'L'Hôtel Concorde, s'il vous plaît.'

Our drivers drove like maniacs. I was nearly broad-sided by a car, and Rocco narrowly escaped almost certain death by way of a truck on a roundabout. It was so bad that he got off his bike and got on another one.

After what seemed like an age, our drivers stopped at a multiplex cinema. 'Here we are!'

'Où est l'Hôtel Concorde?'

'Là!', beamed my driver, pointing at the cinema.

Ah yes. The *Cinema* Concorde. Yep, they thought we wanted to go see a movie at half past five in the morning.

'Hôtel!', I exclaimed, 'l'*Hôtel* Concorde!'

Our drivers talked to each other. One nodded. The other nodded. We sped off into the night.

Half an hour later we arrived at the Hôtel Concordiere.

Which, if you're playing attention, you'll note is *not* l'Hôtel Concorde. I would have been happy to sleep on a park bench at that point, but we had left our backpacks in l'Hôtel Concorde.

It was 6:30am before they found it, just around the corner from where the *sept-place* from Porga dropped us off.

We could have walked it.

To add insult to injury, our drivers were now demanding the equivalent of a month's wages for our unwanted and unnecessary night-time tour of Cotonou.

I told them to go to hell and went to bed. Rocco, being the awfully nice chap that he is, eventually cut a deal with them. Better the production company's money than mine.

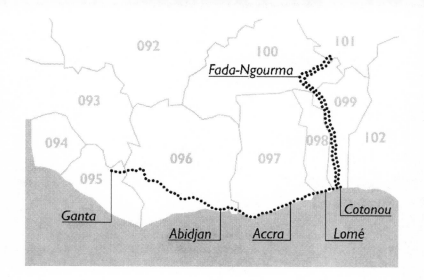

Chapter 20
Fury Road

I got a couple of hours of sleep before I had to be up and ready for **Nigeria**. Now, Nigeria is a notoriously dangerous country and Lonely Planet didn't want their MVP[30] getting robbed or injured along the way.

Their MVP, of course, being Rocco.

They paid for him to fly over Nigeria and wait for me in Cameroon while I travelled overland through Lagos, around the Niger Delta and over the border at Calabar.

If I was arrested, mugged, kidnapped or smashed up in a car accident, I didn't want to be losing my little laptop and my beloved underpants as well, so I only took some money, my camera, my passport and my toothbrush — the rest of my gear I gave to Rocco. With any luck I'd see them again on the other side.

So with just one little bag and two huge balls, I stepped forth alone. *Once more unto the breach, dear friends, once more.*

Here goes nothing...!

It was August 6th 2009. One week earlier there had been riots in Maiduguri over the introduction of sharia law.

NIGERIA 102/200

🏛 **ABUJA**

👥 **155.4m**

💬 **English**

💵 **Nigerian Naira**

💰 **$1,090.75**

Nollywood, the Nigerian movie industry that grinds out up to 200 films a week, is valued at more than $3bn.

Hundreds of people had been killed. This would turn out to be the beginning of the on-going insurgency of the now-notorious Boko

---

30 Editor's Note: Most Valuable Player

Haram.

I had been planning to travel up through Maiduguri on the way to Cameroon, so I was damn lucky not to have been in the wrong place at the wrong time.

I had no choice but to take the southern route into Cameroon — one that skirts perilously close to the Niger Delta, an area infamous for kidnappings, especially of Westerners.

Nigeria gets a bum rap. Admittedly it is the most corrupt nation on Earth, but in many ways it is a victim of circumstance. A British colony for many years, it wasn't long after independence that they found oil.

LOTS of oil.

And with the oil came money. And with that money came corruption. The sheer scale of which is simply mind blowing. An investigation by the government itself came up with the arguably conservative figure of more than one-third of a *trillion* US dollars effectively stolen from the people over the course of 40 years.

To put that into context, that's four times more than all of the foreign aid given to the entire continent of Africa over the same period.

This money resulted not only in corruption being endemic in almost every fact of life but also the pollution of the Niger Delta. Farmers and fishermen saw their livelihoods ruined and took up arms. Thus began a spate of kidnappings, usually of rich "oil men".

But given the choice between being kidnapped by Islamic extremists or angry fishermen and I'd plumb for the angry fishermen every time.

Now thanks to my little episode in Cape Verde, my visa for Nigeria had expired. Furthermore, it was printed, so I couldn't alter it with a biro[31] like I had done with my Guinea visa. To make matters worse, the only place I could apply for a new one was the UK.

I crossed the border with my bribe money ready, but they didn't seem to be bothered that my visa was past its use-by date. In fact I was stamped in with a smile. Nice one Nigeria!

I took a shared taxi to Lagos. The driver, John, was a lovely man, but he did almost kill me several times by driving really slowly and not bothering to look in his mirror before changing lanes on the freeway.

I had been told that Nigerians drive like maniacs, and most do, but John flat out refused to join in with the fast and furious brigade, which was arguably even more dangerous. I thought we were going to get rear-ended too many times to count.

---

[31] Editor's Note: Slang (and registered trademark) for a ballpoint pen.

The journey to Lagos was supposed to take 90 minutes. It took over four hours. But there were mitigating factors, aside from John driving really slowly, the road was bloody awful and the traffic was horrendous. But hey, I got to Lagos in one piece so I'm not going to complain. "Better Late than *The* Late", said a prescient road sign along the way.

In Lagos, I met up with Tony, my CouchSurfing host for the evening. Tony was from Ghana and, from my experience, Ghanaians are some of the most chill people in West Africa, quite a contrast to the constant hustle of Lagos.

We had to search for a while for a place to grab a beer and some food because by the time I got there it was after 9pm and a lot of places were closed. I found it surprising that in the biggest city of the most populous country in Africa places close so early, but there's a reason why — the bloody electricity keeps going off.

The state electric company NEPA (which Tony told me stood for 'No Electrical Power at All') consistently fails to provide a continuous service. Even on Victoria Island, the poshest bit of the city — complete with fancy hotels and high-rise buildings, the grid goes down, and thousands of small personal generators rattle to life.

It was not yet light when Tony kindly dropped me off at the "bus station" the following morning. The "bus station" was located in a dodgy part of town, under a flyover. There I was told I'd find a minibus or "mauler" to Calabar in the far south-east of the country.

One of the drivers, George, asked me where I wanted to go. He told me the bus to Calabar would be along soon, but in the meantime it would be best if I waited in his minibus with him rather than, for instance, mooching around Lagos in the dark under a flyover. He had a point.

Soon enough, though, I was on the mauler to Calabar. I bagged the seat behind the driver (the safest one, or so I've been led to believe) and strapped myself in *tight*. I had heard stories about these minibuses that would make your hair stand on end — they don't call them "maulers" for nothing.

From the outset, it was obvious that my driver was a maniac. He didn't seem to realise that he was transporting 20 people in a minibus. As far as he was concerned, he was driving a muscle car, this was Mad Max and there was a biker gang on our tail.

So the rollercoaster began. Over the course of 200 police checkpoints and 100 smashed cars and trucks abandoned at the side of the road, there were 17 accidents that day (including a petrol tanker that had crashed and blown up) and one accident I even caught on camera as an eighteen-wheeler slammed into the side of a mauler that was attempting to do a U-turn at the bottom of a hill on a motorway.

I swear I'm not making this up.

At one point, we were driving at over 100 miles an hour on the wrong side of the carriageway, overtaking somebody who was *also* driving on the wrong side while hurtling towards a blind corner on the crest of a hill. If anything had been coming the other way, we would have been soup.

I screamed at the driver to slow the hell down and to stop driving like a fool. The fat women next to me giggled. 'Shut up white man', she said, in what I took as a good-natured rebuke — 'this is a black man's road.'

Guinness World Records wanted me to take public transport where available because they didn't want me bribing the driver of a private vehicle to break the law by driving too fast. I tried to bribe this guy to slow the hell down.

All this happened with *The Best of Celine Dion* blasting out of the stereo. Seriously.

While the journey took us perilously close to the Niger Delta region of the country, luckily, an amnesty had come into effect the day before and so there had been a pause in the fighting — a pause wide enough for me to squeeze through without any additional hassle, aside from the sheer balls-out terror of being driven across Nigeria by the bastard child of a thousand maniacs.

One of the more fun aspects of the journey was chatting with my fellow passengers. One of the guys sitting up front spoke Nigerian pidgin, or "Brokin". At one point he advised the driver not to go a certain way as it was (what sounded to me like) 'a no-so-go-ro'. Which is a wonderful way of saying 'it's not such a good road'.

He was right – it wasn't.

After stumbling out of that death machine following my 14-hour-long ordeal, I stormed off in to the night without a word, my fists clenched with rage, and that bleedin' awful *Titanic* song stuck in my head.

I will never — *never* — take a "mauler" ever again.

Unless it was that or the Greyhound. Then I'd not only do that journey again, but I'd climb out of the sunroof as we hurtled down the wrong side of the freeway and declare myself king of the goddamn world.

Since the southern road crossing is "shot to shit" in the rainy season, I was hoping to take the overnight ferry into Cameroon, but had arrived far too late. I was told there would be another boat at 7:30am. And so I found myself unexpectedly stuck in Calabar for the night.

The hotel listed in the Lonely Planet was being renovated, but the guy who was watching over the place, a pygmy named Roland, said I could kip at his gaff if I wanted.

Roland lived in a simple one-room shack on the poorer side of town.

When we entered I couldn't help but point out the two giant, yet obviously fake, spiders stuck to the wall as decoration. Laughing, I mentioned I was arachnophobic. 'No problem', says Roland, kills the two *actually living spiders* with his shoe, gathers up the remains with a dustpan and throws them out of the window.

'All gone.'

Roland went back to work and I went to bed, trying my level best not to think of spiders as big as my hand crawling over me in the night.

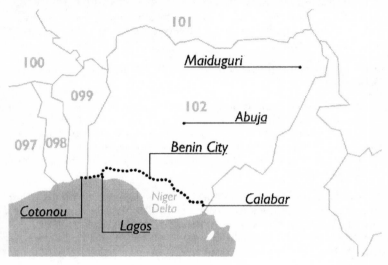

Chapter 21
More Tap Than A Blind Man's Stick

Roland woke me in the morning by firing up his little generator outside the hut. The lights came on and so did the TV. I watched a bit of a bloody awful Nollywood film and then I got ready to head down to the docks to catch this semi-mythical ferry to Cameroon. Amazingly it turned out to be real. The only problem being that it left at 6:30am, not 7:30am.

I got to the port at 7am.

Having missed the boat (in more ways than one), I took a motorbike taxi to the other side of town — from where the "flying boats" depart.

The city centre of Calabar was splendid: grass verges, trees, pavement, road signs, attractive buildings and hardly any litter. The best bit was the truly massive Nigerian flag in the middle of the central park. 'The biggest flag in Africa!', my motorbike driver was excited to tell me.

The "flying boat" was a typical panga fishing boat with an outboard motor. Amazingly, they didn't overload the damn thing (the driver actually told a couple of latecomers to get off) and we were all provided with lifejackets. If only this regard for health and safety extended to the nation's roads.

Racing through the mangrove forests was an exhilarating experience. A natural labyrinth (the mighty Niger river delta-ing out into the sea) separated by thousands of trees standing on their roots as though tiptoeing through the shallow water.

Even the sporadic rain was not enough to destroy the magic — there was ne'er a ripple in the water, save when a boat passed us and the occupants enthusiastically waved to the ginger man with the silly hat.

We passed through the disputed Bakassi Peninsula (claimed by both Nigeria and Cameroon) and within a couple of hours we had arrived at the border town of Ekondo Titi.

Like many of my West African visas, my visa for **Cameroon** had expired. I had been told (by the Cameroonian embassy in London, no less) that I could get the visa extended on the border. However, the border guard was having none of it. In fact, he wanted me to get on the next boat back to Nigeria, take a mauler to the capital Abuja and get a brand new visa. He wouldn't even take a bribe.

It seems in West Africa that you only pay bribes for doing nothing wrong. If you need somebody to bend the rules a little, that's another matter entirely — your money's no good around here!

I waited for an hour for the guy's boss to turn up. They had a conversation in French, the boss shrugged and stamped me in straight away. Maybe the border guard just didn't want the terrible responsibility of allowing a scouser into the country.

So on to my next adventure: the road to Kumba. This road was beyond bad — it was barely even a road — more like a 50km stretch of wet churned-up mud.

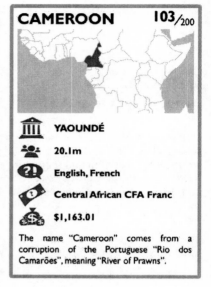

CAMEROON 103/200

🏛 **YAOUNDÉ**

👥 **20.1m**

❓ **English, French**

💵 **Central African CFA Franc**

💰 **$1,163.01**

The name "Cameroon" comes from a corruption of the Portuguese "Rio dos Camarões", meaning "River of Prawns".

We got stuck more than a dozen times. There were kids who made a living by standing at the side of the road and helping push hapless motorists out of the sludge.

One of the other passengers, whose name was Elvis, was incandescent with rage that because of the trouble near the northern border, this was now the main road to and from Nigeria. 'It's the government, they do not care. They do not make it easy,' he said.

They certainly don't.

At one point, the taxi was being physically pushed up a slippery muddy slope by a mob of enterprising children led by a kid named Kingsley. I got out to lighten the load and also to film the shenanigans, hoping somebody would fall over and I could sell the tape to *Africa's Funniest Home Videos*.

But of course the only person who slipped and fell over in the mud was muggins here. That'll teach me!

I reached Kumba at some ungodly hour, but my trials were not yet complete. I still had to get to Douala to meet up with my friend Yaz's brother Hugo who would be providing me with somewhere to stay for the night. The road from Kumba to Douala was much better, but I still didn't arrive until after 1am.

Douala was a threatening place in which to be dropped off at night. My phone was running low on battery and I was worried that I wouldn't get to meet up with Hugo, but his friend Liberty came to my rescue. He gallantly arranged to meet me at the pub (and by jingo, I needed a cold one after that leg of the journey). I gorged myself on tasty barbecue meat from the vendors outside while we waited for Hugo to arrive. Beer, kebab, backpack and mud. I wouldn't have looked out of place at the Glastonbury festival.

Hugo came and took me back to the family home. There I valiantly tried to get all the mud off my trainers, jeans, arms, legs, face, hands and jumper. Although the only thing I really succeeded in doing was making a big muddy mess all over Hugo's guest bedroom. Sorry Hugo!

After a couple of hours of shuteye, it was back on the case. Hugo had only just passed his driving test a few weeks earlier and a combination of him stalling the engine and the relentless monsoon rain resulted in us getting the back tyre stuck in a gigantic pothole at the same time as the car battery died an ignoble death. We had to push the car out of the pothole, uphill, with the rain teeming down and a (very full) storm drain just inches behind our rear tyre. Failure was not an option.

I almost gave myself a hernia, my well-worn Vans slipping and sliding in the wet, but eventually we heaved the car free. I got it push-started and we pressed onto the bus station.

I was supposed to get in to the capital Yaoundé at 4pm, which would have given me plenty of time to reunite with Rocco the cameraman and for us both to catch the 5.30pm train north.

However, I arrived at about 5:15pm.

Sod's law, I got the slowest taxi driver in the country to take me to Rocco's hotel. I had just two minutes to unpack and repack my stuff, fling my muddy clothes at the startled receptionist ('Wash 'em! I'll be back!') and scarper before the train left without us.

In actuality the train didn't leave until 6:20pm, so we need not have rushed. Unfortunately, while Rocco was filming me enter the train station, some light-fingered jackanape made off with his radio mic.

There wasn't a lot we could do about it so we boarded the train and made our way to the *couchette* — our sleeping quarters for the night. The train reminded me of my days travelling around India many years earlier. There aren't too many railways left in sub-Saharan Africa, which is a pity, as there's a certain romance about train travel that can't be replicated sitting on a coach or crammed into a bush taxi.

The train arrived the following morning in the central Cameroonian town of N'Gaoundéré. If we were very lucky, we could make a quick border hop to Chad and get back to N'Gaoundéré in time to catch the first bus south the following morning.

Early that afternoon we made it to the small town of Figuil, a short motorbike ride away from the frontier. I was nervous that we'd get turned back on the Cameroonian side before we were anywhere near the border (like what happened to me in Tunisia), as we didn't have visas for Chad. But I needn't have worried. The Cameroonian border guards were as nice as pie; they stamped us out of the country and we were on our way.

I must confess I didn't really know much about **Chad**. It seems to keep a low profile next to its unruly neighbours Nigeria, Sudan, Libya etc. But the guys on the border were super-friendly and even invited us to go another 10km into their country to get entry and exit stamps as souvenirs.

But time was pressing and I didn't want to push our luck. I had stepped foot in the country and that's all I needed to do. Rocco snapped a few photos of me posing near Chad's blue-yellow-red tricolour flag (*hmm... that flag looks a bit familiar* *cough* Romania *cough* Andorra *cough* Moldova...)

CHAD 104/200

🏛 **N'DJAMENA**

👥 11.37m

💬 French, Arabic

💵 Central African CFA Franc

💰 $813.76

In French, Chad is spelt "Tchad", which is why its Internet domain is ".td".

and then we fanged it back to Cameroon. So long, Chad!

We arrived back at the railhead of N'Gaoundéré at God-knows-o'clock at night, and promptly checked into a nearby hovel for a few hours of overpriced shuteye. At 6am we were at the bus station, bright-eyed and bushy-tailed, ready to roll for another day's slog along Africa's less-than-forgiving roads.

The plan was to head down towards the town of Garoua-Boulaï on the border with the Central African Republic. The Lonely Planet said to think twice about taking this particular road in the rainy season — and oh my giddy aunt, they weren't kidding.

The road ran for over 400km, and alternated from "bad" to "awful" for much of its duration. Every so often our driver asked everyone to get off the bus whilst he deftly manoeuvred across various swamps which were inconveniently located where the road should have been.

At one stage, we went totally off-road after a tip-off that the carriageway up ahead was blocked. Through the jungle in a bus. Hilarious. We got stuck half a dozen times. Good job there were loads of people on the bus to help us out of the mud.

I'm not complaining though, it was quite fun. And we got to really breathe in the raw beauty of Cameroon, something that we didn't get to see much of on the overnight train or while mooching around the dusty border with Chad. The trees were so green, the soil so red and the sky so blue it was as though somebody had been dicking around with the saturation settings on Photoshop.

We hit the border town at around 1am, slung our bags in the Catholic Mission, downed a couple of Cameroon's oversized beers and crashed out for the night.

The next morning, for the princely sum of $10, I popped over the border to the **Central African Republic** and back before Rocco had even got out of bed. Right, where next?

Equatorial Guinea. Ah.

Visas for Equatorial Guinea are notoriously difficult to acquire. Annoyingly enough, Americans don't need one, but us Brits do. On the bright side, Brits don't need a visa for Brazil, whereas Americans have to pay $160 for the pleasure. Ha!

My original plan for Equatorial Guinea was to just do a border hop, but since I would have had to return to the Cameroonian

CENTRAL AFRICAN REPUBLIC	105/200

🏛 **BANGUI**

👥 **4.26m**

💬 **French, Sango**

💵 **Central African CFA Franc**

🚲 **$464.51**

From December 1976 to September 1979, the Central African Republic was called the "Central African Empire".

capital to pick up visas for Gabon and DR Congo anyway, I figured I'd at least try to get my hands on an Equatoguinean visa as well, make it all official.

The road to Yaoundé was nowhere near as bad as the road from the day before. We even had a little space on the bus to stretch our legs. Halfway through our journey we stopped for lunch in a town called Bertoua. While there I decided to get a few shots for the TV show.

While I was filming a tremendously exciting roundabout outside the Obama café, I was approached by two men in plain clothes who claimed to be policemen and demanded to see my passport. I showed them a photocopy of my passport and asked to see their ID. One showed me his national identity card, which didn't tell me much except for the fact that he was in the military. He could have been the bloke who peels the spuds for all I knew, so I refused to co-operate. Luckily a police car was going past, so I flagged it down.

Turns out these guys *were* the police.

Whoops.

'Go get your bags, you're under arrest.'

Oh for the love of God–

Rocco came with me to the police station where the police chief sat flicking through our passports for a good half hour, presumably trying to think of a good reason to extort money out of us.

In the end, they fleeced me out of €20. I was worried having to wait a day until the next bus, so I paid up.

Once we were back on the road, I was fuming. Rocco said 'I feel like a Jew travelling through Nazi-occupied Europe.'

While our experiences with the police in Cameroon were obviously nothing compared to the horror of World War II, in terms of the way they made us feel, he had a point.

Every time they examined our "papers" (which was every couple of kilometres along the road), my mouth went dry. My heart raced. It's terrifying — they have guns, for heaven's sake. Are they going to demand one dollar or fifty? Are they going to throw us in a cell for the afternoon or the night? Or are they going to take us out to a field and shoot us in the back of the head?

After being tapped for another €20 in bribes along the way, we arrived in Yaoundé angry and despondent. Cameroon is a beautiful country and the people are wonderful, and Yaz's family were so good to take me in, but put it this way — we didn't meet any other backpackers on our little trip up and around the country. Not one. Small wonder when men with guns treat us tourists like walking ATMs.

The next day was V-Day. V for Visa — I had to get permission stamps to enter my next few countries. The visas for DR Congo and Gabon were fairly straightforward, but the guys at the Equatoguinean embassy were less helpful and suggested I come back the next day.

Yaoundé has a nice climate; it's up in the hills, so it's surprisingly cool. But as a city, it's all very 70s brutalist concrete office blocks, which isn't as sexy. However, there is a famous boulangerie called *Calafata's* which supplied us with some disgracefully tasty chocolate éclairs.

The next day I returned (as requested) to the Equatoguinean embassy only to be told that all the borders were closed and that they didn't issue tourist visas at all, ever. Wow.

Well, I guess I'd better pack up my stuff and go home then. Cancel the whole thing. I had a good run there didn't I?

Thanks for reading!

Only joking...

I would just have to sneak in.

I picked up my Gabonese visa, but *zut alors!* They had only given me a single entry visa. Which meant I would have to buy another one if I left the country and returned, for instance if I took a boat to São Tomé and back — something I was totally planning to do.

Unperturbed, we headed to the border town of Ambam on the frontiers of Cameroon, Equatorial Guinea and Gabon. On the way we got into numerous spats with the police for all kinds of fictional crimes. My personal favourite was when a cop claimed Rocco's visa was invalid, because he needed "two visas"; one to "arrive" and another to "travel about".

That night we made friends with a local girl called Vivian who said she would help us do the old border hop into **Equatorial Guinea** (the border most certainly wasn't closed). Even better, we wouldn't even have to sneak in.

EQUATORIAL GUINEA 106/200

🏛 **MALABO**

👥 **676,851**

💬 **Spanish, French, Portuguese**

💵 **Central African CFA Franc**

💰 **$13,835.88**

The equator passes through no part of Equatorial Guinea.

True to her word, the next morning Vivian helped us pay a "fee" to the guards. We went to the supermarket on the Equatoguinean side of the border where we bought a big bottle of Spanish Whiskey to celebrate.

When we got back to Cameroon, Vivian's little brother, Kamikaze (I'm guessing that's his nickname) entertained us with a bit of his comedy routine, which involved him pretending to have a mental illness. I didn't think it would go down very well with a European audience, but then again Mr Bean is improbably popular around the world, so who knows?

Vivian came with us to the nearby border with Gabon. Once again, she was a total life-saver as I needed to be stamped out of the country in my second passport (as that had the visa for Gabon in it); however, I had entered Cameroon using my first passport. A bit confusing I know, but Vivian explained what I was doing. They ended up stamping both passports and wishing me *bonne chance*. Result!

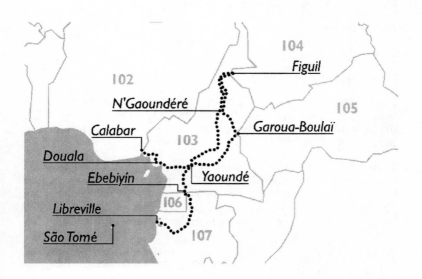

Chapter 22
Behold The Yodelling Pygmies

We arrived in Libreville, **Gabon** several hours later, checked into a hotel and made ourselves at home. The following few days were spent mooching around the country's main maritime hub: Port Mole.

Port Mole was an old-school working port, with fishing boats, tramp freighters, cargo ships and the like, all vying for space along the quayside. There was a real hustle-bustle; junk everywhere, broken down fork-lifts, nets, ropes, chains and anchors, rusting hulks half-submerged in the water — dangers to be avoided.

But there was something rather incongruous about the place. In the middle of all this industry and pollution were three of the biggest superyachts I had ever seen, gleaming white in the oily water.

GABON   107/200

🏛 **LIBREVILLE**

👥 **1.51m**

❓ **French**

💵 **Central African CFA Franc**

💰 **$7,919.71**

In the 1970s, the current president of Gabon, Ali Bongo, released a funk album inspired by James Brown.

I thought maybe Oprah, Tom Cruise and Mark Zuckerburg had come to town.

But it turned out that the biggest yacht was owned by the president of Gabon. The middle one was for his wife and the smaller one was his son's.

Way to rub in the gruelling disparity between rich and poor, Mr President!

I was in Port Mole looking for something that (a) floated and (b) was heading towards the next country on the list, a place most normal people have never heard of: São Tomé and Príncipe, an island nation 300km due west of Libreville.

There were a lot of boats running up and down the coast to Nigeria, Cameroon and the Congos, but nothing going to São Tomé.

I went down to Port Mole every day to check the whiteboard outside the harbourmaster's office to see what was going where. After about a week of this, a battered old tramp called the *Andrea* came into port.

The *Andrea* was scheduled to leave for São Tomé in a few days' time. I was left twiddling my thumbs until then.

At the end of the week Rocco's time was up. Looking back he was one of the best travel buddies I could have wished for. Helpful, diplomatic, professional, great sense of humour and took everything in his stride, even me waking him up after two hours sleep to go trundling through the jungle squished into a bush taxi for 15 hours straight. We're still good mates to this day.

There were very few opportunities to CouchSurf in Libreville, but luckily for me I found a great little hotel down on the beach called the Tropicana. There I met an American travel show presenter called Alex. He was working on the pilot for a show called "The Cure", about alternative cures to modern maladies. He was in Gabon to meet the local tribesmen whose "Bwiti" rituals (involving a potent hallucinogen called Ibogaine) can reportedly cure drug addiction.

A few days later, I returned to the port to check on the *Andrea*. I found out that it was due to leave "first thing Thursday morning" and there may be up to 20 other passengers on board. Where we'd all sit I had no idea. I was also told that the bulk of the cargo would be highly explosive gas canisters. Great!

That Thursday I was up at 6am, eager and excited to get going. I zipped up my backpack and marvelled at how light it felt.

Oh, hang on...

Where are my clothes?

Oh, for the love of God!

I searched my hotel room but they were nowhere to be found. I asked at reception and was led to a grotty room around the back where I found my t-shirts sitting in a bucket, sopping wet.

Did I request a laundry service? No. Did I leave my clothes out with a note saying 'please wash'? No. The maid just took my stuff (most of which was clean and didn't require washing) and threw it in a bucket of cold water for the night.

They had a dryer, so I put my clothes in and tried to at least get them a little dry before I spent 24 hours on a boat. After 10 minutes I took them out and despite now being a little warmer they were just as wet.

Then, as I was grumpily stuffing them into a plastic bag, the hotel manager told me he wanted me to pay for the "laundry service". Crikey, it takes quite a lot to really piss me off, but if you want to give it a go, why not steal my clothes, throw them in a bucket of cold water, and then ask for money for my trouble. At 6:30 in the morning.

Yep, that should do it.

I got to the port for 7am but I wasn't allowed to enter until 7:30am. As soon as the gates were opened I ran to the *Andrea* only to be told we wouldn't be leaving until 9am. While I waited, I was told by one of the other passengers that there were no ATMs in São Tomé, so I ran to the supermarket outside the port, waited for it to open (at 8:40am) grabbed some CFAs out of the cash machine, and ran back to the dock. Thankfully the boat was still there.

I sat down on the stinky quayside and waited. Two hours later I was told the *Andrea* would not be leaving until the afternoon.

So I went to the café at the dock entrance, drank a coffee, did a little work and read a book.

I returned to the *Andrea* after lunch only to be told that the boat wouldn't be leaving until the next day.

Or maybe next Monday.

Perhaps Wednesday.

This was turning into the *Micau* all over again.

After a breakdown that would have reminded a casual observer of Charlton Heston at the end of *Planet of the Apes,* I spoke to the shipping agent, who looked like the guy with the metal claw from *Live and Let Die.*

'What are we waiting for?', I asked, 'The boat is loaded.'

'We're waiting on 600 gas canisters. Tomorrow, no problem.'

'Tomorrow — are you sure? The captain said Wednesday.'

'Tomorrow, I promise you.'

I couldn't go back to the Hotel Tropicana, not after telling them to go to hell in three different languages, and in any case it was an extortionate €25 a night for a thin sponge of a mattress and a cold shower. With no CouchSurfing options and Gabon's first Presidential election in decades due to take place that weekend, my choices were somewhat limited. Elections in Africa seldom pass without incident.

Then came my salvation — Alex the American emailed me saying I should meet him and the Bwiti tribe he was staying with for his television show. He said it was like a hippie commune — utterly hilarious — and, even better, they had a spare hammock for me.

Hell. Yes.

I was picked up from the port in what I can only describe as the Mystery Machine from Scooby-Doo, with what appeared to be *half a bin-bag* full of weed on the passenger seat. Zoinks!

I met Tatayo, the chief of the tribe, a French Keith Richards who came to Gabon in the 1960s and never left. He introduced me to Dimitri, a New York anarchist and ex-heroin addict (also the nicest man you could ever hope to meet) and Justin, a young guy from Chicago who was there for the curative powers of the magic (well, hallucinogenic) tree bark of the Bwiti tribes.

That night, a good thirty or forty of us gathered in the temple for a night of music, dancing and iboga.

Iboga, or Ibogaine as it's known in the West, is a psychoactive drug. It's similar to ayahuasca or peyote. I don't think it's ever killed anyone, but it's very illegal in the United States. Like Kinder Eggs and haggis.

As a rule, I don't do drugs, not just because of the way they make people super annoying (I'm annoying enough, *thank you very much*), but also because of the impact their illegality has on society. Don't get me wrong, I think they should be legal, all of them. But until they are, I don't want to take any part in the building of savage and brutal criminal empires if I can help it.

But since this iboga stuff had come straight from the forest, wasn't illegal and nobody had to die in order to get it to me, I thought I'd give it a go.

They sprinkled a small pile of the brown powder into the palm of my hand, which I had to throw into my mouth all in one go. It tasted awful and my mouth went super dry; so it was a great relief that the next part of the ritual was to take a swig of Fanta, before pouring a little on the ground as an offering. I was told the Bwiti spirits have a fondness for Fanta.

Once everyone had taken their iboga, the main ceremony began. It involved repetitive music played on various local instruments; strings and drums — African rave, I guess. Then the tribe puts their waterpaint on and begins to dance.

Remember the Run-DMC video for *It's Like That?* Well, *it's like that* — boys vs. girls attempting to pull their best shapes for the chief (and the tripped-out audience) and as the night went on the dancing became more crazed and frantic.

No hallucinations for me though. I think you've got to take a lot more iboga to really trip balls.

I have to admit I woke the next morning somewhat perplexed to find myself in a hammock in a Bwiti temple. Not something that happens every day. I said my hearty goodbyes to Tatayo, Dimitri, Justin and Alex and headed to the port.

I needn't have bothered. The *Andrea* wouldn't be going anywhere for a while yet.

Frustrated, I returned to Tatayo's tribe. My only hope now was a guy from Belgium called Marc, who I'd met at the port a few days earlier. He was off work for the next few weeks and he had a sailboat. Maybe, just maybe, he could be my way to São Tomé...

I went to meet Marc at his restaurant on the other side of town. We had a chat and he promised to text me and let me know if it was going to be possible.

Fingers and toes crossed.

That night I stayed with the tribe.

The next day was election day. President Omar Bongo, the longest-standing African "dinosaur" had died a couple of months earlier, so the nation of Gabon had its first chance in over four decades to choose a leader that might not turn the country upside-down by its ankles and shake it until all its money fell out of its pockets.

Out of the 23 candidates running for the post of El Presidente there were three front-runners.

First up, a guy called Obame who I was reliably informed was "a bit of a crook".

Secondly, some dude who might actually change Gabon for the better; you know, redistribute a little of the country's vast oil wealth to the small, impoverished population. I didn't fancy his chances.

Finally there was Ali Bongo, no, not the magician, but Omar Bongo's son and heir to his immense personal fortune, estimated to be somewhere in the region of $1 billion.

It's amazing what $1 billion will buy you. Ali Bongo was *everywhere*. Every single lamp-post (working or not) had Ali's face posted on it, giant TV screens beamed his mug all over Libreville like some Orwellian nightmare, entire buildings had immense posters of him down one side. T-shirts, badges, pens, lanyards, baseball caps, skirts, (yes, skirts) you name it — *Ali* was there.

It probably would have been cheaper just to bribe the 300,000 people he needed to vote for him with free gummy bears for life. Although it wouldn't be much of a surprise if he did that too.

Everybody knew he was going to win. Not only was he the former president's son and the richest man in the country, he was also (at the time) defence minister. He controlled the army. He had it in the bag even if nobody voted for him. The worry was whether the people of Gabon would accept it.

So when Tatayo suggested we get out of town for a few hours, I jumped at the chance. He was going to a nearby woodland in the Mystery Machine with the rest of the tribe introduce Justin to the spirits of the forest and gather leaves and herbs for his upcoming initiation ceremony.

Bwiti is the third main religion of Gabon (after boring old Christianity and Islam) and is inextricably linked to iboga. The already-initiated will generally just eat a handful of the magic powder in a night. However, an initiate has to eat iboga until he or she pukes. And then eat some more. And more. And more. And when the initiate physically cannot swallow any more, the tribal elders might even shove some up their bum. Tatayo *might* have been joking about that. Or maybe not, who knows?

Then comes an elaborate dance staged by the entire tribe designed to freak the hell out of the initiate so that their consciousness leaves their body and goes for a trip around the universe, peeks into the Total Perspective Vortex / Untempered Schism, gets all funky with the spirits of his or her ancestors, while down on Earth their physical body pukes a little more.

The ceremony takes a week of preparation. Afterwards you can look forward to a three-day hangover.

It's certainly a lot more exciting than Sunday school.

After a nice walk through the forest we officially introduced Justin to the forest. Justin was covered in mud and leaves, washed in a river, and then covered in more mud and leaves. I was just glad to be out of Libreville's urban sprawl for a few hours, taking in the sweet tropical woodland air. Lovely.

We got back to the commune late that afternoon. Not long afterwards my phone beeped.

Text Message Received.

It was Marc.

Tentatively, I pressed Open. The text listed a few good reasons why he couldn't go to São Tomé.

It was a no.

I was devastated. After what happened in Cape Verde, I had little faith in the *Andrea* going anywhere, ever.

That night Tatayo blasted his favourite album around the compound. It was a CD of a Gabonese pygmy tribe's harmonic yodelling (for want of a better word). It was wonderfully bonkers, a bit like The Flying Picket's cover of *Only You* as sung by Alvin and The Chipmunks.

Something they got wrong in *The Lord of the Rings*, but kinda got right in *The Wizard of Oz* — people born with proportionate dwarfism often have shorter vocal chords. The pygmies I met in Nigeria and Cameroon sounded like they had been huffing helium.

Although to be fair, Sam Gamgee's "I can't carry it for you, but I can carry you" line wouldn't *quite* hold the same emotional impact if said in a squeaky voice.

Monday began with a telephone conversation with the guy who looked like the guy with the metal claw from *Live and Let Die*. He was now saying the *Andrea* would leave the following Thursday.

The highlight of the day was setting Justin on fire. As part of the cleansing ritual he had to undergo before his big initiation later in the week, Justin had to dig a hole, light a fire, throw a load of sweet-smelling leaves on it, sit over the damn thing wearing a large black cape and, erm, *roast* for half an hour.

The smoke emanating from his black cloak made him look like some sort of evil wizard. If he had worn a crooked hat, it would have been perfect.

Later that day I found myself twiddling my thumbs. 'Sod it,' I thought, 'I'll text Marc again.'

Most of his reasons for saying no had to do with work and time constraints, but he was thinking of doing the trip anyway the following year with one of his friends — us going over could make a nice little recce[32]. I told him about the *Andrea* and he texted back suggesting we meet up to talk some more, which we did.

The results of the election had not been announced, but already all three front-runners were claiming victory. Consequently, nearly all the restaurants in town (including Marc's) were closed in case of trouble..

With his restaurant shut, Marc had no particular reason to stay in Libreville for the next few days.

'Hmm, do you think you can get me a visa and a GPS device?' he asked.

'I know I can,' I replied.

'Okay. Screw it - let's go to São Tomé.'

---

[32] Editor's Note: This is British slang for reconnaissance or reconnoiter.

The game was afoot.

That night Justin and I prepared for the arrival of Alex the American's film crew by daubing chalk and charcoal on my face and body. The plan was that when they got there, Justin (already whited-up and wearing a bird's nest on his head from his Bwiti initiation) would run over to the minibus in a panic, pleading for help. I'd then jump out of the bushes with a whip and a big net and scream 'NUMBER 43!! BACK IN YOUR CAGE!'

I guess you had to be there.

The next morning I had me a mission: find a handheld GPS receiver for the trip to São Tomé. It wasn't going to be easy to find specialised sailing gear; half of Libreville was still closed.

I was at the big Mbolo Supermarket when it opened at 9am, but all they had were GPS loggers like the one I already carried with me; no display, no use.

I rang Marc to see if he was having any joy. Sadly not. The Gabon Meca (where the guys at the supermarket had suggested I go) was a damp squib and the nearby Michele Marina was closed for the next week.

I headed to Port Mole for some advice. Steve the Nigerian fishmonger said he knew of a place. What's more, he'd take me there. He left his shop, jumped in his car and opened the passenger door for me. 'C'mon, let's go!'

Steve drove me all over town. We found a handful of places that were open, including a Yamaha shop that sold boat engines, but GPS receivers were nowhere to be found.

We had almost given up when Steve remembered a shop that *might* sell GPS devices. The place he took me to was so hard to find that even when we were inside I wasn't sure we were there. No sign, no indication other than that it was chock full of sailing kit, fishing kits, and...

Oh yes...

Global Positioning System receivers!

We had done it. GPS gadget in hand, Steve took me back to the dock; I thanked him profusely. What a legend! He just smiled, shook my hand and went back to work. I can't emphasise enough how much *The Odyssey Expedition* re-affirmed my faith in humanity.

I headed over to the São Toméan embassy to meet Marc. As I had predicted, he would get his visa at 11:30 the next day. I already had mine.

Marc was jubilant.

São Tomé, you tricky little bugger, here I come.

That night, Alex's film crew treated Tatayo, Dimitri and I to a bite to eat at the Sunset Beach hotel next door to the commune. His crew included a doctor who was studying the medicinal effects of iboga. He was also an ex-New York gang member. Crazy world.

After printing charts and getting supplies, Marc and I set off on his boat, the *Reol,* at around 2pm the next day. Into the Atlantic Ocean for what would be the last time of *The Odyssey Expedition.*

The *Reol* was tiny — just 10 metres in length, even smaller than the pirogue to Cape Verde. We plotted a course due west along the equator itself.

Marc had worked in Africa for many years, and his wife was Gabonese. His speciality was mining, so we had a good old chat about this mysterious substance I kept hearing about in passing: "coltan".

Short for 'colombite-tantalite', it's in your laptop, it's in your smart phone, it's in your flat-screen TV. Like Frank Herbert's "spice", coltan makes the modern world go round. It's as sought-after as it is rare, and over 65% of the world's supply of it is in Congo, where it has been fuelling conflicts for years. Think *Blood Diamond* but on a much, much larger scale.

That night Marc caught a huge fish, too big for us to eat in one sitting. Unfortunately, we didn't have a stove on board, so we had to do a Gollum and eat the thing raw. Although we did marinate the big guy in vinegar for 30 minutes. It was actually pretty good — at first. A little later on I puked my guts up. I still hated sailing.

It was the beginning of September. The midday sun was almost halfway on its journey from the Tropic of Cancer (June) to the Tropic of Capricorn (December), which meant the solar radiation got pretty intense along the ol' equator.

Luckily, there was plenty of wind and that wind took us all the way to the little island of São Tomé in less than 48 hours.

São Tomé. Wow. What a diamond in the rough. We pulled in at around 5pm, but without proper charts we had no idea where. I found out later that it was a place called Agua-Tzi about halfway down the island. We sailed into a little bay and dropped anchor.

The dingy trip to land resulted in me getting my shoes utterly drenched, but at last I was standing on the soil of São Tomé, albeit with rather wet feet.

In many ways, I felt like São Tomé was the ying to Cape Verde's yang. Both were former Portuguese colonies, but São Tomé was everything Cape Verde was not. Lush, green, clean white beaches, gorgeous old architecture, a tall, narrow volcano that stands proud in the middle of the island like a backdrop from *The Flintstones* and the friendliest people you could ever hope to meet.

Upon our unorthodox arrival, the locals raced out to meet us. One guy, Molo, offered not only to store the dingy in his home but also helped us get on the bus to the capital.

São Tomé and Príncipe is really undeveloped, even by African standards. Its population of 193,000 scrapes by with just $25m of foreign aid and $5m from cocoa exports. It has no ATMs, no electrical grid, no sewage system, and only gets on average 20 visitors a week — but the potential! The soil is rich and fertile, there are miles and miles of unspoilt beaches, and, best of all, it never gets cold.

When Marc and I returned to Agua-Tzi several hours later, we saw, to Marc's horror, that the tide had gone out and his boat was marooned on the sand. The *Reol* had a retractable keel (which we had retracted before disembarking) so she wouldn't tip over, but we hadn't raised the outboard motor before we left.

SÃO TOMÉ & PRÍNCIPE 108/200

🏛 **SÃO TOMÉ**

👥 173,240

❓ Portuguese

💵 São Tomé and Príncipe Dobra

💰 $1,134.11

Male gold-diggers beware! Marrying a São Toméan women does not mean you have any legal right to her money.

The weight of the entire sailboat on the motor's bracket would have snapped it off the back transom, damaging the motor and the ship.

But this was São Tomé. The locals from the village, led by Molo, had run over to the boat, lifted the outboard motor out of the water and locked it in the raised position to prevent it being damaged.

São Tomé, you rock my world.

At around 2am the tide came back in. Marc and I pushed the *Reol* back into the water. We both got sodden wet, but we made it out. Thank heavens for lovely people and retractable keels.

That night we made tremendous progress back to Gabon.

The *Reol*, bless her, was a simple craft — a manual rudder, no inboard motor (just a little outboard)[33] and sails that were past their sell-by

---

[33] Editor's Note: An inboard motor is enclosed within the hull of the boat, while an outboard motor is mounted onto the outside.

date.

That being said, we covered over 60 nautical miles (110km) before midday, which was awesome going.

That afternoon we attempted to use the spinnaker sail. Marc's method of installing it was a little unorthodox (he had never done it before) but it worked a treat, increasing our speed by a good few knots. By nightfall we were over halfway back to Libreville.

The next day I awoke before daybreak and found myself staring transfixed over the sea, which was more silver than I had ever seen it. We could have been floating on an endless lake of mercury. A thin line of gold drew a path towards the rising sun which beckoned us back to Africa.

After a few hours spent plodding along at around 4 or 5 knots, Marc threw out the spinnaker again and soon we were cutting through the waves like a hot knife through butter.

You may not consider travelling at ten miles an hour to be very exciting, but when you are sitting on the back of a boat, clinging to the rudder for dear life, struggling to keep *dead on* a bearing of 90° lest the boat goes one way and the sail goes the other (which would cause the boom to swing across and hit you in the head so hard you'd probably never wake up), you realise that you're corralling two unstoppable forces of nature with just a couple of sheets and a plank of wood. It's all marvellously ridiculous.

Later, after the sun had set and before the moon had risen, clouds obscured the stars and the GPS ran out of power. Marc was asleep below decks and so it was just me and the *Reol*, a tiny speck of light in a literal ocean of darkness. I couldn't see the sea, the sky, the horizon, land, rocks, islands, anything — the only thing keeping us from being lost at sea with little in the way of emergency equipment was the ship's compass.

I kept a heading of 90° due east and pushed on into the night.

When we reached the bright lights of Libreville it was midnight. We anchored down and waited until first light. In the morning, we pulled into Port Mole.

The mission complete, Marc and I shook hands and went our separate ways. What an amazing guy.

Of course, the *Andrea* still hadn't left.

Later Tatayo and the gang gave me a lift in the Mystery Machine to the PK8 area of town from where the shared taxis left heading south towards the border with Congo.

While I was on my way to São Tomé, Justin had finished his initiation.

He said it was an incredible experience, but didn't find himself floating on a cloud above the entire universe. Maybe he needed a bit more iboga shoved up his bum. I bid a fond adieu to Dimitri, Alex, Justin and, of course, the irrepressible Tatayo. If you ever find yourself stuck in Libreville for a few days, you know where to go.

The first leg of the journey south (to Lamberéné) was remarkably pleasant. It felt good to be properly back in the Southern Hemisphere again.

Once I reached Lamberéné I was herded onto the back of a pickup truck, along with two other guys, a shitload of bananas and several bags filled with dried fish. We hurtled south so fast it made my toes curl.

Speeding along the sealed road was admittedly exhilarating; but once it ended and the dirt track began, it was nothing short of torture. The driver didn't slow down to accommodate the sorry state of the road. In fact, I think he may have even sped up.

After the first hour one of the guys got off so it was just me and another guy — Anisé — clinging onto the pick-up truck for dear life. We found it was easier to stand and lean forwards, gripping the metal bar behind the cab, even if it did mean getting covered in dust.

After the second hour, as if to add a little more comedy value to the situation, the truck driver stopped to load even more bananas, some more fish and, oh yes, a live goat! So not only did I have to worry about falling out or the driver crashing, I now had to worry about getting goat shit all over my shoes.

It began to rain, something I pointed out to Anisé. He shook his head.

'It can't rain, it's not the rainy season.'

I admired his optimism.

For the rest of the journey, the driver maintained a solid 100kmph no matter how many potholes he hit. The vibration from the road's corrugation made my eyeballs shake. My vision flickered like an old movie. With one hand holding the back rail with a vice-like grip, I tweeted my progress every few minutes so the folks back home could share my terror in real-time.

At 8pm we reached the border town of N'Dendé. I jumped out, my legs shaking from their five-hour ordeal.

That night I crashed out early in a cheap n' cheerful guest house, genuinely happy to still be alive. I remember thinking, 'well, that's São Tomé out of the way, nothing can stop me now!'

Of course I had no freakin' idea what was about to happen to me in my next country: Congo.

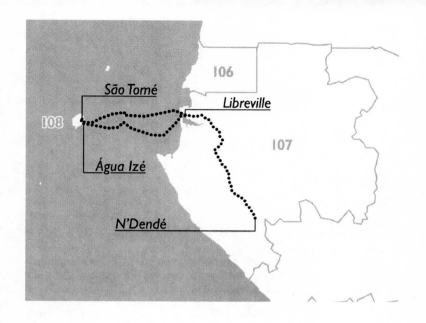

Chapter 23
Free Hugs

'There are places in this world where the safety net is suddenly whipped away, where the right accent, education, health insurance and foreign passport — all the trappings that spell "It Can't Happen to Me" — no longer apply, and your well-being depends on the condescension of strangers.'

– Michela Wrong, In The Footsteps of Mr. Kurtz

I was up at 5am the next morning. It wasn't until 7am that I found a bush taxi to the Congolese border. Although when I did find one, instead of heading to the frontier, the driver spent an hour driving errands around town and then kicked me out of his car. Turns out he wasn't going to the border after all.

I waited by the side of the road for an age before another bush taxi finally turned up. I squished myself inside.

An hour or so later I was in the queue waiting to get stamped out of Gabon. I got chatting to a Spanish guy, Javier, who was waiting to get stamped in. Javier worked for *Médecins Sans Frontières* and after his latest stint, he had decided to ride his motorbike from South Africa to Spain.

It felt like I had met a kindred spirit — someone else who had been through the emotional rollercoaster that is overland travel in Africa, and somebody who still had a long way to go. We were meeting half-way, he was going up and I was coming down.

We swapped good road/bad road stories and general advice. Worryingly, Javier had originally wanted to travel up through Angola, but just couldn't get a visa. Apparently, obtaining one in Africa is next to impossible. Unfortunately for me, my Angolan visa had expired.

I shook my fist in the vague direction of Cape Verde.

We handed over our passports and were told to wait outside. Javier was called back into the office first. I sat outside on the concrete plinth of the Gabonese flag. After a few minutes I was called inside. It was only when I picked up my backpack that I saw to my horror that I had been sharing the plinth with a spider a good 30cm in diameter. To this day, my toes still curl at the memory.

Freshly stamped out of Gabon, I wished Javier well on his journey and marched into country number 109: **Congo**.

Okay here's where it gets a bit confusing, so pay attention. The Republic of Congo is on the north side of the river Congo. The Democratic Republic of Congo is mostly on the south. The Republic of Congo used to be a French colony, while the Democratic Republic of Congo used to be Belgian.

To make things a little easier, I'm going to refer to the Frenchie northern Republic of Congo as "Congo" and the southern Belgian-y Democratic Republic of Congo as "The DRC".

The rest of this chapter takes place in the former French Congo, north of the river.

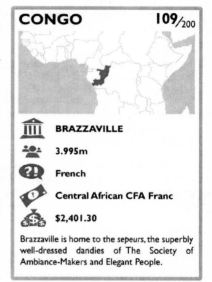

CONGO 109/200

🏛 **BRAZZAVILLE**

👥 **3.995m**

💬 **French**

💵 **Central African CFA Franc**

💰 **$2,401.30**

Brazzaville is home to the *sepeurs*, the superbly well-dressed dandies of The Society of Ambiance-Makers and Elegant People.

Once I had finally cleared the border shenanigans on the Congo side, I hopped a motorbike to the first town over the border and arrived at about 3pm. I was hopeful of getting some kind of bush taxi south to the city of Dolisie that day.

No chance. There was no transport south until the next morning. It had taken me an entire day to go a little over 50km. There was nothing else to do but sit in the only café and update my website while getting deafened by the almighty din blasting from the gigantic speaker stack a few feet away. I wouldn't mind but I was literally the only person there.

The next morning, the woman who ran the guest house woke me to tell me the bus to Dolisie was leaving. I jumped out of bed, quickly gathered my things and ran outside.

But there was no bus. Only a cattle truck with loads of people on board slowly making its way out of town.

'Est que le bus?', I asked the woman.

'Oui', she confirmed.

I grimaced and ran after the "bus", clambering on board the back while it was still in motion. People shuffled up to allow me to sit at the end of the left-hand bench.

The "bus" was a 50-year old cattle truck with open sides. It was carrying a staggering 73 people and their luggage, 14 live goats and several chickens. Under my feet were two freshly butchered cow's legs, still with their hide, blood oozing from the wounds and attracting flies like an open latrine.

The "road" was a dusty track peppered with potholes. It was also corrugated. Every time the driver put his foot down I could feel the fillings shaking loose in my face. The dust was ubiquitous. It covered my bags, my hat, my clothes — it covered my face and got into my lungs.

As if that wasn't bad enough, the truck was seemingly rigged to blow its filthy black exhaust in the faces of those unfortunates (including me) sitting towards the rear.

I made do with a wet-wipe held over my mouth until it became too dirty and I had to sling it and pick up a new one. Each one lasted less than ten minutes. If you've ever used a sanding machine on floorboards, you'll have some idea what it was like.

And there were children — babies on board.

It was worse than the pirogue to Cape Verde, worse than the bush taxi through Guinea and worse than the mauler ride across Nigeria .

But was it as bad as the Greyhound? In retrospect, no. Nobody went out of their way to be nasty to me and it only cost $10.

After over 100 miles of suffering, the "bus" broke down a mile or so north of the town of Kilbangou, about half-way to Dolisie. No surprise there. I decided enough was enough and I set off on foot to see if there were any other transport options. I was accompanied by a local guy named John. He was a teacher in Dolisie and was wearing a suit, which would now require one hell of a dry-clean to get rid of all of the dust.

We walked for a couple of kilometres until a bush taxi came along. We flagged it down and reached Dolisie that afternoon.

Before the civil war a decade earlier, Dolisie was the retreat of the moneyed elite, a leafy town with beautiful old buildings. The war saw the end of that. It was still leafy, but a lot of the old buildings had been reduced to rubble.

The train line was a dilapidated single-track affair, despite being the main route from the capital, Brazzaville, to Pointe Noire, the country's only port. I asked at the station what time the next train left for the capital. Not today, not tomorrow — the day after tomorrow. Sod that.

There were no shared taxis that went all the way to Brazzaville, but there were some that stopped at the next town along the way, Nkayi. After a pleasant dinner with John, I wished him well and headed east. Once again I found myself crammed into a bush taxi carrying far too many passengers. I taxi-hopped at Nkayi and made it all the way to the town of Modingo, where I spent the night.

I found a little hotel that was recommended in the Lonely Planet and after three showers and a hot bath I finally felt clean again.

I stayed up most of the night copying my tapes and backing up all of my files onto an external hard drive, in case my laptop and/or camera got stolen the next day. I had been warned that the road from Modingo to Brazzaville was notorious for banditry.

In the morning I walked to the parking lot where the vehicles taking passengers congregate. There I met Thomas, a Congolese transvestite and medical doctor. He wore the most phenomenal red nail varnish. I asked him if he got much grief for wearing a dress in what is a pretty conservative country. He said, 'Nah — most people around here are too confused when they see me to give me any hassle.'

The good Dr Tom then found me a ride in a big old truck that was taking passengers to the capital. He even managed to get me a seat in the cab. My "passenger seat buddy" was a friendly soldier, complete with AK-47, to ward off any would-be dandy highwaymen. It was strangely reassuring.

We spent the day bouncing down the shambolic dirt track that was the main road from the port to the capital. It was dark when we arrived at the city of Kinkala, the last big town before Brazzaville — and the start of the sealed road. That was when the nice soldier guy left us.

Something you should know about overlanding it through West and Central Africa: the worst time to travel is between 7pm and 11pm. This has nothing to do with banditry, the state of the roads or even the lack of streetlights. It has to do with the police.

Palm wine is cheap and devilishly alcoholic, and the policemen manning the ubiquitous checkpoints tend to have a good few swigs of the stuff throughout the day.

The upshot of which is that by around 7pm they're usually pretty drunk. With decidedly un-pretty assault rifles.

We arrived at the police checkpoint outside Brazzaville at 8pm. At first everything seemed quite straightforward until they asked me to get out of the cab so they could rifle through my belongings.

After finding a good few miniDV tapes in my backpack they decided that they wanted to see what was on them. I picked one at random and played it to them. It was footage of Steve, the lovely Nigerian guy from

Port Mole driving me around looking for a GPS device. The policeman was convinced it was in fact Ali Bongo, the new president of Gabon.

'What? Do all black people look the same to you?!', I asked, laughing.

He didn't laugh back.

Shit.

Before I knew it, my phone had been confiscated and I was being stuffed into a sequestered car with four policemen (me and three others in the back, all armed). I was being taken to see "the chief".

These guys weren't screwing around.

I was hauled into a police station and invited to sit down opposite the chief of police. My tapes were stacked on the cluttered desk that lay between us. Ten armed officers stood behind me gawping and jostling like a bunch of schoolboys who've found a dead animal and are psyching each other up to poke it with a stick.

I was tired, I was grumpy, I was sick of being asked the same inane questions over and over. My name, my nationality, which football team I supported...

The chief explained that they wanted to see what was on my video tapes. I knocked the stack of tapes over. 'Frigging well watch them then.'

Yeah. Shouldn't have done that.

Really shouldn't have done that.

The chief, face like thunder, told me to stay put. He left the room and took his entourage with him. My phone may have been confiscated, but after the Cape Verde debacle I had made sure to always carry a spare. I quickly tapped out a tweet that I had been arrested and waited for the cavalry to arrive.

The cavalry took the form of Christophe, the guy who was supposed to be hosting me that night. He arrived with his flatmate Max. Max suggested to the police that they retain my passport and my tapes, and let me go — the reasoning being that I couldn't really go anywhere without my travel documents.

'Non', was the rather succinct reply.

So then: onto Plan B.

Christophe and Max managed to get a phone call to the British embassy in Kinshasa (in the DRC) and explain the situation. There's no British Embassy in Brazzaville, only an Honourary Consul. The guy I spoke to, a rather posh chap named Holgar, told me that they would "do all they could" to get me out, "as soon as possible."

It wasn't *particularly* reassuring.

Christophe and Max eventually gave up trying to reason with the police. They promised to come and see me in the morning and headed home. It was past midnight. Weirdly, the "chief" pulled a bottle of Scotch out of his drawer and offered me a tipple, an offer I took him up on. He told me it was all a matter of "procedure" and I'd be released the next day, so I might as well make myself comfortable on the tiny two-seater couch in the corner of his office.

I curled up into a ball and allowed the exasperation of it all to sing me to sleep.

The following morning Max returned to the cop shop and once again attempted to reason with the police. They were having none of it. After a couple of hours of fruitless mediation, I was taken outside and stuffed into a 4×4. I resisted on the grounds that they wouldn't tell either Max or myself where they were taking me. In the end, Max said he'd follow them and not to worry, they promised they'll let me go soon.

I was taken to another police station — this one much larger (and even more horrible) than the last. I was hauled in front of another "chief" (turns out chiefs are ten-a-penny in Congo) and the conversation went a bit like this:

'Why am I here?'

'It's a matter of procedure.'

'So you do this to all tourists then?'

'No.'

'Just me?'

'Yes.'

'Why?'

'It's a matter of procedure.'

Kafka much?

I was taken downstairs and left in a room to twiddle my thumbs. As the day dragged on, it became increasingly clear that they had no intention of letting me go before dark, even though I was told repeatedly that I had not committed a crime, my visa and passport were in order and that I was — apparently — "free". Not free to walk out the door though.

Around 7pm, my bags were brought into the room and my camcorder, tapes and mobile phone were plonked down on the desk beside me. Since I had *literally* been left to my own devices, I took the opportunity to call Mandy.

She was concerned — obviously there was a feeling of *déjà vu* after what happened in Cape Verde — but I explained that if they were serious about me having committed some sort of crime they wouldn't have given me access to all my stuff.

At that exact moment, seven policemen burst into the room, ripped the mobile phone from my ear, proceeded to violently relieve me of my hat, my shoes, my socks, my belt, my T-shirt and everything in my pockets. They even ripped the glasses from my face.

I was then frog-marched out of the room, my arms twisted behind my back. The cell I was thrown into was like somewhere you might wake up if you were a victim of the Jigsaw Killer from the movie *Saw*. Dirty concrete, blood smeared all over the walls, no lighting.

In that dark, filthy, stinking, mosquito-ridden cell, the world out of focus, semi-naked and afraid, I curled up into a ball, rocked forwards and backwards muttering over and over 'what the f---? What the actual f---?' as the tears streamed down my face.

I awoke at dawn. I had spent the night on a damp, dog-eared piece of foam. I was covered in insect bites.

Angry and distressed, I started banging on the cell door and screaming at the top of my lungs for them to let me the hell out.

I was ignored for hours.

Late that afternoon, three policemen came to the door looking for Hugs.

My surname had proven difficult for a lot of non-English speakers on my journey, what with that silent "gh" in the middle. I usually explain that it is pronounced "hews" to rhyme with "rhythm and blues" or "BBC News". In this case, I couldn't be arsed correcting them, so the Congolese police just called me "Hugs".

I was told that if I calmed down I would be allowed to speak with the chief. I was given some food, but I didn't eat it. Did I mention that they took my shoes and socks? Even the thought of having to use the stinking shit-covered squat toilet in the cell — a toilet that didn't look as if it had *ever* been cleaned — in my bare feet filled me with way more dread than starving to death. In any case, there was no toilet paper or running water. Not going to happen. I figured if I didn't eat, I wouldn't need to shit. Thus began my Congolese hunger strike.

An hour later I was given my t-shirt back and was taken to a filthy little office on the other side of the police station where I sat down with yet another "chief" — my third to date.

He asked me a bunch of simple questions, the answers for which were readily available in my passport which he held in his hand. Ten other policemen looked on — there's apparently not much crime for them to fight in Brazzaville.

'Monsieur Hugs, what are you doing in Congo?' asked the chief.

'I'm trying to travel to every country in the world without flying and I'm raising money for the charity WaterAid, I've just been to Gabon and next I'm going to the DRC — you can see I have the visas in my passport.'

'Yes. I have read your website' said the chief, surprisingly. 'You are doing a good thing. May I ask, what do you intend to say about Congo?'

I took a deep breath.

'I'll say it's a wonderful place filled with wonderful people. Can I go now?'

'Soon.'

'How soon? Suis-je un criminel?'

'No, you are not a criminal.'

'Un terroriste? Un homme d'espionnage?'

'No, you are not a terrorist. Or a spy. You are a free man.'

'I'm free to leave?'

'You are free, you just cannot leave.'

I had somehow found myself staying at the Hotel California, Congo style.

The chief promised to have me out "as soon as possible".

'Today?', I asked.

'Yes yes today.'

I was escorted back to my cell. Day turned to night. At around 9pm I gave up thinking I was getting out and fell asleep on my floor sponge. *Such a lovely place.*

The next day was a Sunday and like all good Sundays it passed agonisingly slowly. Nothing to read, nothing to write — just me and my thoughts. The police station was empty. Everyone was at church, apparently.

My daydreams centred on two things — developing the idea of an *Indiana Jones* film set in Africa and attempting to suss out a way of escaping this infernal place.

Luckily for me, the police had missed something when they stripped me of my possessions — my secret wallet containing a tiny Swiss army knife, €80 and a credit card. I figured that if I could get out it would easily be enough to pay a fisherman to take me over the river Congo to Kinshasa. I even worked out the direction of the river by observing the shadows as the sun passed overhead so I'd vaguely know which way to run.

I tried all of the bars on the windows, but they weren't going anywhere. There was a missing bar in the window above the toilet, but it would mean I would have to climb over the stinking pile of shit that was spread out all over the floor. In bare feet.

In any case, without my glasses I couldn't see much. Anything over a foot away was out of focus, so the plan was only to be enacted if things became really desperate. Running barefoot along the streets of West Africa is not recommended even when your vision is 20-20.

The one thing I didn't think about was food. Staying for the weekend in a tiny room that smelled like a rotting corpse kinda puts you off your din-dins. Just think: Congolese detention cells could be the new fad diet.

I wasted the rest of the afternoon carving a copy of the periodic table into the cell wall with my little knife and then kicking the hell out of the metal cell door with the soles of my feet.

I did so much damage to the door that the next day it took the three policemen over half an hour (and a crowbar) to get damn thing open.

When they did get it open I braced myself for a beating, but instead they gave me my glasses back and told me to come with them.

I was escorted to a small room on the right of the police station's large entrance hall. The room had a bunk-bed, and if I climbed onto the top bunk I could see people coming and going through a little gap where the partition wall didn't quite reach the ceiling.

After a few hours, a smartly-dressed woman arrived at the station. I called to her from across the way. She smiled and gave me the thumbs up followed by the international two-palms-down signal of "stay calm".

The woman met with some police officers and then disappeared into an office. A few hours later she came to see me.

Diplomacy is a delicate game so all I can tell you about her is that she worked for the British Embassy. I'll call her "Mrs X".

'Okay — first of all', said Mrs X, 'stop screaming and shouting and banging doors.'

'But I haven't done anything!'

'I know that, they know that, but this is Congo. There is little stopping them from taking you around the back, beating you to death and claiming it was an accident.'

Not a lot you can say to that. I promised her I'd calm down.

The woman continued. 'We're going to get you out. It may not be today, but if not it will be tomorrow.'

'What if they don't let me out tomorrow?', I asked.

'I requested for you to be moved to this room instead of the cell. I won't be hard for you to get out in the night when there's nobody here. I will get you a map so you know where to go; we can give you asylum.'

'Are you kidding? I've got no shoes.'

'Let's cross that bridge when we get to it. Now all we have to do is go to the chief's office and run through your footage with him.'

'Which chief is it? I've met so many.'

It turned out to be a chief I had not met before. Let's call him "Chief #4".

So we sat in Chief #4's office for a couple of hours, fast-forwarding through every single one of my tapes that I had filmed over the previous month. I hoped to goodness that I hadn't accidentally filmed anything that would arouse their suspicions — a shot of a policeman perhaps, or a government building, an airport, a border post or a Cameroonian roundabout.

Once we were done, I was taken back to the bunk-bed room. Mrs X stayed with the chief.

A few hours later a police officer came in with my "paperwork" — four copies of a 16-page report of what was in my bag and why I was in Congo. I had to sign every copy in several different places. The fact that it was all in French meant it could conceivably say pretty much anything, but it all appeared in order, so I signed it.

Mrs X came back to see me. Apparently my "situation" was now in the hands of the Minister of Justice. Not only that, but the President had also been informed.

'The President of Congo?'

'Yes.'

'Has he not got anything better to do?', I asked.

'It would appear not.'

Mrs X let me use her mobile phone, so I called my parents and then Mandy to let them know I was all right. Apparently my incarceration had made the BBC News over the weekend.

'They say I'll be out tomorrow morning', I told them. 'We'll see...'

Before Mrs X left she handed me something that was akin to a bucket of KFC to a starving man: two copies of National Geographic magazine and a little flashlight. After *five days* of nothing to read, write or watch it was manna from heaven.

That night I stayed up for hours reading the Nat Geos from cover to cover. Words — lovely, beautiful, words.

I woke up before dawn to find that the guy who had been guarding the door had disappeared. So I went for a walk around the station — it was empty. I was strongly tempted to run away, but I had no map and no shoes. I returned to my bed, hoping that I wouldn't regret the decision not to just leg it.

In the morning I kept an eye on the front door thinking that Mrs X would be back any minute.

By noon, I became despondent. Mrs X was nowhere to be seen. Where was she?

By now they had detained me for six days without charge. Let's just say my patience was wearing thin.

Late that afternoon Mrs X emerged from one of the offices. She had arrived before I woke up and spent all day petitioning yet another police chief (number 5!) for my release. I would later find out that she had told him that she would not leave his office until I was set free.

Go Mrs X!

After several phone calls that culminated in the President of Congo personally telling the police to let me go, the police had relented. Mrs X gave me the good news.

'Let's get out of here.'

We walked across the police station and into an office. My backpack, my laptop and my video camera were all there. Everything was catalogued, and I was asked if anything was missing. All the important stuff was there, although I never did see my plastic spork again.

I put on my shoes, grabbed my bags and, being typically British, muttered an apology for wasting everybody's time. I instantly regretted doing that — needless to say I didn't receive a word of contrition in return.

Back in the UK, my dad was asked by reporters if, given this was the second time I had been detained without charge, I would be giving up and coming home.

Dad just laughed. 'Don't be silly', he told them, 'my son's no quitter.'

A policeman held the front door open for me. As I stepped outside into the bright afternoon sun, my hat was finally reunited with my head.

The show was back on the road.

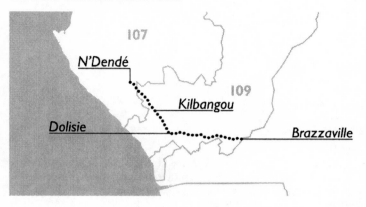

Chapter 24
We Are Nowhere And It's Now

Mrs. X drove me to her rather luxurious family home in the diplomatic area of Brazzaville. I was greeted with a glass of Baileys on ice beside the swimming pool. I hadn't washed, eaten or gone for a dump in a week. It was a bit like popping out of a sewer into a cocktail party.

I downed the Baileys and, excusing myself, made my way to the bathroom. A shit, shower and shave later and I emerged feeling like a new man.

That night I met up with Christophe and Max and went for my second pizza of liberation. Embarrassingly enough, I couldn't finish the damn thing. I guess my stomach had shrunk. The beer was more than welcome, though. That night I chatted with Mandy for hours before sleeping in a proper bed in a proper house. Bliss.

The next morning, I was met by Parul, the Vice-Consul from the British embassy in Kinshasa. She would be escorting me into my next country: the **Democratic Republic of Congo**. I later found out that while I was in jail she had come across the river from DR Congo and tried to see me, but the Congolese police wouldn't let her.

DEMOCRATIC REPUBLIC OF CONGO 110/200

KINSHASA

60.49m

French

Congolese Franc

$301.93

The uranium used in the bomb that was dropped on Hiroshima came from The Democratic Republic of Congo.

After what was possibly the most straight-forward border crossing since I left Europe (a travel buddy with a diplomatic passport is like a cheat code for all this palaver), Parul and I headed over to the Angolan embassy only to find that it had closed early. I'd have to return the next day to try to get the visa that everyone was telling me I couldn't get.

With my appetite back, we grabbed a cheeky Nando's. That evening I was invited to watch a screening of Sacha Baron Cohen's *Bruno* at the British embassy. Afterwards I was picked up by Michael, my CouchSurf host in Kinshasa. He was a Belgian working for *Operation Damien*, a charity that worked with lepers and TB sufferers in Africa.

In another bit of hilariously bad timing, the next day, September 17th, was "Angolan Heroes Day", so the embassy was closed.

'Oh well,' I thought. 'I probably needed a few days of R&R after all of last week's bollocks anyway.' So I spent the day strolling around Kinshasa. It's pretty much what you'd expect it to be for a nation that's historically been given the shitty end of the stick: messy, impoverished, lots of concrete, lots of traffic, homelessness, malnourished kids, tin shack shantytowns.

In the olden days it was known as "Kin la Belle" (Kin The Beauty). Now they call it "Kin la poubelle" (Kin The Bin), because of the enormous amount of garbage stinking up the streets – just one of a great many issues the Congolese government seems utterly ill-equipped to deal with.

I found a little old brick church and sat inside for a while, enjoying the cool silence.

Reading up on the history of The DRC is heart-breaking. King Leopold II of Belgium annexed the entire region — an area the size of Western Europe — in the 1880s, pledging to "improve the lives of the native inhabitants".

Of course he had no intention of doing that.

Instead he set about enriching not the Congo Free State, but himself, at the cost of the lives of an estimated 10 million Congolese — half the country's population.

He never even visited the place.

After growing public disgust at what was happening in Congo, the Free State was handed over to the Belgian government in 1908. They did a better job, but that's not saying much. The indigenous people were still treated like dirt.

When independence was declared in 1960, the country was almost immediately plunged into crisis until the military dictator Joseph Mabuto took over, changed the name from Congo to Zaire and ran the place as a kleptocracy for over 30 years until his ignominious downfall in 1997 (when the fallout from the 1994 Rwandan genocide spread across the whole of Central Africa like a cancer). Mabuto went into exile and the resultant wars left an estimated 5.4 million dead.

Remember that "coltan" stuff I was discussing with Marc on the boat to

São Tomé? Conflict minerals like coltan helped bankroll those wars. Although peace was declared in 2003, sporadic fighting continues in eastern DRC to this day.

That night Michael and I went for a beer and I learned first-hand just how eye-wateringly expensive DR Congo can be. You'd be lucky to get a meal for less than US$15, and if it wasn't for CouchSurfing, I'd be staying in a grotty, health & safety-baiting room for at least US$75 a night.

The next morning I was back at the Angolan embassy. Third time lucky! Not only was the embassy open, I found out that there was a chance — *an outside chance* — that I could get a new visa, since I already had one issued in London. But I'd have to return after the weekend to find out.

You didn't think it would be *that* easy, now did you?

Later on in the day, I was invited to a barbecue at the British Embassy. There I met with Laure and Alex, a French couple that I had made contact with through CouchSurfing. Laure was one of only two female pilots in the DRC and Alex worked doing logistics for *Médecins Sans Frontières (MSF)*.

They dragged me (oh so reluctantly!) out for a Friday night of irresponsible drinking in the dives and grottos of Kinshasa. I met a stack of people all working for NGOs[34] or charities and probably consumed one or two too many glasses of obscenely overpriced lager.

Michael was working until late and would be working again tomorrow so unfortunately he didn't join us, but he left a key out for me, and after a quick ride around town in an MSF 4×4 (MSF employees are not allowed to go around town without a chaperone), I finally found his flat. Not bad considering I was so drunk I could barely find my arse with both hands.

On the Saturday night, I was invited to a house party with Alex and Laure. We sat in the garden talking, drinking and eating until the wee small hours. On our way back to the MSF compound, we stopped off at another friend's house and promptly indulged in a bit of why-not-throw-yourself-in-the-swimming-pool shenanigans. I slept the night on Alex and Laure's floor.

After a great weekend, Monday was my prescribed day of action. I headed to the Angolan embassy first thing in the morning, armed with my passport, my old visa, my letter of invitation, my onward flight ticket (just for show), photos, photocopies, vaccination certificate, and a nice, shiny new $100 bill.

There was no rhyme or reason as to who was "served" first, so I just

---

34 Editor's Note: An NGO is a non-governmental organization. It is a "not-for-profit" organization that is independent from states and international governmental organizations.

stood in the middle of the room looking lost until somebody came to help me. They looked at my stuff and said that I needed a letter from my embassy confirming that I wasn't an escaped serial killer or something.

I jumped a "taxi" to the British embassy. Really it was a private car, but since there are no real taxis in Kinshasa, it makes pretty much every car that isn't covered in UN stickers a taxi.

At the British embassy, I very nicely asked Parul to sort me out with a letter of introduction, which she did. I said my thanks and headed back to the Angolan embassy.

There I was taken into a back room. I handed over everything and hoped for the best. They told me to come back in the next day.

I headed over to see Alex at his workplace and we set about trying to fix my laptop.

When the police in Brazzaville had decided that I was a spy, they thought they'd do the honourable thing and rifle through my laptop files. In doing so they had somehow dumped a ruddy great big virus onto my hard drive. My only hope to get rid of it was to re-format the drive, wipe all the data and for Windows to be re-installed.

Lucky I backed up all my files onto a separate hard-drive the night before I left for Brazzaville, eh?

After a few hours, thanks to Alex, my little lappy was almost back in business. I just needed a few more drivers and a copy of Office that wasn't in French.

Alex and Laure were going out for dinner with friends so that night I stayed at Michael's place and watched a bunch of movies. The next day I returned to the Angolan embassy, fingers and toes crossed. I hung about for an hour or so before somebody came to help me. I was taken into that back room again and — *miracle of miracles* — was given my passport back with a shiny new Angolan visa in it.

It was only a transit visa, and it only gave me five days, but my word! Everybody I had spoken to said it couldn't be done. I headed over to MSF HQ waving my passport around like I had won a golden ticket for *Willy Wonka's Chocolate Factory*.

The bus to the Angolan border leaves very early, so I had missed the one for that day. That night, Alex, Michael and I headed out for a Chinese meal and a few drinks.

Alex picked up the tab for all of us, which after taking me out drinking, fixing my laptop and putting me up for the night was way above and beyond the call of duty. I couldn't thank him enough.

Not for the first time I took a moment to consider that the good things that had happened thus far on my adventure massively outweighed the bad.

I said my goodbyes to Michael and headed back to Alex and Laure's for some shut-eye. Alex even arranged for an MSF 4×4 to pick me up in the morning — I'd be taking the first bus to the Angolan border at 5am, which (of course) didn't leave until 9am.

It wasn't all bad though. I got a seat all to myself and wasn't squished like a sardine. Even better, the driver's mate distributed sandwiches and Cokes to everyone on board.

It's the little things...

At the border I didn't run into any of the hassles alluded to in the Lonely Planet. It did take me an hour to get stamped out, but only because the guy with the stamp was having his lunch. Apart from that, I got over the border without any problems or bribes. DR Congo, you may have a lousy reputation, but I think you're great. I'll be back. Other Congo, not so much.

I crossed into **Angola** and found myself in the village of Noqui, which I would come to assume was how you said "Nowhere" in the local language.

With no typical public transport options to take me the 400km to the capital Luanda, I had to take a truck-taxi, like in Congo, laden with people in the back. It took the truck about five hours to clear the border, and by the time it arrived in the middle of Nowhere, it was already 9pm.

'How much to ride in the cab?' I asked.

'One hundred.'

'Kwanza?'

'No, dollars. US.'

ANGOLA 111/200

LUANDA

18.93m

Portuguese

Angolan Kwanza

$3,988.68

From fighting the Portuguese to fighting each other, Angola was at war for over 40 years from 1961 to 2002.

Forget Norway or Japan. Angola is, hands-down *the* most expensive country in the world. A can of coke is $4, the cheapest, grottiest hotel is at least $80 a night and a single piece of chicken from the side of the road will set you back $6.

I haggled him down to a (still a rip-off) $70, and I thought we were on our way. *Thought.*

We parked up and went nowhere. I fell asleep in the cab, the thirty-odd people in the back of the truck had to sleep under the stars.

I was roused at 6am. We started moving! We got as far as the edge of Nowhere before we were all told to get out.

Apparently, they were going to pick up some sand. The truck drove off, back towards the border with the DRC. An hour or so later they returned, the truck now filled with sandbags. 'Where's everyone going to sit?', I asked.

'Don't worry, we're taking it off', came the reply.

I helped offload the sand onto the side of the road, and then when we were done I grabbed my bag, ready to get going — only to watch the truck drive off again in the direction of the border to pick up some more bloody sand. When they eventually returned, it was midday. Again, I helped them unload the sand.

'Can we go now?', I asked, acutely aware of my rather tight time limit in this country of just five days, one of which I had already squandered waiting for this truck to leave.

'Yes,' came the reply.

'Right now?'

'Right now.'

We didn't set off for another hour.

The truck was something from the 1950s, probably built in Stalin's Russia. I was squished in, three people on two seats, *well worth $70*. We drove for a few miles. Then we stopped, did a U-turn and made our way back to the middle of Nowhere.

We hung about for another hour while they did something or other. Then finally, almost 24 hours after I first crossed the border into Angola, we started moving.

Well, I say moving. Don't let that fool you into thinking that we were going anywhere fast. We weren't. The road, such as it was, bore more resemblance to a dried-up riverbed. Our average speed was a steady 15 miles an hour. Plus, we stopped every five minutes for little or no reason and broke down several times.

As the day wore on it became obvious that I wouldn't be getting to Luanda that night. I was beginning to panic.

What if I didn't get to the border with Namibia before my visa ran out? I had been thrown in jail twice without even committing a crime. I shuddered to think what would happen to me in Africa if I actually, you know, *broke the law*.

Night fell, we parked up and I slept a second night in the truck cab. Again, I was awoken at 6am; why, I have no clue. We didn't set off until after nine.

Apart from the magnificent silver-bark trees, the landscape was remarkably unappealing. Charred by war and slash-and-burn farming, much of the countryside was blackened and barren. Angola has a lot of flat, fertile lands, but because its government is wearing oil goggles (a whopping 1.4 billion barrels exported every day), they're not particularly interested in farming. Which is a shame, as otherwise Angola could easily feed itself and those around it; but as in many resource-rich, cash-poor countries, a mixed economy is not a priority.

We reached the Mbenzi-Congo junction around lunchtime and the road improved immeasurably, but before we could really get anywhere we were pulled over by the police.

Some of the people in the truck were from Congo and didn't have the necessary paperwork to be in Angola, so there was a bit of a kerfuffle going on. I hid in the cab, sinking into my seat, but eventually, one of the policemen saw me and ordered me out.

I handed over my passport — 'look, I've got a visa'. One of the policemen told me to come with him and motioned to his motorbike. He muttered something in Portuguese and then said a word that made my blood run cold.

'Chief.'

No. Not more chiefs. Not again.

I walked slowly back to the cab to get my bags, my legs shaking.

It couldn't happen again. It couldn't.

I took a deep breath — if they arrested me, I was truly stuffed. My phone hadn't been picking up a signal since I crossed the border and the Congolese police had kept my spare Nokia. On top of that, nobody knew where the hell I was. I should have been in Luanda yesterday.

It crossed my mind to just leg it, but given the horrific number of landmines still dotted around the countryside in Angola since the end of the civil war in 2002, I thought better of it. I picked up my bags.

The policeman wanted some money for petrol for his bike, so I gave him a couple of dollars. One of the truck passengers spoke a little bit of English so I appealed to him. 'Help me.'

He spoke to the policeman in a local language. After a bit of an animated discussion, the cop gave me the two dollars back. 'You can go.'

That passenger may well have saved my life. But at that moment he was taken away to be deported with some of the other men, women and children from our truck. I never even caught his name.

'What now?', I asked the driver. He merely shrugged and walked off down the road with his mate, leaving me, the truck and the few remain passengers (mostly breast-feeding Angolan mothers) behind. After about 20 minutes a pick-up truck rumbled past. I ran into the road waving like a loon. 'Can you take me to the next town?'

'Sure — get in', said the driver.

Damn that $70, I just had to let it go.

The town was just a mile or so down the road, and — even better — the actual coach to Luanda was due in half an hour.

The guys in the pick-up sorted me out with something to eat and drink. I was given some barbecued bush meat cooked at the side of the road. It tasted like a cross between pork and chicken. I hope to hell it wasn't monkey.

The bus arrived bang on schedule. I paid the fare and took my place sitting next to the driver on the metal hood that covered the engine. You'd think for the $50 it cost me I'd get a seat. Peter, the driver, spoke good English and was a big jolly man who took the terrible road in his stride. He did the trip down to Luanda four times a week.

In contrast to Captain Slow in the truck, Peter thundered along as if potholes, adverse cambers and the dense clouds of dust were mere glitches in the computer game he was playing. By dinnertime, I was confident that we would reach Luanda before midnight. Peter let me use his phone to call Emilio, my CouchSurf contact, and I asked him to e-mail Mandy to let her know that I was still alive.

Peter treated me to a dinner of fish, rice and beer at the side of the road and we were about to head off again when there was a problem with the engine. The driver's mate spent an hour or so fixing a hose that had split. He used cigarette filters, superglue and rubber strapping. I'm not even joking.

Soon enough, we were back on the trail, but Africa was to have the last laugh. After being stopped at the checkpoint for over an hour (everyone had to get off the bus and have their details taken down), when we got back on board Peter and his mate couldn't get the damn bus started again.

After yet another quick fix-it job, we trundled on for another hour until something else broke and we pulled over on the side of the road. I curled up on the engine block and fell asleep.

I awoke resoundingly not in Luanda. We hadn't moved all night. Peter was nowhere to be seen. I got off the bus and flagged down a passing 4×4. I asked the driver if he could give me a lift. 'Get in mate, no problem.'

The 4×4 took me all the way to the minibus park outside Luanda where I said my thank yous and jumped a minibus the rest of the way. That'll be $20 please! I arrived in Luanda at 11am. I had travelled just 275 miles in three days and I had over 750 miles left to go before I hit the border with Namibia.

I contacted Emilio, my CouchSurf host. Heroically he came to pick me up through Luanda's perennially grid-locked traffic.

Emilio was a French guy who had been living in Africa all his life. He grew up in Brazzaville, Congo, lived in Conakry, Guinea and even stayed in Cape Verde for a bit — all my favourite places! His knowledge of Africa was second to none.

He worked in logistics, like Alex and Michael in Kinshasa. Running logistics in Africa? These people are madder than me.

I grabbed a sandwich ($15) and we headed over to Emilio's flat. After sleeping on buses and trucks for three nights, a shower was more than welcome. All things being equal, I would have pressed on south, but the buses only left in the early morning and Emilio was hosting a house party that night, so I elected to stay in Luanda. It wasn't a difficult decision. I love house parties.

I met a stack of cool people and drank more than I possibly should have. I was a little giddy at the prospect that in just a couple of days, I would be out of West and Central Africa. As the Scissor Sisters once sang, *it can't come quickly enough.*

With just 37 hours left to get out of the country, Emilio's driver, Yuri, picked me up at 5am to drop me off at the bus to Benguela, a town halfway to the Namibian border.

Once again, the bus didn't leave until 9am, so I was once again duped out of a decent night's sleep. My ticket cost a whopping $60, but at least this time the road was decent and I had a proper seat all to myself. I arrived in Benguela in good time, it only taking a few hours to cover the same distance that had just taken me three days.

In Benguela, I hopped on another coach only to discover that I would have to wait until the coach was full before it left. With shared taxis you can be waiting several hours for the seven or eight passengers needed to set off.

This coach needed another *FORTY* passengers.

I waited a few hours, but with only a trickle of passengers turning up, I demanded my money back and found myself a small taxi-van that was heading south. A taxi-van which shoehorned twelve people (and their luggage) into a space designed for eight. I had pins and needles all the way to Lubango, the next big town, 250 miles from the border. We arrived just before midnight.

Thankfully, the driver of the van said he'd help me find somewhere to stay for the night, which turned into a bit of a mission and we drove to four different hotels before I found a room.

Well, I say "room", but it was little more than a broom closet. The door hit the bed as I went in. It was filthy, no windows, no toilet, no shower, no television, no AC and I had to be out by 6am. It was half-past midnight when I arrived. If it was a room in any other country, I would be loath to hand over a fiver.

It cost $50.

The next morning I was on the 6.30am bus to the border with Namibia. It didn't leave until 9am. If you're seeing a (rather frustrating) pattern here, you're not the only one.

The journey was tinged with tension — my visa expired *that day*. According to my Lonely Planet, the border closed at 6pm. The bus was scheduled to get in at 5pm. And, so far, Angola and "being on time" had been queer bedfellows indeed.

Every time we stopped, I found myself jiggling my legs, chewing the inside of my mouth and repeatedly looking at my watch.

I couldn't hack being detained again. Not after Congo. Unhelpfully, the road from Lubango to the border was only decent for the first few miles. After that, it was (yet another) dirt track. Although on a positive note, they were building a new road, so these days you can no doubt do the taxi run from Luanda to Windhoek in less than 24 hours.

After a few hours, I had a horrible thought. What if the border closes 6pm *Namibian* Time? Namibia is an hour ahead of Angola. That would mean that the border would close at 5pm my time. I dismissed the thought as silly. Why would a bus running to a border town be scheduled to arrive just as the border closed?

We arrived at the border town of Santa Clara that afternoon. I sauntered off the bus and I asked the first person I saw which way it was to the border. The guy pointed down the road, but said 'I think it's closed'.

'What?'

'It closes at 5.'

I looked at my watch. It was 5.10.

Oh for the love of God...

I ran the 500 metres to the border. Backpack, laptop bag, camera bag, baking heat, dry mouth, kicking up dust. As I approached the checkpoint I could see a man shutting a big metal gate, closing off the road for the night.

Arms outstretched, sweat pouring down my face, I screamed out to the guy '*WAAAAAIT!!!*'

He saw me and held the gate open a crack. When I reached him I gesticulated wildly and spouted something it being an emergency. Miraculously, he let me through.

I ran to the emigration window as fast as I could and slapped my well-worn passport against the glass.

'Please, my visa expires tonight.'

The woman wordlessly took my passport, sighed and turned her computer back on.

I may have danced a jig.

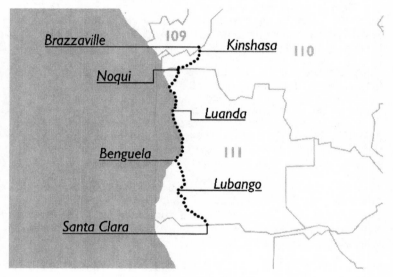

Chapter 25
The Nuns Of Gaborone

Stepping into **Namibia**, I was overcome with a feeling of exhilaration. I had done it. I had taken on every country in West and Central Africa and won. A 10,000 mile obstacle course over hell and high water; a game of cunning, endurance and a great deal of luck.

For the next few weeks I'd be back on the beaten path, on the well-worn tourist trail through Southern Africa. Good roads, frequent and scheduled buses, no squishing into bush taxis, maybe even some air-conditioning.

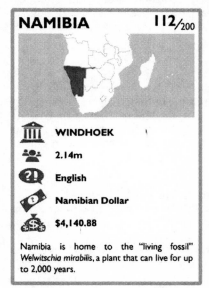

NAMIBIA 112/200

🏛 **WINDHOEK**

👥 **2.14m**

💬 **English**

💵 **Namibian Dollar**

💰 **$4,140.88**

Namibia is home to the "living fossil" *Welwitschia mirabilis*, a plant that can live for up to 2,000 years.

It was the end of September 2009. Thanks to that little spell in jail, I had been to just four new countries in the last month. Now I was in Southern Africa I was hoping to tick another *ten* nations off the list before the end of October.

Namibia was once a German colony, but after losing The First World War, Germany also lost its African "possessions".

South West Africa, as it was then known, fell under the rule of South Africa. South Africa clung on to the place until March 1990, making Namibia one of the youngest nation states in Africa, after Djibouti (and subsequently South Sudan).

Even though it had been 90 years since the end of rule from Berlin, I found that many Namibians still spoke German, and it wasn't unusual to hear local people speaking English in remarkably thick German accents.

Namibia has the highest gem quality of diamonds anywhere in the world and enjoys a stable government, a mixed economy and a free press — things that are sadly in short supply in West and Central Africa.

As I entered the border town of Oshikango, I met up with Cliff, a Namibian guy who had been on the bus with me from Lubango. He had taken a "less official" route into Namibia.

As the bus to the capital, Windhoek, would not be leaving until the next morning, we went for a beer. Less than a dollar for a 750ml bottle of Carling.

That's more like it.

Cheers!

On the way to the capital I saw warthogs, antelopes and water buffalo. We stopped at service stations fully stocked with everything a growing boy needs. As night fell, an electrical storm reared up ahead. The landscape was vast, forbidding and beautiful. This is the country where, years later, they would film *Mad Max: Fury Road.*

The bus pulled into Windhoek terminal around 9pm. I made contact with Tashia, on whose couch I would be surfing for the night. Namibian born and bred, she worked in real estate since the diamond industry (her former employer) took a nosedive after the financial crisis of 2008.

She also presented the sports bulletins on Namibian television, which is pretty damn cool.

It was a comfortable night on Tashia's couch, interrupted only by the once-an-hour shrill of my mobile phone alarm waking me to change the video tapes that I was uploading onto my laptop. I would be going to DHL later to send the tapes to Lonely Planet in Australia and I didn't want to let them go (especially after what happened to me in Congo) without making sure I had them all backed up.

In the morning, Tashia left me to my own devices. Soon I had all of my tapes uploaded and I was ready to go. The bus for South Africa left in the evening, so there was no rush. Tashia came back around lunchtime — her kid had fallen ill and had been admitted to hospital. Nothing too serious, but the doctors wanted to keep him in for observation. Tashia's dad (a huge Liverpool FC fan) dropped me off at the coach offices on the way to the hospital.

I tried to buy a ticket for the Intercape Mainliner bus to Johannesburg/Pretoria, but they were sold out. The lady who was serving me suggested that I get the first bus as far as Uppington (the first major town over the South African border) and then chance my luck that there'd be a spare seat on the connecting bus.

I then asked where DHL was. The lady said it wasn't far and then offered to drive me over there.

I nearly fell over.

This level of customer service was not something that I was expecting. It doesn't exist in America; it certainly doesn't exist in the UK. Intercape Namibia you get a gold star *and* a jelly baby. You hear that, Greyhound?

SOUTH AFRICA 113/200

🏛 **PRETORIA, CAPE TOWN, BLOEMFONTEIN**

👥 **50.22m**

❓ **Zulu, Xhosa, Afrikaans, English, Northern Sotho, Tswana, Swazi, Sesotho, Tsonga, Venda, Ndebele**

💵 **South African Rand**

💰 **$5,658.43**

In South Africa it is illegal to sit less than two metres from a person of the opposite sex if they're wearing nothing but a swimming costume.

So the tapes were mailed off to Lonely Planet in Australia (I didn't get much change from my $100) and soon I was on my merry way to Uppington, South Africa.

My main task in **South Africa** was to get a new passport. Africa has conspired to fill my little burgundy booklet with as much ink as possible. I had *eight* different stamps for Gabon alone. Considering I only (officially) entered that country once, that's some feat. When I entered Togo for just three hours I lost three good pages of my passport in the process.

I have a strong suspicion that the wives of African border officials have to make do with the couch while their husbands spend the night in bed cuddling up to their little stamps.

I crossed the border around 4am, reaching the pleasant town of Uppington later that morning. Luckily, somebody didn't turn up for the connecting bus, so I managed to snag the last seat all the way to Pretoria. One of the many advantages of travelling alone.

I got chatting to a couple of South African guys on the bus, Jared and his mate. Apparently, Pretoria is the capital of the 'Boerewors Eaters'[35], Johannesburg is just as dangerous as everyone thinks it is, and Cape Town is the best bit. Sadly, I wouldn't be seeing Cape Town on this trip — but I'd be seeing a lot of the other two.

By the time we got to Joburg, it was dark. The first thing that greeted us in the murder capital of the world was, yes, a murder. A body bag at the side of the road, police cordon and two police cars, their lights flashing.

---

[35] Editor's Note: Boerewors is a type of South African sausage. The name is derived from the Afrikaans words boer ("farmer") and wors ("sausage"). Boerewors must contain at least 90 percent meat and no more than 30% fat, and always contain beef, as well as lamb, pork, or a mixture of lamb and pork. The other 10% is made up of spices and other ingredients.

I'll be pressing on to Pretoria now, thanks.

Arriving at around 9pm, I checked into the backpackers on Glyn Street, nice and close to the British High Commission.

A little tired after my marathon coach journey from Windhoek, I was planning on an early night — but first I wanted something. Something dirty. Something wrong.

I wanted KFC.

You don't miss something until it's gone. Until I hit Southern Africa, I hadn't passed a single outlet of the Colonel Sanders' greasy deep-fried 11-herbs-and-spices chicken for my whole 10,000 mile journey down from Morocco. And as much as I like to bemoan American fast food culture, there are times when only a KFC will do.

After completely devouring a few pieces, I was walking back to the hostel when I realised I could do with a drink to wash all that chickeny goodness down. I dropped in to a bar called Cool Runnings, a log-cabin style affair with good music playing.

Now, drinking on your own is sad. Even when I'm travelling on my own, it's a rare occasion that I'll go into a bar without company. If I do, I'll always be armed with my trusty laptop or a book to read. The same rule applies to restaurants and cinemas. Although in a cinema, having a book doesn't really help.

That being the case, I merely intended to swig down a bottle of the local grog and then return to the backpackers and go to bed. But I got chatting with the staff and the regulars, and got invited on a night out in Pretoria followed by a house party. Pretoria is known for being a heavily Afrikaans city, yet I found myself partying with people from all different backgrounds and ethnicities. It gave me a lot of hope for the future of South Africa.

After 40 minutes of sleep (it was a good night) I was up and searching for the British High Commission. I walked around in circles for half an hour in the bright, crisp Friday morning air before I found the place. The was no sign and no flag – I guess that would have made it too easy.

I was served by a Scottish lady, who informed me that my new passport would take ten days to come through. I explained what I was doing and asked (nicely) if they could do me a rush job. 'Okay then, Monday.'

I even got to keep hold of my old passport for the weekend, so I could hop over the border with Botswana while I was waiting.

These "embassy" things are great! Every country should have one.

I then set out to find bus times to Gabarone, the capital of Botswana. Nearly all of the buses were full, unless I headed over to Joburg, which I didn't fancy — Pretoria is a nice place and I felt safe there, so I decided to take a bus the following morning, a Saturday.

The folks at Lonely Planet had set me up with an interview on South African Breakfast TV on the Monday, so I had to be back Sunday night at the latest.

That evening, I went to watch *District 9* with Andy, a British guy who was also staying at the backpackers. It was pretty cool watching a sci-fi movie that was set a few miles down the road, doubly so that it was one of the best films of that year.

Later, we headed over to Cool Runnings for another big night out with my new Pretorian friends. I woke up the next morning in my dorm bed clutching my camera and laptop, with no idea how I had managed to get back to the hostel in one piece.

I threw my clothes into the laundry to pick up on Monday (along with my new passport) and headed to the bus station.

The bus would be getting in to Gabarone really late, and Botswana is terribly expensive, so I opted to get off at the little town of Zeerust, the last South African town before the border, and spent the night there.

I stepped off the bus into the dark (in more ways than one) and asked the first person I met if there was a guesthouse in town.

Luckily, there was, but unluckily I had to walk a kilometre down darkened side streets to get there. As I've already stated, South Africa has a bit of a reputation when it comes to crime, and here I was walking down a deserted side street in a town I had never heard of looking for a guesthouse I don't know the location of, weighed down with a camcorder, a laptop and all and sundry. It was a tense few minutes, but soon I was breathing a sigh of relief in the Good Hope Guesthouse.

My hosts were a wonderful Afrikaan girl called Nenien and her boyfriend. Nenien's parents ran the guesthouse, but were away attending a music festival. We whiled away the evening sitting in the communal room chatting, drinking and watching telly. They let me stay for free and made me a steak dinner. The steak was the biggest I've ever seen.

Oh South Africa, you little charmer you.

Up at 6am and down to the nearby service station where one goes to cadge a lift to the border. I found myself waiting until 9am before (finally) a minibus came and picked me up.

Botswana is arguably Africa's biggest success story. It has had both free and fair elections and a stable economy since independence. While pretty much every other country on the continent has had to endure dictators, war, famine, apartheid, genocide and/or dizzying levels of corruption, Botswana has generally kept its head down and got on with things.

That might seem a little counter-intuitive after all that I've said about it being difficult for landlocked nations to avoid falling into the poverty trap, but Botswana has an ace up its sleeve. An ace of diamonds.

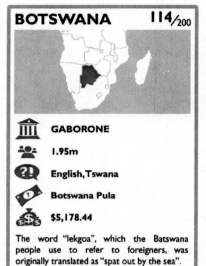

BOTSWANA 114/200

GABORONE

1.95m

English, Tswana

Botswana Pula

$5,178.44

The word "lekgoa", which the Batswana people use to refer to foreigners, was originally translated as "spat out by the sea".

A handful of diamonds will net more profit than a ton of copper, and you don't need to rely on somebody else's seaport to get them wherever they need to go — you can simply fly them out. Consequently, Botswana is doing all right.

My original plan had been to take the bus from Windhoek to Gaborone and then Pretoria, crossing the Kalahari in the process, but the bus schedules had not tallied with my hopes and dreams. And so unfortunately my trip to Botswana became nothing more than a border hop. As I needed to hurry back to Joburg for this TV interview at 6am, I didn't have time to check out the capital, so I clocked my GPS and headed back from whence I came.

On the way back to Zeerust I found myself chatting with a couple of nuns. Carmel, the older nun, was originally from Ireland and still hadn't given up her Irish lilt, even after nearly forty years of living in the capital of Botswana. I was just overjoyed at meeting real-life Nuns of Gaborone. I love that movie!

Back in Zeerust, I picked up my bag from the Good Hope Guest House, said my fond farewells and then worried about how the hell I was going to get back to Joburg. After enquiring at the local Shoprite Supermarket, I found out that there were no coaches until the following morning. Bugger.

I headed to the nearest petrol station. There was a minibus there and I asked if they were going to Johannesburg. Yep, they were, but they were full. 'Hey — I'm a little desperate,' I said, looking all needy.

'No worries bro, just walk up the road and there's a bunch of minibuses, just take the next one that fills up. They all go to Joburg.'

Why did nobody tell me about these things?

Later, I found out why. The minibuses that buzz around South Africa are not recommended for tourists. Too dangerous, they say! Too dangerous? Bah! I've done the *Lagos to Calabar Mad Max Fury Road Minibus Rally* without a functioning safety belt, travelled down the *Camino de la Muerte* in a bus held together with sticky tape, and crossed 300 miles of open ocean in a goddamn wooden fishing boat!

I spit in the face of danger and eat impossible for breakfast! I say good day to you sir! Good day!

I flung myself onto the next minibus with gay abandon. I feel it's my duty to inform you that they're *bloody fantastic.* Not only do they cost a fraction of the price of the big coaches, they're twice as fast and you don't have to put up with bizarre evangelical programming or bloody Tyler Perry films on the telly, because there are no tellys! Huzzah!

We got to Joburg so fast it made my head spin. My driver was Zulu and wearing a full headdress, massive earrings, the lot. He tried to teach me how to say words with the Zulu click, represented in Roman letters by a "!". It's trickier than it sounds.

When we hit central Johannesburg everyone but the driver and I got out. I found myself in a minibus in a traffic jam in the middle of murder central with my bags on my lap and a door that wouldn't lock.

I should mention it was also getting dark.

I'm not usually this paranoid, it's just that the entire time I was in South Africa everybody was always going on about how dangerous it is. People talk about not stopping at traffic lights in case you get "jacked" and your side-mounted flame throwers are out of propane.

The driver and I were stuck in traffic for 40 minutes. It felt like the longest 40 minutes of my life. When I finally got off the bus I ran straight towards a taxi, jumped inside, *go go go!*

I had arranged to meet my friend David at the old Sundeck Bar in the Norwood area of town. David was a mate of mine from Liverpool who had been living in Joburg for the past three years.

While I waited for David to arrive, I got chatting with a guy called Matthew from Zimbabwe who, like thousands of his fellow countrymen, can only return home when Robert Mugabe is no longer president.

Imagine being exiled from your home and having to wait for a man — one man — to die or be killed or even *just damn well retire* before so you can return to your life, your family, your friends and everything you know.

But the thing is, if dictators like Mugabe retire then they lose their diplomatic immunity. That's one of the main reasons these dinosaurs refuse to be shunted off to a nursing home.

When David arrived we caught up over a pint before heading over to his house. I instantly saw the appeal of living down here. To rent a place like this in London, you'd have to be earning Brewster's.

One of David's mates was celebrating his birthday that night, so we picked up David's girlfriend Jenna-Lee and headed to the bar on the top floor of the swankiest hotel in town. After five months of slumming it, I felt somewhat out of place with my dirty t-shirt and ripped jeans (not a fashion statement, believe me!) but the beer and pizza went down a treat.

David's mates were cool, although the stress of living in a city with such a bad reputation for crime had obviously taken a toll. Their main concern was that the biggest political party, the ANC, regularly got over 75% of the vote. 'What's to stop them pulling a Zimbabwe?' they asked.

The brutal seizure of white-owned farms by Mugabe's thugs was still fresh in everybody's mind.

I was told it was like living at the foot of the volcano. The soil may be rich and fertile, but you never stop thinking about the volcano.

In the morning David graciously hauled his ass out of bed at the crack of dawn to take me to the *Sunrise* studios.

Soon enough I was on the couch in front of the cameras nattering about my adventures thus far with the presenter, whose name was also Graham (I think he spelt it "Graeme", but you can't have everything).

It was one of those days when I thought, 'I love my job!' Who else gets to bum around the world for a living? All the crap that I crawled through to get to South Africa seemed worth it, and it put a spring in my step for the task ahead: the next 86 countries on the list.

David dropped me in the middle of Joburg and, after a fond farewell, I headed to the massive central bus station. I mooched about for half an hour and was recognised by a couple of people— 'Were you the guy on *Sunrise* this morning?'

Ah, my first brush with infamy.

Soon I had boarded a bus for Pretoria. Brilliantly enough, nobody asked me for a ticket or anything, so I managed to bag myself a free ride. Christ knows, I needed a free ride. I had been too scared to look at my bank account since Cape Verde.

Pretoria. Ticket for that night's bus to Durban. New passport. Backpackers. Breakfast. Laundry. Pub.

When I got to Cool Runnings, it seemed that everyone had seen me on the telly that morning, and everyone wanted to buy me a drink. It's my solemn duty to inform you that I didn't put up too much of a fight.

One minute it was 3pm, the next it was 7:45pm.

'Shit and giggles!', I exclaimed, 'my bus leaves in 15 minutes!'

One of the guys offered to drive me to coach station. We made it in double-quick time, tyres screeching around corners. I was the last to board. The lady taking my ticket accused me of being drunk. I muttered an apology, got on board, sat down, opened my laptop and fell asleep.

I actually didn't want to go all the way to Durban — I wanted to get off at a place called Pietermaritzburg; not too far from the Sani Pass — the border with little landlocked Lesotho, the next country on my list.

By some weird voodoo, I just so happened to wake up at 4:19am as we were approaching Pietermaritzburg.

From there I took a minibus to the border town of Underberg and booked myself to go up the mountain in a shared 4x4. The deal is you go up in the morning, check out a typical Basotho village, grab a bite to eat at the highest pub in Africa and get back to Underberg for about 4pm. I was joined on the adventure by Dr Daniel and his girlfriend, a trauma surgeon and nurse combo from Germany.

Lesotho is completely surrounded by South Africa, which doesn't make much sense when you see it on a map, but when you see it in real life you go, 'ahh!' This is because it's a country way up in the mountains, like Andorra.

The track up the mountain was as beautiful as it was perilous. I was glad we were in a 4×4 and our driver (an ex-copper, no less) seemed to know what he was doing.

As I drew the sweet mountain air into my lungs, I felt like a smoker who had finally kicked the habit — fresh, clean, renewed and ready to take on the world. Around us were towering giants of stone, peppered with crystal-clear waterfalls trickling down to the rocks below. Out of the 4×4; no motors, no engines, no constant vibration. Just me and my mountain fortress in the sky.

The Sani Pass is only a few kilometres, but it's uphill all the way. The road isn't sealed and there are no crash barriers. After a couple hours of switchbacks and inclines that would make your head spin, we reached the border, a mere formality, as my crisp new virgin passport enjoyed its first glob of ink — an exit stamp for South Africa.

Once in **Lesotho** we went to check out the mountain lifestyle of the Basotho people. The village we saw was quite charming — thick mud-brick walls and thatched roofs. Before they start to build a home they cunningly place a huge flattened stone under the dwelling, so the fire in the middle of the hut radiates its heat along the floor.

As much as I loved the organic architecture, the poverty in Lesotho was not a joy to behold. With 45% unemployment, many of the men end up working in mines in South Africa and are away from their families for up to six months at a time. Many of them return HIV positive. With limited resources, getting to grips with the scale of the HIV epidemic in Lesotho is a monumental task — 30% of *all adults* are infected.

LESOTHO 115/200

🏛️ **MASERU**

👥 **1.99m**

💬 **English, Sesotho**

💵 **Lesotho Loti**

💰 **$858.73**

Lesotho is pronounced *Lee-Soo-Too*, the people are called Basotho *(Baa-Soo-Too)* and their language is called Sesotho *(See-Soo-Too)*.

After our trip to the village we all fancied a drink. Luckily for us, a mad scouser (yes, we get everywhere) had set up a pub at the top of the pass — not just any pub, but the "highest pub in Africa", no less.

There I met another intrepid English overlander who had left his home the previous February in order to cycle from London to Cape Town. That ascent was tough enough in a 4x4. I couldn't imagine doing it on a push-bike. What can I say? Brits be *cray-cray*.

After lunch, we began our descent (which was even hairier than the climb) but soon enough, we were back in merry old Underberg just in time for me to catch the 4pm(ish) minibus to Durban.

I checked into the Durban Backpackers just after dark.

The next morning I set off to do some chores that I had been putting off for far too long. The first of which was to get my tooth sorted. You recall that I had lost a chunk of one of my teeth just before the start of the journey? I paid for it to be fixed in Barcelona, only for the filling to fall out a few days later in Western Sahara.

So I plodded to the nearest dentist, getting an appointment for 11am.

I then headed on foot towards the city centre, with an eye on getting a taxi along the way. Did I mention how difficult I found it to hail a cab in South Africa? Like God and Santa Claus, South African cabs just don't seem to exist. In Pretoria, for example, there are three (and there are only ever three) waiting at the bus station, but should you stand outside one of the biggest shopping malls in the city, you'd be lucky to catch a cab before Halley's Comet makes its return in 2061.

In hindsight (which is always 20-20), I should have gone back to the backpackers and got them to ring a private-hire, but that would have meant walking back uphill; sod that.

So I ended up walking all the way from Durban's leafy suburbs down towards the city centre. I was crossing a busy intersection when I noticed I was being followed. I hitched my little canvas bag (containing, amongst other things, my camcorder and passport) up on my shoulder and walked a bit faster.

So did my shadow.

All I could think is that if stayed close to the road, I'd be all right. But the guy was gaining on me and after all I had been told about South Africa's crime epidemic, daylight robbery seemed like it would be a common occurrence.

I was walking as fast as I could without fully running. I could hear my heartbeat thumping in my ears. Suddenly, a vehicle screeched to a halt just in front of me. It was an ambulance.

The back doors flew open.

'Get in.'

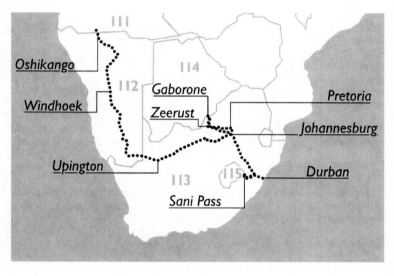

Chapter 26
Zim Zam Thank You Mam

I leapt on board the ambulance and we sped off, leaving my shadow in the dust.

'Have you any idea how close you were to being mugged just then?', asked the uniformed medic.

Apparently, I was being followed by a chap who was rather notorious for that kind of thing. The driver — a female paramedic — and the guy who opened the back doors (a medical student) may well have just saved my life.

I thanked them profusely. They dropped me in the city centre. I bought myself a new pair of jeans and headed back to the dentist's.

This time, I took a taxi.

The dentist had a look at the gaping hole in my lower right first molar and put it bluntly. 'I could fill it, but it would just fall out again — we'd be best making you a crown.'

'How long will that take?'

'About 15 minutes. We have a 3D printer.'[36]

Be still my beating heart.

And so, in the back room of the dentists, I watched it happen before my very eyes! The 3D scan of my broken tooth was converted to 1s and 0s and was piped (presumably by magic) into a machine the size of an office printer *that totally made it real*. A new tooth was forged, buzz-cut from a porcelain cube by two diamond-tipped drills and plenty of water.

Once the crown was glued in place, my tongue glided over my swanky

---

[36] Editor's Note: Technically it's a CNC milling machine and not a 3D printer and I thought you should know that I know that.

new bit of dental wizardry with unrestrained glee.

I returned to the backpackers, mouth still numb and weird.

I needed a bunny.

Not a hopping floppy-eared bunny, but a Durban bunny, chicken tikka masala served in a hollowed out half-loaf. It may sound a bit mad, but that's only because all works of genius sound mad at first. It works, by God it works.

I got to the minibus "depot" at 2pm only to discover that the last bus for Swaziland left at 1:30pm. If it wasn't for that damn bunny! Gutted, I returned to the backpackers for another night.

So, up early and off to Swaziland. No not Switzerland, but **Swaziland**.

As countries go, Swaziland is pretty tiny. In fact, I was planning to pass straight through on the way to Mozambique. However, I had heard a rumour that Mozambique was no longer giving out visas at the border.

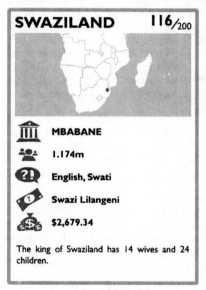

SWAZILAND 116/200

🏛 **MBABANE**

👥 **1.174m**

💬 **English, Swati**

💵 **Swazi Lilangeni**

💰 **$2,679.34**

The king of Swaziland has 14 wives and 24 children.

Thinking "better safe than sorry", I hung a left at Manzini and headed to the capital Mbabane.

There I met Lilianna, originally from Portugal, my CouchSurf host for the evening. It was early afternoon and I figured that I had loads of time to sweet-talk the embassy into giving me a visa asap.

Only the rumours were false! Balderdash and twaddle! I *could* get a visa on the border.

Had I played my cards right, I could have been in Maputo, the capital of Mozambique, by now. But I had blown it all on a bunny!

'Well,' I thought, 'I'm here now so I might as well make the most of it.' Lilianna took me to see Sibebe Rock, Swaziland's equivalent of Uluru, the second largest freestanding rock in the world (after Uluru).

That evening, we headed into town for a bit of live music. A guy singing with an acoustic guitar with his mate on bass. Great vibes, cool blues, swinging rhythm and kick ass rock n' roll.

Lilianna then took me to a quiet little restaurant that rustled up some good, old-fashioned Swazi scran. My eyes nearly popped out of their sockets, there was so much food. And by Christ, it tasted good.

Great geology, great music, great food? Swaziland, you may be one of only six absolutist monarchies left in the world, but you certainly know how to put a smile on this ginger travelling monkey's face.

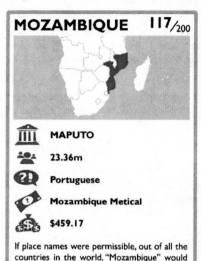

MOZAMBIQUE   117/200

🏛 **MAPUTO**

👥 **23.36m**

❓ **Portuguese**

💵 **Mozambique Metical**

💰 **$459.17**

If place names were permissible, out of all the countries in the world, "Mozambique" would give you the highest score in Scrabble.

I arrived in the capital of **Mozambique** the following afternoon and bought a ticket for the 4:30am coach up north. At the time buses in Mozambique were not allowed to travel overnight, so I checked into the Base Backpackers and got my head down for the night.

I wanted to get to the city of Tete in northwest Mozambique that day, but with the roads being what they were, there was no chance of making it before midnight. I chose instead to stay in the city of Beira on the coast. It may have been 100 miles out of my way, but Mandy had found me a CouchSurf host there and I had been doing this long enough to know it would beat the alternative.

Responsibility for building roads in Mozambique lies in the hands of regional governors. Which means you'll be hurtling along a lovely smooth strip of asphalt at 100 miles an hour when WHAM you cross a state boundary and suddenly you're up to your ears in dust and cattle. That was the road from Inchope to Beira.

I ended up seeing very little of Beira, it was already dark I when I arrived and I was beyond tired. I felt dreadful as we ate dinner, barely keeping my eyes open, but my host Flore was terrific company — a wonderful French hippy who had been living in Mozambique for many years. At 11:30pm I retired to the couch. One minute later I was fast asleep.

Up again at 5am and on the bus to Tete. All I wanted to do was sleep, but the driver's terrible music was set to "eardrum shattering". Earplugs made no difference. The babies on the bus were just as unhappy as I was about the situation — screaming and bawling like their lives depended on not having to listen to shit music cranked up to 11 at the crack of goddamn dawn.

The bus arrived in Tete that afternoon and not a minute too soon. I was met at the station by my CouchSurf contact, Guilherme. Gui was originally from Brazil and worked at Tete University teaching finance. He told me that if I wanted to do a border hop to Zimbabwe that day I'd get stuck at the border for the night, which didn't sound too appealing.

So instead I ditched my bag at Gui's place and we went for a hike in the hills surrounding Tete.

There I was treated to some great views of the mighty Zambezi, the fourth longest river in Africa, which rises from its source in the DRC through Angola and Zambia, touching the panhandle of Namibia, meeting the northern border of Zimbabwe at the Victoria Falls before flowing through Tete and out into the Indian Ocean.

That night we ate at a little restaurant on the banks of the grand old river.

The following morning I took the first minibus to the border with Zimbabwe. Along the way we stopped at the town of Changara to pick up more passengers. As their luggage was being loaded, most of it sitting on the road behind the minibus, the driver inexplicably slammed the bus into reverse, squishing a load of bags, caving in a subwoofer and leaving a birthday cake with a tyre mark down the middle of it.

The police tried to arrest the driver for reckless driving (and wanton destruction of a birthday cake), but the driver did not want to be arrested, and I was left squatting at the side of the road, 70km from the border, waiting for all the hullabaloo to sort itself out.

This all took place amidst the backdrop of some big fiesta, so while the driver and the policeman screamed blue murder at each other, the rest of the town was singing hallelujah and clapping hands. It was all rather surreal.

After a good half-hour of people shouting at each other in a language I don't speak (others joined in, of course), we recommenced our journey and arrived at the border before noon.

I told the guy with the exit stamp I intended to purchase a "day pass" into Zim. He said 'okay' and stamped me out of Mozambique.

But when I got to the Zimbabwean side of the border, I discovered (too late!) that in order to get my hands on a day pass the Mozambique border guards needed to stamp a separate piece of paper, not my passport. I went back to the Mozza side and asked them to stamp the bit of paper for me. They refused. I returned to the Zim post, but they told me there was nothing they could do. To get in I'd have to get a full-fat visa, and that would be a whopping $55.

Sod that!

Oh well, I had passed the sign saying "**Zimbabwe**", so technically I had crossed the border. I would have liked to have seen a bit more of Zim, but never mind, they don't hand out Guinness World Records for "getting to know a place".

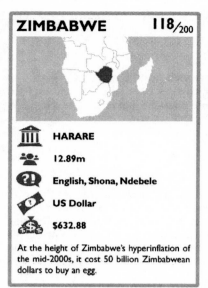

ZIMBABWE

🏛 **HARARE**

👥 **12.89m**

❓ **English, Shona, Ndebele**

💵 **US Dollar**

💰 **$632.88**

At the height of Zimbabwe's hyperinflation of the mid-2000s, it cost 50 billion Zimbabwean dollars to buy an egg.

I headed back to Moz only to be told that as they had stamped me out I had to go to Harare, the capital of Zimbabwe, and get a new visa for Mozambique. That would take five days. I had a multiple-entry visa. Was this guy taking the piss?

'But I've got no luggage, no clothes!' I had left my backpack at Gui's.

The nasty stamp man shrugged. 'I don't care.'

I put $20 in my passport and handed it over to him. He shook his head.

Oh for Christ's sake...

I put *another* $20 in the passport. This time he took the money, threw it in his secret money drawer and crossed out the exit stamp with a biro. I should have just done it myself.

The return trip to Tete was a little uncomfortable to say the least. The locals here call minibuses 'two-mores', because there is always room for two more. You'd be amazed at the contortions people put themselves through to squeeze into a space that simply doesn't exist, can't possibly exist, but-then-it-somehow-does exist — it defies the laws of physics.

Gui was a little surprised that I was three hours late getting back, but there was still time for me to make it to Malawi that day. I said my fond fare-ye-wells and crammed myself into yet another minibus bound for the second border crossing of the day.

I didn't get what you might call a racing start. The 1km long bridge across the Zambezi was being repaired and so the traffic was horrific. But we picked up speed after the river and arrived at the frontier just after nightfall.

There was the usual hustle and bustle at the border. I found myself taken under the wing of a woman from Zimbabwe called Mel, who was travelling to Lilongwe, the capital of Malawi, with her mum and her family. She told me she would be setting up a new life for herself in Britain very soon, far from the tyranny of Robert Mugabe. Mel saw me through the all-too familiar border procedures; the female border guard didn't even give my crossed-out exit stamp a second glance, she just stamped me on my way.

After cruising into **Malawi** (no visa necessary yay!), Mel and I shared a bush taxi to the nearest town. We then waited in the long distance bus park, the fringes of which were lit by the lights of the market stalls which surrounded it. After half an hour, the coach to Lilongwe rucked up.

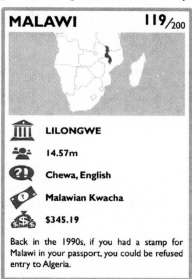

MALAWI 119/200

🏛 **LILONGWE**

👥 14.57m

❓ **Chewa, English**

💵 **Malawian Kwacha**

💰 **$345.19**

Back in the 1990s, if you had a stamp for Malawi in your passport, you could be refused entry to Algeria.

I texted Jason, my CouchSurf contact for Lilongwe, telling him I'd be getting in around midnight and offered to stay in a backpackers instead. He texted back to say it was cool for me to stay at his regardless.

As things turned out, the bus didn't get in until 2am. Jason came to pick me up.

'You owe me a drink', said Jason in his charming Colorado drawl. I most certainly did.

The next morning, we chatted over some rather excellent coffee. Jason was a Peace Corps volunteer for a couple of years in Malawi and decided to stay on and set up a business in Lilongwe.

He told me that Malawi was a great little place; it may be landlocked but it has decent roads, good internet, reliable electricity and the people are exceptionally warm and welcoming.

Two hours north of Lilongwe is a town called Jenda, right on the border with Zambia. If I high-tailed it up there during the day I could pop over the border into Zambia, have a cup of tea, return to Jenda and wait for the 7pm international coach from Lilongwe to Dar es Salaam in Tanzania to arrive — it should be rumbling through Jenda sometime around 9pm.

Concerned that tickets for the big bus to Tanzania might sell out, I bought mine before I left Lilongwe.

I boarded the minibus to Jenda at 11am but by 12:45pm we were still sitting in the carpark.

When we did set off I quickly discovered that I had inadvertently jumped aboard the slowest bus in the world.

By 4pm we were not even halfway to Jenda. And then something weird happened. The driver stopped the bus and told everyone to get off, which we all did.

'So you're not going to Jenda then?', I asked him through the window.

'No. Bye!', He sped off into the distance, suddenly having found third gear.

I got on another bus which was somehow even slower than the first. It was six o'clock before I reached Jenda, which I thought was a border town. It certainly looked that way on the map.

The minibus dropped us all off a good kilometre away from the battered old pick-ups that do the border run each day.

'How much to the border and back?' I asked when I got finally there.

'Forty dollars, US.'

'Forty dollars?! How far is it?'

'Thirty kilometres'

I took out my Lonely Planet and looked at the map. Something wasn't right — Jenda looked like it was right on the border. But what could I do? If I didn't go straight away, it would mean missing tonight's coach to Dar es Salaam. They don't run every day and that ticket wasn't cheap either. Another concern was that I didn't have enough local money to pay the guy, I only had an American $100 bill, which would be difficult, if not impossible to change into Malawian *wibbledeewees*.

'What time does the border close?', I asked.

'Seven.'

I looked at my watch. It was 6:15pm. 'Have we got time?'

'Yeah. Yeah, lots of time.'

By now it was getting dark. My driver, Terry, had failed to mention that he only had half a headlight which would vary in brightness depending on how hard he pressed down on the accelerator. His mate had to stand in the open back of the pickup and shine a torch at the road ahead so we could pick our way along the track.

Needless to say, progress was slow.

I wondered whether it was an unwritten law that all roads in Africa that lead to a border must be constructed in such a way that puts off all but the most intrepid (or desperate) of commuters?

It wasn't until much later when I reviewed the data from my GPS logger that I realised that the road ran parallel to the border. I could have got out at any point along the track, walked *a few metres* over to the left-hand side of the road and I'd have been in Zambia.

But you know, hindsight is always 20/20. We pressed on to the actual border crossing, arriving not before 7pm, but at 8:30pm.

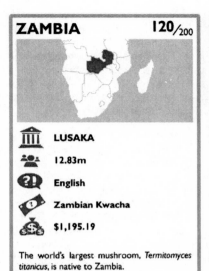

ZAMBIA

🏛 **LUSAKA**

👥 **12.83m**

🗣 **English**

💵 **Zambian Kwacha**

💰 **$1,195.19**

The world's largest mushroom, *Termitomyces titanicus*, is native to Zambia.

Malawi and **Zambia** seemed to share what was an open border, not one of those with a big wire fence around it (like Zimbabwe) so getting "in" was no sweat. I even had a chat with the lone border guard. He told me that I could buy a visa if I wanted one, but for $50 it wasn't worth it. In any case, I had to get back to Jenda.

Short of a Harrier Jump Jet turning up and offering me a lift (which would somewhat break the old "no flying" rule), there was no way we'd make it back to Jenda before the bus to Tanzania rolled through at 9pm. And so I was left banking on it being late.

I harangued Terry to drive as fast as his clapped out pick-up could. We made much better time on the way back than we did on the way there, a feat that was doubly impressive since, you know, we couldn't see the road.

It was 9:50pm when we got back to Jenda. It was then that I dropped the slight bombshell that I had no way of paying Terry unless he knew somebody who could change my $100 bill.

Luckily he did, and within five minutes, I had a HUGE stack of Malawi *blurghelflorgs* in my hand. (The biggest note in Malawi is worth about $3.)

I paid Terry and ran as fast as I could to the police checkpoint on the edge of town. I arrived all out of breath. I asked the policeman if the bus to Tanzania had passed through.

'Not yet, no... oh, here it is now', said the policeman, pointing at the large vehicle trundling towards us.

The bus stopped. I climbed aboard. I hadn't even taken my seat before we cleared the checkpoint and tore off into the night. Had I arrived 30 seconds later I would have missed it.

Magic.

I crossed the border of **Tanzania** on the morning of October 14th. Eight countries and a new passport in ten days. I was one happy little backpacker.

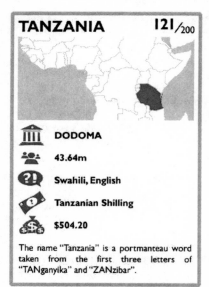

🏛 **DODOMA**

👥 **43.64m**

🔤 **Swahili, English**

💵 **Tanzanian Shilling**

💰 **$504.20**

The name "Tanzania" is a portmanteau word taken from the first three letters of "TANganyika" and "ZANzibar".

What I was less happy about was my seat on the coach. I had to sit in the middle of the back row. There was no back window and so there was no way I could see — much less film — any of the exciting Tanzania stuff that was no doubt whizzing past.

What's more, the entire nation had seemingly decided to embark on a whole new programme of road building just as I showed up, turning a projected 12 hour journey from the border into a prolonged 20-hour slog. Still feeling guilty about keeping Jason in Lilongwe up all night waiting for me, I opted to find myself a hotel for the night.

The following morning I headed down to the port to do business with people who do business in great waters. The next four countries on my list, the Indian Ocean island nations of Comoros, Madagascar, Mauritius and Seychelles, would require a boat.

I spoke to a shifty-looking guy who was hanging around the dock gates, and asked him if there any boats going my way. He led me to the back of a nearby café and there I met a shipping agent called Mbuyi. He had a cargo ship leaving for Comoros the day after next and it was taking passengers.

'And then how do I get to Madagascar?' I enquired.

'No problem', he said, 'boats go every day.'

I looked around for the hidden cameras.

'You're joking, right?'

It couldn't be *that* easy — it just couldn't be.

'Really? It's that easy? I just buy a ticket and away I go?'

'Yep.'

Wow.

This freed up the rest of the day somewhat. I took a stroll around town, taking in the cityscape of Dar es Salaam along the way. Not the most fragrant of towns is old Dar, but the people are friendly enough and there's enough Indian influence to ensure the food is tip-top.

My CouchSurf host was a softly-spoken Canadian guy named Dylan. We met for lunch at his place of work — The International School, on the Msasani peninsular, north of town.

I was introduced to few of Dylan's colleagues over lunch and figured we'd get a good weekend out of this crowd. After the *Micau* and the *Andrea*, I wasn't particularly convinced that this boat would be leaving on schedule.

Unfortunately, (for me, at least) the following week was half-term, so everybody (Dylan included) would be heading out of town for a few days. This mass exodus of Dar didn't fit in which my social plans, but hey-ho, I hoped to be well on my way to Comoros by then.

That evening, Dylan and I headed over to the Irish Bar. A couple of Maasai warriors in full regalia (spears, the lot) worked the door. In a way it made total sense. Nobody in their right mind messes with the Maasai... you better have ID.

I ordered a curry and a lager. So there I was in Africa, eating Indian cuisine, drinking Danish beer, in an Irish pub with Maasai warrior bouncers. If that doesn't sound like a fabulous night out I have no idea what you're doing reading this book.

These good times aside — it was time to face some cold hard facts. My dream of completing this journey in a single year had already been crushed somewhere back in West Africa. I was sure I could complete the task I had set for myself, just not in one trip around the Sun.

So the next day I spent a good few hours chatting with Mandy, trying to work out a new goal: how were we going reunite at some point. The vague plan was that she was going to come and meet me at the end of the year. But where? This was going to be hard to coordinate.

The most perfect thing would be for us to meet up in Egypt. The reason being that we *met* in Egypt, outside the ridiculously situated KFC opposite the Sphinx, back in the heady summer of 1999.

The problem was that there were at least 10 countries between me and Egypt, and some of them were islands. Given past experience it didn't sound *impossible*, but it certainly sounded improbable.

After Dylan got back from school we dropped in on a mate of his for a couple of drinks. Then Dylan and his mate dragged me (not exactly kicking and screaming) to a casino, were we whiled away a couple of hours playing blackjack with what seemed to be half the Chinese population of East Africa.

Once we were all gambled out, Dylan must have decided that I simply wasn't drunk enough because before I knew it he whisked me away to a nightclub where I danced until I could dance no more.

The next day was a Saturday and I was raring to go. But I'm not even going to tease (the whole "I thought it was leaving!" shtick is getting old). Of course the boat wasn't leaving. Let's cut to the chase — I didn't get on the boat until Monday.

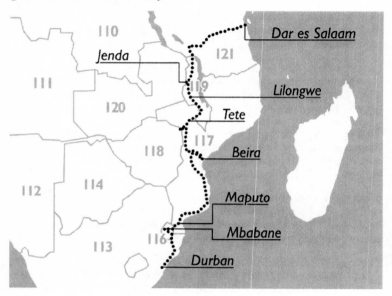

Chapter 27
Drink Your Way Around The World

First thing Monday morning I returned to the booking agents and they took me over the road to the port. Only, the guard on the gate didn't want to let us in. So me and my fellow passengers (there were dozens of them) made do with squatting at the side of the road. A few hours later we finally were granted access.

And there she was: the *Shassiwani II*. God knows what happened to the first one. A great big rusty stinking overloaded mess of a cargo ship. At least half a century old and looking just about as seaworthy as house brick.

I was told to wait on the quayside as the boat wouldn't be leaving until the cattle was loaded. Cows. Fifty of 'em. After a good few hours they finally arrived and were guided around the quay and onto the boat. What I didn't know at this point is that we'd all be sleeping on the deck *next to the damn cows*.

With the cattle loaded, I figured we'd be leaving within the hour, so I boarded the *Shassiwani II* and looked around for instructions, advice, anything. Nothing doing, I headed up the stairs onto the top deck.

Oh. My. God.

Over one hundred people lying cheek-to-jowl on scraps of foam, bits of cardboard, bags of rice. In the sweltering heat, the stink, the rotten feet, the squalor was on a scale that I had, as yet, not experienced. Well, not since I got off my last Greyhound bus.

Remember the banana boat to Barbados when I had to sleep on the greasy metal floor in the galley? Add another 100 passengers on board and you might just get an inkling of what conditions were like on the *Shassiwani II*. Uncomfortable doesn't even begin to describe it. And my cabin? What cabin!? No, I had to make do on the floor like everybody else. Well that was $225 well spent.

A skinny, long haired, snaggle-toothed Chinese guy caught my attention. His name was Lee. He had left China 12 years ago and was fulfilling his dream of cycling to every country in the world. So far he had been to 140 worldwide, including Somalia. He too had been arrested in Congo without charge, but his embassy sprung him after just *two* days, the lucky badger.

Lee was a welcome distraction from the nightmare that was unfolding all around me, but his halitosis felt like part of a wider conspiracy to make me hurl all the way to Comoros.

By 10pm we still hadn't left port. 'When are we going to leave?' I asked a guy who looked like he might know. 'It's just a problem with passports', said the crewman, 'we should be gone by midnight.'

Ha!

Since he had his own roll mat, Lee kindly donated the filthy bit of foam he was sitting on to be my bed for the night.

In the morning I awoke and rubbed my eyes. Either this was the smoothest boat ride of all time or we weren't moving.

I sat up and confirmed the awful truth — I had just spent a night cramped in a greasy corner on a damp bit of foam on the floor of the floating equivalent of a cockroach-infested storage room from *Ramsey's Kitchen Nightmares* for no reason whatsoever.

We were still in port.

Even more frustratingly, every time I asked when we were leaving I was told "in 30 minutes", which meant I couldn't even leave the boat and go for a coffee or something in town. If I had known it would be Tuesday afternoon before we left I would have spent the weekend visiting Zanzibar.

It was 6pm before the engines were *finally* put in gear.

The *Shassiwani II* was a floating circus of grot. The smell, the garbage, the insects, the livestock (which were allocated more room than us humans) — it was a LOT to stomach. It was like the terror of the pirogue to Cape Verde mixed with the squalor of the jail in Congo.

After three incredibly uncomfortable nights, we arrived, battered and bewildered, on the island of Grande Comore, the main island of **Comoros**.

Getting off the boat was a scrum, "customs" consisted of a line of officials set out across the road like riot police. Immigration charged me $100 to get in. So much for my visa being included in the price of the boat ticket.

However, the immigration guy was reasonably friendly and told me there were two boats leaving for Madagascar the day after next.

'Will they be as bad as the *Shassiwani*?', I asked.

The immigration guy looked at the boat and laughed. 'No. Not so bad.'

The guys at immigration accepted my US dollars, but everywhere else was Comorian francs or euros only. Nowhere would change my money and the damn ATMs didn't work. I walked around the city of Moroni for two hours with all my bags in the tropical heat before I found a bank that was open and would allow me to withdraw money over the counter.

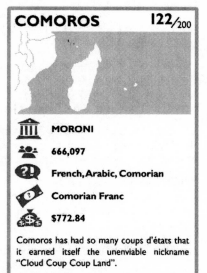

COMOROS 122/200

🏛 **MORONI**

👥 **666,097**

💬 **French, Arabic, Comorian**

💵 **Comorian Franc**

💰 **$772.84**

Comoros has had so many coups d'états that it earned itself the unenviable nickname "Cloud Coup Coup Land".

Exhausted and exasperated, I went into a nearby internet café, but before I could even log on a couple of guys turned up claiming to be police.

'Passeport s'il vous plaît.'

Given that neither of them was in uniform and their non-photographic ID consisted of a laminated bit of printed card that I could knock out in five minutes on *MS Paint,* my passport was staying in my secret pocket stuffed down the front of my trousers, thank you very much.

Instead I showed them a photocopy of my passport, my letter from the British Embassy in Kinshasa that said I was a good egg (in French!) and my European Driver's License.

But that wasn't enough for them.

Here we go again.

They tried to bundle me into a random car, but I had no evidence these guys were anything more than a couple of grifters with fake IDs. After being almost kidnapped in Bolivia a few years earlier by two guys pretending to be police, I'm rather cagey about getting in random cars at night in a foreign city just because a couple of blokes tell me to.

I flat refused and headed back into the internet café. One of the "policemen" made a phone call.

'The chief is coming.'

Soon enough, the "chief" turned up. He had the same crappy ID, but if this was a set-up it was getting rather elaborate, plus I had plenty of witnesses in the café. He inspected my passport and was satisfied I wasn't an illegal immigrant coming from the UK to claim benefits and steal jobs. I breathed a huge sigh of relief and got back to my Internetting.

I sent a tweet to let the folks back home know that I was still alive. Mandy contacted me to let me know that there were no CouchSurf hosts in Comoros. Well, there was one, but he was on another island.

So that night I stayed in the cheapest hotel I could find, a tiny hovel with a cold bucket shower.

The next day I ran into Commissioner Madhi, the helpful port official from the day before. He was on his way to midday prayers on the back of a scooter. He waved at me from across the road, told me he'd be back in half an hour and to hang on for him, which I did.

When he got back, he told me that the shipping agents were closed for the day, it being a Friday in a Muslim country, but I could get a ticket to Madagascar in the morning if I got there at 8am.

Madhi also informed me the ship people would ask for €155, since I was a Johnny Foreigner, but as there were two boats going the next morning, I'd be able to haggle them down to €80. Commissioner Madhi was a top bloke.

I thanked him and headed back to my grotty little guest house, stopping on the way to say hello to Lee the crazy Chinese cyclist, who was sat drinking a Fanta. He was planning to hike up to the big volcano in the morning. If I was around for the weekend, I would have joined him, but there was no way I was missing those boats. The next may not be for a fortnight.

Moroni was not particularly pleasant. There was far too much litter on the ground and the drains didn't seem to drain anywhere, and just stunk up the place with an odour most foul. It reminded me a lot of Cape Verde, only without the whole prison-and-getting-stuck-for-six-weeks malarkey.

There was a big sign on the downward curve of the road as you head towards the Friday Mosque which lays claim: "Mayotte: the fourth of the Comoros Islands." Unfortunately for the other three (Grande Comore, Moheli and Anjouan), Mayotte has other ideas, twice voting overwhelmingly to stay a part of France. Hardly surprising when you consider that the GDP per capita of Mayotte is about 12 times more than that of Comoros. That and all the coup d'états, corruption and dengue fever that Comoros is infamous for, I'd choose to stay with France as well.

It doesn't matter how hot it is outside, a cold shower in the morning is always a pain, doubly so when there's no running water and you have to give yourself a "bucket shower" from a large water container that might as well have a little sign next to it reading "Mosquito Motel —

Vacancies".

I headed down to the port, half-believing that the boat would be leaving that day, but bracing myself for disappointment if it didn't.

But what's this? Not only did I manage to snag a ticket for €90, but soon enough I was on the boat. Less than an hour later the ship, the *Mojangaya*, was actually leaving port! OMG!

As we departed I looked back at wretched old *Shassiwani II* — after three days in port its cargo was *still* being unloaded.

The *Mojangaya* couldn't have been more different from the *Shassiwani II* if it tried. First, it was clean. Second, there were only ten passengers (not over 100) and we all had comfortable padded bench seats to sleep on, like upper class tramps.

Around 48 hours later we arrived in the port town of Mahajanga on the west coast of **Madagascar**.

It's fair to say that I liked Madagascar from the start. The port staff came on board, sprayed the boat down with disinfectant (always reassuring) and stamped me into the country with nay a murmur of discontent over the fact my Madagascar visa was in my old passport, not my new one.

My next mission was fairly straight forward. I needed to get to the town of Toamasina[37] on the east coast before 5pm the next day. This was because I had to get myself to the Tropical Services Travel Agency in order to buy myself a ticket for the ferry to my next country, Mauritius. Yes there was an actual proper scheduled ferry. Wonders never cease.

MADAGASCAR 123/200

🏛 **ANTANANARIVO**

👥 **20.5m**

❓ **Malagasy, French**

💵 **Malagasy Ariary**

💰 **$417.18**

The British accepted the imposition of a French protectorate over Madagascar in return for British control of the tiny island of Zanzibar. Why? Saffron. Worth more than gold.

Now Madagascar is a bloody big place, the fourth largest island in the world. To get from west coast to east coast, I'd have to travel over 700km via the splendidly unpronounceable capital city of Antananarivo. Or as the locals call it, "Tana".

Arriving at the chaotic *taxi-brousse* area at 10am, I discovered that the next minibus for Tana wasn't until 5pm. The Golden Rule of Africa is

---

[37] Author's Note: AKA Tamatave

never travel at night, but I had no choice. If I stayed in Mahajanga until morning I would miss the ferry to Mauritius and it wasn't scheduled to return for two weeks.

The next day as we were coming into Tana on the overnight bus, I imagined myself writing a letter to Santa Claus thanking him for everything Madagascar.

Lovely and tropical, but with big green mountains so that it doesn't get too hot. Spectacular views, beautiful scenery and great hiking tracks. Unspoilt palm-fringed beaches where you can sling your hammock and read a book in the shade. Gorgeous buildings made of wood, local stone or charming handmade bricks. Flora and fauna found nowhere else on earth.

Cool people, no hassle from the police. Yes, you need a visa but it won't cost you anything. Women carrying things on their heads and little old grandmothers speeding down the mountain on wooden go-carts. It's cheap as chips; a pizza and a beer for less than the price of a Happy Meal in the UK. And best of all, the men wear these cool trilby-looking hats, so you feel like you're in a 1930s detective story.

A quick bus swap in Tana and then it was on to Toamasina, arriving early that afternoon.

The agency that sold the ferry tickets told me I could go as far as the French island of Réunion, which was a stop on the way to Mauritius, but I'd have to get off there as the onward voyage was sold out.

The ticket was quite expensive, but at least I knew that I would get a proper cabin this time, not a dirty slice of foam in some floating nightmare like the *Shassiwani II*. There was even a bus service direct to the ferry. Amazing!

The following morning, I had a bit of time before the ferry departed so I took a trip to the nearby lemur sanctuary.

Lemurs are one of my favourite animals on Earth. A primate, cut off from their cousins in Africa and Asia for over fifty million years, they are undoubtedly the cutest little critters one could ever hope to feast one's eyes on. Drawing on the best bits of cats, dogs and monkeys, there's an vast array of different species and breeds — including the famous ring-tailed lemur, the pygmy mouse lemur (the smallest primate in the world) and my favourite animal of all time ever, the dancing sifaka.

The sanctuary was several shades of brilliant. Yes, it had a few other animals knocking about, but I was just there for the lemurs, those lovely little lunatics. A bunch of them were allowed to run free around the sanctuary, so now and again you'd hear a rustle up in the trees. You'd look up to see a family of these weird little guys hurling themselves from branch to branch with reckless abandon.

As I was leaving, a tiny lemur was walking along the fence at the side of the path. I even managed to touch the little critter. Which in hindsight wasn't such a great idea — turns out they stink of piss. Which is probably a good thing as it put me off stealing one to be my new travel buddy.

The ferry was called the *Trochetia* and it was great — just what they need in the Caribbean. It was a good-sized mixed-purpose vessel with a bunch of decent cabins at the back and space at the front for containerised cargo — the best of both worlds. What's more, it had a bar, the beers cost a euro each and the food was pretty good.

I got chatting with a guy from Mauritius who spoke English with a Scottish twang as he had lived in Glasgow for a good few years. He was an engineer working on the boat and he had some good news for me — the ticket agents were talking out of their backsides. There were definitely spaces on the *Trochetia's* onward journey to Mauritius. I just had to visit the ship's agents in Réunion and get myself a ticket.

I went to bed happy that (all being well) I'd be in Mauritius before I knew it.

The next day the ferry arrived in **Réunion**, my sixth and last overseas territory of the year.

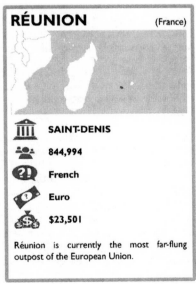

RÉUNION (France)

🏛 **SAINT-DENIS**

👥 **844,994**

❓ **French**

💵 **Euro**

🛵 **$23,501**

Réunion is currently the most far-flung outpost of the European Union.

The ship would be in port for a good few hours so I arranged to meet with Mickael, the chap who we planned would host me through CouchSurfing when I returned back through Réunion after ticking Mauritius off the list.

We grabbed some lunch in the rather charming capital city of Saint-Denis. Mickael was a web designer who worked in advertising. Originally from France, he came to Réunion three years previous, liked it and stayed. I could see why. The island was beautiful and it boasted one of the "safest" active volcanoes in the world. You can even climb it — if you are brave enough.

Mickael and I arranged to meet again upon my return the following Monday — three days hence. (Aren't scheduled ferries great?!) Then it was back to the port for the relatively short trip from Réunion to Port Louis, the capital of **Mauritius**.

The next day I stepped off the *Trochetia* and onto the 124th country of *The Odyssey Expedition*.

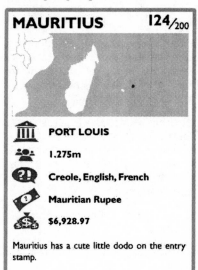

MAURITIUS 124/200

🏛 **PORT LOUIS**

👥 **1.275m**

❓ **Creole, English, French**

💵 **Mauritian Rupee**

💰 **$6,928.97**

Mauritius has a cute little dodo on the entry stamp.

It was October 31st. I started the month in Namibia and ended twelve African nations later in Mauritius. It had been a damn good month.

The *Trochetia* would be returning to Réunion the next day so I checked into a cheap little hotel in Chinatown for the night.

After a hearty breakfast with the cheerful owner I strode out onto the streets for a walking tour of the city of Port Louis; a place where people speak French, write English, eat Indian, look Afro-Chinese and drive on the left... my kind of town.

I trekked up to Fort Adelaide, perched upon a bluff overlooking the city. The royal crown above the gateway bore the monogram 'WR IV'. That's special code so cleverclogs like me know it was built in the 1830s.[38]

After a mooch around the ramparts I ambled down the hill to the natural history museum, but I found it closed, which was a real shame as Mauritius was home to the most famous extinct bird in the world, the dodo[39].

With no natural predators on the island, over the millennia the dodo lost its ability to fly. Then humans turned up with their big clod-hopper boots and wiped all these weird looking birds out. A few centuries later, the curator of Oxford's natural history museum felt that his stuffed dodo specimen was looking a bit tatty, so he threw it on a bonfire. It was only his quick-thinking assistant who saved what would prove to be the *only preserved dodo in the world* from the flames. Now presumably even more dog-eared than ever before, it went back on display for the public's viewing pleasure, where one day it was spotted by a bloke called Charlie Dodgeson; aka Lewis Carroll.

By inserting the dodo as a character in his *Alice* books, Carroll secured the dodo's place in the public imagination and one of the cuter stamps in my passport was the one I got from Mauritius – it's got a little dodo on it.

---

[38] Editor's Note: William IV was King of England from 1830-1837.
[39] Author's Note: *Deadasus dodous*

Speaking of stamps, I had more luck at the Blue Penny museum as it was actually open. I have to admit I got a little distracted with the spectacular old maps on display and almost forgot what I came to see — a couple of stamps.

As any philatelist worth their salt knows, one of the most valuable stamps on Earth is the *Mauritian Post Office Blue*, followed by the *Post Office Red*. Two little iddy-biddy scraps of paper printed, apparently by mistake, in the 1840s. The rumour is that they were supposed to say "Postage Paid" down the side, but actually said "Post Office". They were recalled and burnt, but not before the Governor's wife posted off a load of invitations using the misprinted stamps.

There are only thought to be 26 of these stamps in existence. Most of them were postmarked; there are only five in the world that were never sent through the mail, and two of them — a One Penny Red and a Two Penny Blue — were bought by a consortium of Mauritian businesses in 1993 for a staggering amount of money and put on display in their own purpose-built museum. To give you some idea of their value, the museum cost less to build than the stamps cost to buy.

These two tiny bits of paper are now possibly the most valuable objects on the entire island. To protect their colour, they are only illuminated for a few minutes every hour, and then only one at a time. Seeing them in person didn't give me a teardrop-on-the-face-of-eternity moment, but each to their own, I guess.

A trip to Port Louis wouldn't have been complete without a visit to the *Champ de Mars* racecourse that dominates the eastern end of the city. The Mauritius Turf Club is the oldest horse-racing club in the Southern Hemisphere and the second oldest in the world.

When I got there, I found to my delight that it was a race day. I thought I'd try my luck.

Using an age-old strategy that has never failed to let me down in the past, I placed a bet on the favourite (to recoup my bet should he win) and picked another that was around 20-1. The favourite was called *Power of Poseidon* and the 20-1 outsider was called *Cut Em Up*.

I climbed the stands to watch the spectacle — just once around the course, but that's all it took. *Power of Poseidon* failed miserably, but *Cut Em Up* romped past all the others and finished in first place.

Hell yeah!

I strode over to the turf accountant to collect my winnings — nearly €100 worth. It was time to go to the pub.

I found a place called the Keg and Marlin down by the waterfront. I was waiting to order when I noticed the "Drink Your Way Around The World" board at the end of the bar with a few dozen name-plates on it.

'What do I have to do to get my name on that thing?' I enquired.

'You have to drink twenty beers from twenty different countries', said the barman.

'In one night?!'

'No — over six weeks.'

'Has anyone ever done it in one night?'

'Of course not.'

Well... in for a penny (red)...

'I'll start with a Guinness.'

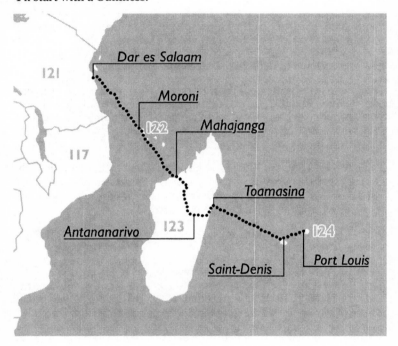

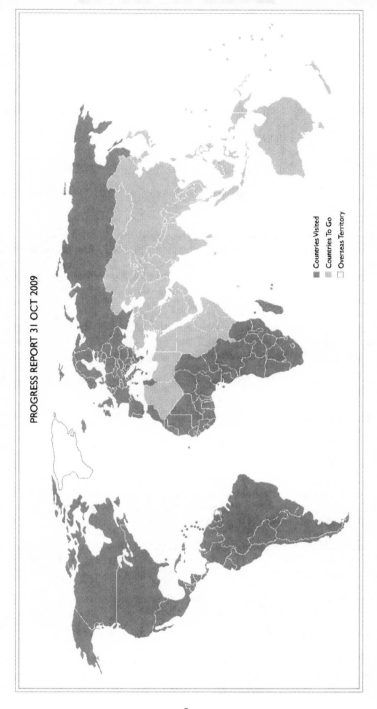

PROGRESS REPORT 31 OCT 2009

Countries Visited
Countries To Go
Overseas Territory

287

Chapter 28
Here Be Pirates

By midnight it was all over. The bar was closing, I downed the last of my twenty drinks and Oliver the barman signed and dated my form. I hadn't felt this accomplished since I managed to complete the *Curry Hell Challenge* at the Rupali Restaurant in Newcastle several years earlier. I don't think I had been as drunk since then either.

I was five sheets to the wind in an unfamiliar city, clutching a bag that contained my laptop and my camcorder. Any sensibly-minded type would retire to his hotel, job well done, and fall into a deep intoxicated slumber. But where did being sensible ever get me?

I set off to find a nightclub in Grand Baie, a few miles north of Port Louis.

That was the last thing I remember.

I still have no idea how I managed to get back to my hotel. To be perfectly frank I have no idea how I am still alive.

I awoke at 3pm, realising that at 3pm I was supposed to be on board the *Trochetia* for the trip back to Réunion. I rubbed my eyes, waited for the room to spin at a more reasonable pace, then headed for the shower. For once I was thankful that it was cold.

After saying my exceptionally fuzzy farewells to the owner of the guesthouse, I stumbled my way through the (merciful, refreshing) rain and took a taxi that was being driven by a rather garrulous driver.

He talked and talked, but all I could do was grunt and hope he didn't take the corners too fast. Thankfully the *Trochetia* was a bit late leaving port. One good thing about transportation in Africa — you can usually rely on its unreliability.

Once on board I calmly walked to the bathroom and did an reasonably good impression of the little girl from *The Exorcist,* although, unlike her, I did manage to get all my chunder down the loo.

My head then rotated 360 degrees and I did a weird backwards spider walk back to my cabin, hissing at anyone who came near.

I curled up in bed and fell fast asleep.

The next day I waved goodbye to the good ship *Trochetia* having just about cleared the hangover from my system. I then made my way from La Port to Saint-Denis, the capital of Réunion.

The ferry ran a bit of an odd schedule. It went back and forth between Réunion and Mauritius every other day, but it only did the trip to Madagascar once every two weeks. This meant returning to Réunion was the easy bit, but I'd have to figure out another way of getting back to Madagascar. I hoped I hadn't painted myself into a corner.

So again I met up with Mickael, only this time I'd be staying with him for a few days until I figured out a way off this (albeit rather delightful) rock.

Now if anybody could figure out a way of getting me back to Madagascar within the week, it was my friends Dino and Lorna. It was time to reactivate Team Odyssey!

And this time, we had a secret weapon — a friend of Lorna's called Thierry. A native francophone, he worked to sweet-talk the wonderful folks at CMA-CGM, the French shipping group (one of the biggest in the world) into allowing this dishevelled ginger monkey to hitch a ride on one of their ships.

A couple of days later we had our first lead. A cargo ship called the *DAL Madagascar* was scheduled to leave Réunion "soon", bound for Madagascar. Lorna suggested I go to the CMA-CGM offices at the port to find out more.

The next morning I did just that.

'Oui', said Audrey the lovely shipping agent, 'there is a ship called the *DAL Madagascar*, it's in port today and it's going to Madagascar, but it's stopping in Mauritius first, is that okay?'

A trip back to Mauritius? I wasn't going to argue with that!

'When does it leave?' I asked.

'Today at 4pm.'

'Amazing!'

And then I thought of something. Oh hell. *I didn't have a visa for Madagascar*. Even worse, I had been told they can take up to 48 hours to come through.

After the Cape Verde debacle I had come to understand that you can't just expect to turn up somewhere without the necessary paperwork.

Audrey printed me out a crewlist with my name on it, I thanked her and ran for the bus to Saint-Denis, 20km away. As I was approaching the bus stop the bus zoomed past me. I shouted and whistled, but he just kept on going.

It was hot as hell and I did not find the twenty-minute wait for the next bus very amusing. Nor did I find the massive traffic jam on the approach to Saint-Denis tickling my funny bones. By the time that I got to the Madagascan embassy, it was already way past midday. I explained the situation to the lady on the front desk, but she didn't really understand what I was blithering on about. Luckily for me, the Consul himself was in attendance — and spoke good English.

He told me that it wasn't necessary for me to get an advance visa for a single trip of less than 30 days — I could get one upon arrival, but since I was there they gave me a visa anyway.

Oh, and best of all — it was free! I love Madagascar!!

Within five minutes, I was skipping out the door, my passport now furnished with a lovely new Madagascan visa.

I looked at my watch. I had less than an hour to get back to Mickael's, pick up my gear and race back to the port.

I hopped on the next bus that looked like it was heading in the right direction. I got off about a kilometre from Mickael's house and ran. As I was approaching the front door — hot, sweaty, out of breath — with less than 30 minutes to get back to the port — my phone buzzed. It was Audrey, ringing to tell me that the *DAL Madagascar* had been delayed and would not be leaving until the next day.

Phew!

I immediately headed back towards the city centre to buy a new pair of shoes — all my adventures thus far had taken their toll on my poor little Vans. My left had a whopping great hole in the sole and my right had lost all its stitching around the front, leaving it flapping about like it was trying to tell you something.

That night Mickael's housemate Matilde and the boys from next door came over for a great big French feast. We sat in the back garden laughing and joking and stuffing our faces with garlic and cheese and all that great stuff I had been missing while travelling around Africa. Afterwards, we made a little funeral pyre for my old pair of Vans. I saluted their contribution to the cause.

In the morning, Mickael's neighbours popped back over for a farewell breakfast, which sort of spilled over to a farewell elevenses and then a farewell lunch. Mickael's friend Pierre drove me to the bus station for midday, leaving me plenty of time to get to the port before 2pm.

Or so I thought.

In the event, the next bus to the town of Le Port wasn't for another 45 minutes, and then we got stuck in a traffic jam getting out of Saint-Denis.

I didn't get to Le Port until 1:45pm. But my troubles were not over. I couldn't find a taxi and so was forced to hike a good couple of miles from the town of Le Port to the port itself.

And then, like a proper chump, I went to the wrong gate.

Now the port complex is the size of a town itself and the correct gate was a couple of miles away. With all my bags, I had no hope of making it for 2pm — the deadline had already passed. I called the ship to let them know that I wasn't going to make it, but thankfully the Captain got the shipping agent to come and pick me up. Thank You Captain.

Captain Jens-Uwe welcomed me on-board. After I had signed the usual letter of indemnity, I was shown to my cabin (nice!) and I settled in for the night. Lorna, Dino, Thierry, Audrey, CMA-CGM; take a bow.

The next morning I found myself back in Mauritius. We came into port around 10am and by midday I was walking the streets of Port Louis. I hoped to drop into the National Museum this time, but instead I spent most of the afternoon in a branch of HSBC trying (and failing) to get HSBC to unblock my telephone banking.

I spent the remainder of my sunny afternoon in Mauritius sending another batch of video tapes via Fed-Ex over to Lonely Planet in Australia.

By the time I had finished my chores, it was 5pm and the museum was closed. I headed back to the boat, checking in along the way at the Keg and Marlin to see if my name had been added to the *Drink Your Way Around The World* board yet. Sadly not. I'd just have to return to Mauritius at some point.

The following morning we were already well on our way to Madagascar on board the good ship *DAL Madagascar*.

We had a change-over of captains in Mauritius and now we were under the command of a surprisingly sprightly (and wonderfully foul-mouthed) 67 year old German seadog named Klaus. Captain Klaus asked the second officer, Yuriy, to show me the "pirate map" of the Indian Ocean. It had all of 2009's pirate incidents (thus far) marked on it: sightings, attempts, hijackings.

Oh crappy-la-la.

There were so many I couldn't believe they had all happened in less than a year. It included one particularly ominous marking — "OUR SHIP ATTACKED" — dated April 2009 (the same month as the hijacking of the *Maersk Alabama*).

Apparently the ship was sprayed by bullets fired from AK-47s and hit with a rocket-propelled grenade — but the *DAL* managed to outrun the pirates.

Captain Klaus told me that after the stop in Madagascar, they'd be blacking out all the windows "like it's the f---ing war" and gunning it at full speed — 24 knots — in a bid to avoid any future confrontations.

Looking at that map I saw that I had a problem. A very big problem. The "High Risk Area" (HRA) for piracy ran from the east coast of Africa to the west coast of India, the Arabian Peninsula to a few miles north of the top of Madagascar.

The next place I needed to visit, The Seychelles, was stuck slap bang right in the middle of the HRA.

With things being as they were, it was highly doubtful I could hitch a ride on a cargo ship. To make matters worse, cruise ships visiting the Seychelles were few and far between (a handful each year).

I thought perhaps I could convince a yachtie to take me to Farquhar Atoll, part of the most southerly group of islands in The Seychelles archipelago.

The Farquhar Group lay just 175 nautical miles north of Madagascar, but it was right on the southern edge of the HRA. It would be a long shot, to be sure, but I had struck lucky before with Captains Johnny, Milan and Marc.

We arrived in Toamasina a day earlier than expected, which was a pleasant surprise. I said my thanks and goodbyes to Captain Klaus and the crew before racing down the gangway, and jumping back onto the terra firma of good ol' Magadascar.

The CMA-CGM shipping agent, Ricky, gave me a lift to the *taxi-brousse* area, where a minibus was helpfully leaving for the capital.

Once back in Tana I checked into a cheap little place and treated myself to a great big pepper steak in a posh restaurant. It cost less than $7. Did I mention how much I love Madagascar? Because I *really* love Madagascar.

The next day I was up at 6am for the 7am minibus to the northern port town of Diego Suarez[40] on a wing and a prayer I could find a yachtie up there who would take me to Farquhar.

But the 7am bus didn't even turn up until 8:30am. I paid my money,

---

[40] Author's Note: AKA Antsiranana

climbed on board and was told the bus would be leaving "very soon".

By noon the bus still hadn't moved. I grew rather agitated and demanded to know why we weren't going anywhere. That's when I discovered we wouldn't be leaving until 3pm.

'Okay, give me my money back.'

The bus tout seemed less than keen on that idea.

Luckily there was a policeman walking by. I hopped off the bus and I explained the situation.

He simply shrugged.

Colonial legacy that. Bleedin' Frenchies, coming over here, teaching people how to *shrug*.

I kicked the minibus and got back on board. If I had known the bus was leaving at 3pm I would have had a lie-in and explored the city a bit.

We didn't leave until 7pm.

I arrived in Diego Suarez 26 hours later. The place was deader than Dillinger. I walked into the Belle Vue hotel (indeed it did have a nice view) slapped some Malagasy ariary[41] on the desk and bought myself a room for the night.

The next day I went on a recce around the town. Wow. When the Lonely Planet said that Diego Suarez is sleepy, it wasn't kidding. There were a total of two yachts in the bay, a couple of fishing boats, and that was about it.

I asked Thierry from Team Odyssey to call up a few French-speakers on my behalf. One guy, Francis, said that he might be able to help.

Francis put me on to somebody who owned a catamaran in Nosy Be (a hilariously-named island off the east coast of Madagascar).

Thierry spoke to this catamaran chap and he confirmed my worst fears — nobody, absolutely *nobody* was sailing anywhere *near* the Seychelles anymore. It was just too damn dangerous.

A couple of French yachties were shot dead earlier in the year as French forces made a bungled attempt to rescue them from their captors.

With military gunships patrolling the shipping channels in the north up by Yemen, the pirates had been pushed down south towards The Seychelles. Even the run to Comoros was looking increasingly fraught.

Bear in mind, the pirates were not striking out of Somalia; they were

---

[41] Author's note: The currency of Madagascar

using uninhabited islands and captured freighters as bases.

And just two weeks earlier Paul and Rachel Chandler, a British yachting couple, had been kidnapped just 78 nautical miles off the coast of The Seychelles.

They wouldn't be released until a year later.

At this point of my adventure, Seychelles was a bust.

But that didn't mean all hope was gone. Boats left for The Seychelles from other ports — Mombasa in Kenya, Salalah in Oman and Fort Kochi in India.

Cruise ships were rare, but not entirely out of the realms of possibility — after all, I had hitched a ride on one before.

I'd get there someday.

Just not today.

With The Seychelles off the menu it was time to return to continental Africa.

I called Mandy and we hatched a plan together. We would meet at the KFC by the Giza pyramids on New Year's Eve.

If getting back to Comoros and then onto Dar es Salaam was as easy as my outward journey, I could be back in Africa by mid-November.

This would give me six weeks to saunter through the remaining countries in Africa (most of which I did not need an advance visa to visit) on my way to Cairo.

After all the travelling I had done over the past year, it didn't sound like too much of a stretch.

I took an overnight minibus back down to Mahajanga, the port for Comoros, my stepping stone back to Africa.

The music on the bus was as bad as it was loud but at least the stars were bright and clear. I felt like a fool for not just staying on the *DAL Madagascar* — its next stop was Mayotte, the French island in the Comoros chain. I would have been there by now.

The bus arrived in Mahajanga around 11am. I headed straight to the port. I slogged around in the noonday heat with all my bags visiting shipping offices: MSC, CMA-CGM and the like, but it there were no boats to be found.

Then I had a bit of luck. I found the agency for the boat I came in on, the *Mojangaya*. Its sister ship, the *Liege*, was supposed to be leaving a few days ago, but had been delayed. I was told that "it should be going

294

to Comoros tomorrow."

Emphasis on the word "should".

That night I stayed at the Chez Karon hotel in the north of Mahajanga, lovely wooden cabins on a quiet beach. I dined on lobster that cost less than a couple of cans of Coke in Angola. Madagascar, I love you.

I ran down to the port bright and early on the morning of November 14th, eager to jump on the boat for Comoros.

But it was not going anywhere. 'Try again tomorrow.'

I checked back into Chez Karon.

From bitter experience, I can firmly say that the only thing worse than waiting for a boat to leave is being told every day that the boat will leave "tomorrow".

If they had told me it would be another week I would have explored Madagascar a bit more, gone for a hike or something, joined a travelling tribe of musical lemurs, I dunno.

Although I have to admit that when it finally did depart (several days later), the little *Liege* was a treat, especially compared to the goddamn *Shassiwani II*. I had a desk with a power socket (I could work!), I got my own bed (amazing!) and the sea was calmer than Bob Ross on Xanax. Nice.

Once back in Comoros, Commissioner Madhi asked how long I was planning to stay. I told him 'as long as it takes to get a boat back to Africa.'

He looked downcast. 'There are no boats on the schedule. Not for a week at least.'

That was bad enough, but then when I looked on the noticeboard outside the port, the only ship leaving before Christmas was — the goddamn *Shassiwani II*.

Kill me now.

Oh well, if it meant I could make my date in Egypt, I didn't have much of a choice.

The first thing that you notice on your arrival in Moroni is that there is litter *everywhere*. At one point I saw some people in the back of a low loader and thought for one (idiotic) second that they were cleaning up the trash. Ha, no. They were just shovelling loose garbage *off* the truck and dumping it onto the side of the road.

The second thing you'll notice is the price of everything. While not quite up there with Angola, it definitely gives Norway a run for its money.

Imagine a dirty, cobweb-filled room with an unfinished concrete floor and a bed that's second hand from the local jail. The electrical sockets hang dangerously out of the wall and the door handles fall off with gay abandon. The communal "shower" is a bucket of cold mosquito-infested water which you must scoop up in a plastic jug and pour over yourself. The floor is so filthy that when you walk from the bucketroom to your bedroom the soles of your feet will look like you've just clambered over a coal pile. You can forget about TV, air-con, mini-bar or room service; and breakfast — of course — is not included. The only things that are complimentary are the ants. And spiders. And mosquitoes. This is the palatial Pension Faida hotel.

The asking price for such princely lodgings? Three dollars? Five would perhaps be a little much. Ten would be outright extortion. Fifteen would be taking the piss.

It was $20. A night.

On top of that, the beer was so expensive I could only drink half a pint before I blew my daily drinking budget. Food wasn't cheap either, SIM cards were a whopping €15 (pretty much everywhere else in Africa they were €1) and because there are no ATMs, every time I needed more money it cost me €15 in bank charges — and you can't change Comorian francs into anything useful (like US dollars) once you leave the country.

The third thing you notice is that the people are rather pleasant. Yes, the service was diabolical and if I got my camera out all the locals would invariably scowl at me, but that aside, there are a lot of good people in Comoros. I never felt conscious about my stuff and was happy to leave my laptop out in the café while I used the loo — it was that kind of place.

'Well', I thought, 'if I'm going to be here for a week, I might as well climb that damn volcano.'

Mount Karthala is an active volcano and at 2,361 metres is the highest point of Comoros.

To get up there you have to start before daybreak. I was with a guide and another climber, an older guy from France.

Unfortunately for me, by 6am my leg started to hurt. It was probably connected to spending a good portion of the year being crammed into uncomfortable positions for hours on end.

By 10am I didn't think I could go on. At 11am I collapsed. I tossed my video camera to my guide and asked him to get some nice footage of the summit and then come back for me.

I fell asleep on the mountain. A foolish thing to in the noonday sun of a tropical island. UV rays, you know? When the Frenchman and the guide returned two hours later my face was horribly sunburnt, and on top of that I would have to spend the next five hours limping down the mountain.

I spent the next four days peeling strips of skin off my sunburnt face, which I found strangely satisfying. Like popping bubble wrap.

I went back to the port every day to check the noticeboard. Nothing was coming in, nothing was going out. I wondered how the island managed to feed itself.

One day I was arrested for the crime of owning a camera. I didn't have a photo permit (possibly because they don't exist) and a toad-faced gendarme was trying to drag me down to the airport and stick me on the next plane out of his country.

Luckily, Commissioner Madhi and the nice chaps at the port calmed him down. They explained that I was desperate to get off the island, but I couldn't fly. They promised the policeman they'd put me on the first boat to Africa, which is exactly what I wanted.

When that "first boat" would be, nobody had any idea.

After ten days in the godawful Pension Faida, I was done. At the suggestion of a friend I checked out the Itsandra Hotel, 4km north of Moroni, the best hotel on the island. Nice views, lovely staff, private beach and free wi-fi. Bliss.

Of course I couldn't afford to stay there.

Happily, Fanja, the friendly hotel bartender, took me under his wing and said I could crash at his place.

I ended up staying with Fanja for the best part of a week in his one room shack in the local village next to the Itsandra Hotel. We watched far too many awesomely crap action movies and reggae music videos for two guys who weren't even remotely stoned.

By December 7th I was still on Comoros. Even if the boat left that day, I would have only three weeks to get to the pyramids.

A boat didn't leave that day. Or the next day. I was told there might not be a ship leaving for another *week*. Mandy had already booked her flight from Australia to Egypt.

Time was running out.

While I fretted about how the hell I was ever getting off this rock, I met Alice, Daniel, Keith and Stephanie, a group of international adventurers who were on their way to Mayotte to meet up with the boat they were due to crew on — a replica of a 2,600-year-old Phoenician vessel that had been built by a British guy in order to re-create the first circumnavigation of Africa.

My new Phoenician friends invited me on a tour of the island, the highlight of which was the discovery that, yes, Comoros has lemurs too! I met one called Rambo. The lowlight was our local guide, Joseph, who was so hilariously miserable he could have given Morrissey on a wet Wednesday in Manchester a run for his misery.

For the next few days, Alice, Daniel and Stephanie kindly allowed me to sleep on the floor of their hotel room.

My final days on Grande Comore involved getting up bright and early, finding out if any boats were going to Africa (spoilers: no!) and then heading up to the Itsandra Hotel to nurse a small glass of beer and abuse their free internet connection.

Also to be found hanging out at the Itsandra were some members of the US Navy. A bit of a new initiative for them. Instead of bombing the shit out of everything, the US had started sending their military to underdeveloped nations to help small community projects. One of the guys, Don, treated me to dinner and even let me use his hot shower (he wasn't in it at the time). After three weeks of cold bucket showers it was the sum of all bliss.

Then, finally, on December 15th, more than six weeks since I drank my way around the world, a beat-up old passenger/cargo ship called the *Simacom* readied to depart for Tanzania.

I bought a ticket and clambered on board, steeling myself for my greatest challenge yet: getting from Dar es Salaam to Cairo through ten African nations without flying in just two weeks.

The race was on.

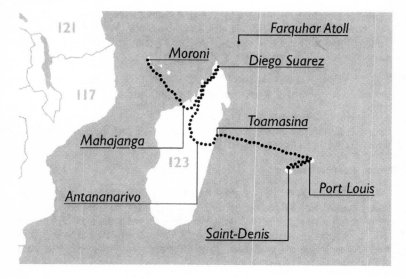

Chapter 29
The Pyramid Scheme

The *Simacom's* on-board entertainment was a tiny CRT screen covered in soot and smudges at the far end of the hold. Throughout the two-day journey it played every Bond movie in reverse order, beginning with Casino Royale (2006) and ending with Dr No (1962). While Pierce Brosnan's tenure as 007 got better and better (unlike in real life) I busied myself working out how in hell I was going to make it to the pyramids by December 31st.

To say it would be a tall order would be an understatement. I would be arriving back in Tanzania on Thursday December 17th. I had just 14 days to get to Egypt via Rwanda, Burundi, Uganda, Kenya, Ethiopia, Somalia, Djibouti and possibly Eritrea and Sudan.

I hoped that, despite Band Aid's best efforts, they *didn't* know it was Christmas time... because then the buses wouldn't be running.

Although I could get a visa upon arrival for Tanzania, Rwanda, Burundi, Uganda, Kenya and Egypt (and Eritrea and Somalia were possible border-hops), I would have to get visas in advance for Ethiopia, Djibouti and Sudan.

My visas for Ethiopia and Djibouti I could pick up in Nairobi, the capital of Kenya.

Sudan was another matter entirely. According to my copy of Lonely Planet, getting a visa for Sudan from Nairobi wasn't possible; and getting one from Addis Ababa, the capital of Ethiopia, would be a bloody nightmare — the process could take up to six weeks. I had two weeks. And ten other countries to visit.

I took the executive decision to skip Sudan *for now*. My main focus had to be getting to Egypt for the end of the year or else Mandy would have my guts for garters and for the rest of the journey I truly would be alone.

But how could I skip what was (at the time) the biggest country in Africa without flying?

Fortunately, Team Odyssey had my back. Dino had found a cargo ship, the *CMA-CGM Turquoise*, scheduled to leave the port of Djibouti on December 26th.

It would be stopping in Saudi Arabia and then — all being well — arrive in Suez in Egypt in the early hours of December 31st, leaving me plenty of time to meet up with Mandy for a New Year's Eve reunion at the pyramids.

Dino spoke to CMA-CGM and things were looking positive for me to climb aboard, so long as I could reach Djibouti in time.

That left nine East African countries to tear through in just nine days.

BRING IT!

I hit the soil of Africa like a man possessed. Within a good hour of arriving back in Dar es Salaam I was on a bus to the capital, Dodoma.

That night I stayed in a grotty guest house, bracing for an early start the next day. It was barely dawn when I hailed a cab and jumped inside. 'Bus station please'.

My driver shrugged.

'Bus station. *The bus station?* The station for the *bus?*'

Nope. This guy didn't have a clue what I was banging on about.

Now I'm not so culturally insensitive that I think everyone around the world speaks English. After all, the first language of Tanzania is Swahili and there are over 120 regional languages spoken around the country. Having said that, it's not like there are that many destinations in Dodoma that a random backpacker might want to go to at that time in the morning — it was much too early for the pub, the cinema, the local sex dungeon and "bus" is not that uncommon a word. So I tried some variations.

'Buus station?'

Nah.

'Bes station?'

No.

'Bis station?'

Eh?

'Bos station?'

Try again.

'Bas station?'

Hmm...

'Baas station?'

A big toothy grin spread across the driver's face. 'Ah! The *baas* station!! No problem, I take you there', he said with a wink.

By the end of the day I was well on my way to Rwanda. I crossed the border of my 125th country on the morning of December 19th.

Ah, **Rwanda** — what a breath of fresh (mountain) air! For a place that has become synonymous with images and tales of the horrific genocide that took place in the mid-90s, it's fair to say that it has moved on a pace or two. This tiny country in the heart of Africa has managed to not just get itself back on its feet, but also defy expectations to become what I felt was one of the nicest, tidiest and most pleasant places on the entire continent.

The infrastructure was well-maintained, the roads had refreshing lack of potholes and the streets were closed to traffic for an hour each week so people

RWANDA 125/200

🏛 **PORT LOUIS**

👥 10.53m

❓ Kinyarwanda, English, French

💵 Rwandan Franc

💰 $504.19

The famous mountain gorillas of Rwanda sleep in large nests made of sticks and leaves. The young ones make them in the trees.

could pick up litter. Seatbelts were mandatory (and so taxi drivers don't take offence when you put them on). And when I jumped on the back of a motorbike the driver gave me a crash-helmet to wear — there was a sizable fine if I refused.

There are those who firmly believe that being forced by law to wear safety equipment when doing something dangerous is an affront to their civil liberties. These people are idiots. Having travelled through some "Lands that Health and Safety Forgot" (Bolivia, Nigeria and India—to name a few), it may be exhilarating, but it's hardly the best way of doing things.

By early afternoon I had passed through the Rwandan capital of Kigali and had made it all the way to the border with **Burundi**, Rwanda's twin brother to the south.

Since declaring independence from Belgium in 1962, Burundi has had a rough time of it. While not as well-known as the problems that have afflicted Rwanda, the legacy of the European colonial strategy of "divide and rule" in this tiny nation is something that has wreaked havoc since independence, with numerous atrocities committed by both sides of the Hutu-Tutsi divide. A divide that seems shockingly arbitrary to an outsider such as myself.

Rwanda has taken the sensible option of making it illegal to force somebody to declare which tribe they belong to. (Before the 1994 genocide this information was printed on their ID cards, something that made it easier for the machete-wielding militias to find and kill their "enemies".) But Burundi still insists on highlighting the difference, which may well store up trouble for the future.

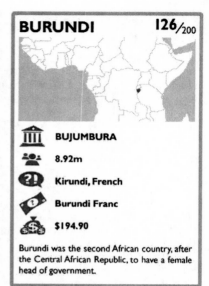

BURUNDI 126/200

🏛 **BUJUMBURA**

👥 **8.92m**

❓ **Kirundi, French**

💵 **Burundi Franc**

💰 **$194.90**

Burundi was the second African country, after the Central African Republic, to have a female head of government.

To buy a visa for Burundi would be $100, and as much as I would have liked to have travelled down to the incredibly-named capital city of Bujumbura for the day, all I could think about was how much I needed to get back to Mandy before the stroke of midnight on December 31st. So, along with a bunch of other countries — Suriname, Panama, Belarus, Central African Republic, Equatorial Guinea etc. — all I got to see was the border zone.

'Ah well', I thought to myself, 'these countries are not going anywhere — I can always return when I'm not trying to set a brand new Guinness World Record.'

So then. Back up to Kigali and hardly time to brush my teeth before I was on an overnight bus to Nairobi in Kenya, via mighty Uganda.

Since I've done it dozens of times on this journey, it's probably worth explaining the process I go through when crossing a border.

I emerge from the bus, groggy and bewildered after a few hours of broken sleep. It's far too early and the border is about to open for the day. I take all my bags with me and leave nothing on the bus, just in case. Sometimes touts will try to "help" me by telling me where to go in exchange for a few dollars, but I prefer to suss things out by myself. Border formalities are fairly standard and I usually have a bus-full of people to follow.

There will invariably be a complex made of concrete. Somewhere inside will be a room in which I can (hopefully) get stamped out of the country I am in. A form will need to be filled out. Profession? I usually go for "teacher", keeps me out of trouble. I never put "journalist", "TV presenter" or "adventurer", that would be silly. By now I know my passport number off by heart. Some forms want my parent's names, some want my place of birth, still others want to know my religion. I once put "none" on a form to enter Bangladesh which I think made their heads explode. These days I just lie and put "C of E", just to confuse them since nobody seems to know it means "Church of England".

Also, it pays to have a pen.

Of course there is a queue. There is always a queue. If I'm lucky it's early morning, but if I'm unlucky it's noon, swelteringly hot and the queue snakes out of the door. And no, not all British people like to queue. I certainly don't.

After between ten minutes and three hours of waiting I'll be face-to-face with a border official. Smile, I always smile. Sometimes they demand an exit tax. This is super annoying, especially if I've purposefully used up all my local currency since, you know, I'm leaving an' all. I ask if they accept dollars (they usually do).

As my passport fills over time, blank pages become very precious. I don't want a tiny exit stamp in one corner ruining my ability to obtain a full-page visa further down the road. So I ask them (nicely) if they can stamp the page that already has stamps on it.

If I'm lucky...

Boom! That's it, I'm stamped out. But I'm only halfway there.

Now it's time to head on over to my shiny new country. Usually the two border posts are just a few hundred metres from each other, but depending on the level of animosity between the two nations they can be miles apart — in which case, walking through No-Man's-Land will not be an option and I'll have to catch a lift in somebody's car.

There's invariably a river so I'll probably find myself crossing a bridge. There will be a line of trucks on the bridge waiting for inspection. Most will all have left their engines on (for some reason) even though they're stationary. There will be toxic black smoke belching all over the road. I hold my breath as best I can and cross the bridge.

On the far side will be another complex of dispiriting concrete buildings. I find the one marked "entry" and head on in. The lady or gent with the stamp will be the first person I'll meet from that country and their attitude can greatly influence how I end up feeling about the place. First impressions count. Fingers crossed I don't get a grumpy sod.

There will be another form to fill out, maybe a visa to purchase. Sometimes I have to go to another building to get the visa. Sometimes I have to get an entry stamp and a customs stamp after an official has rifled through my bag.

Top tip: Put all your dirty underwear on top. This usually puts them off looking too hard.

Occasionally I'll have to be seen by a doctor, or walk through a temperature scanner to ensure I don't have a fever. That's all right — if I've got Ebola, the last thing I want to do is spread it far and wide.

After queuing and queuing and queuing (and quite possibly being extorted a few times along the way), I will eventually be released back into the wild, free to go about my business.

Now here comes the hard bit.

In my pocket is a mishmash of currencies — dollars, euros, local currency from whatever country I'm leaving and maybe some Great British pounds if I'm feeling fruity. Now I need to change those worthless kwanzas into worthwhile kwacha.

There are always a bunch of guys on the border flapping around large wads of filthy lucre, and I mean physically filthy. They might rip me off, they might not. The bills might be fake. Who knows? Either way, I need to be on my toes. I get out my phone, use it as a calculator and play them off against each other. But it's still early and beastly hot and I've been standing in a queue for the last 90 minutes with my backpack on — working out fair percentages in languages that I don't speak in order to exchange currencies I can't even pronounce. This isn't the easiest of endeavours. If I'm lucky there will be a bureau de change. But sometimes I get a better rate from the touts. It often pays to read the "Entering The Country" section of your Lonely Planet.

After the money changing ordeal I check to see if my phone still works. The reason for this is that I might need a new SIM card. Somebody will be selling them at the side of the road, usually for just a dollar or two — the same price that it would cost to receive a five-second phone call on my home SIM so it's definitely worth it.

Then I either wait another hour for my bus to cross the border or, if I arrived by taxi, attempt to get into another taxi to the nearest bus station. I say "attempt" as this procedure is not always as straight-forward as one might imagine as the modern convenience of the taximeter (invented in 1891) has not quite permeated a surprising proportion of the modern world.

I don't know the going rate, haven't quite got to grips with the local currency, and am not quite sure how far I'm going, how much I should pay or how much that is when I convert it back into dollars, euros or pounds.

Top tip: I find a bunch of taxi-drivers and ask loudly how much it is to the bus station. It's kinda fun to let them fight it out amongst themselves, then go with the lowest offered fare. Of course, try not to get stabbed in the process.

In this case I would be getting back on the bus from Rwanda as it was going straight through **Uganda** on its way to Nairobi in Kenya. At the Ugandan entry desk I asked for a transit visa. They told me it would be $50. I asked how much a normal visa was. 'Also $50.' I didn't think this was very fair.

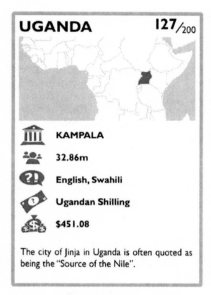

UGANDA 127/200

🏛️ **KAMPALA**

👥 **32.86m**

💬 **English, Swahili**

💵 **Ugandan Shilling**

💰 **$451.08**

The city of Jinja in Uganda is often quoted as being the "Source of the Nile".

After reluctantly stumping up the half ton, I was stamped in. I swapped my Rwandan francs for Ugandan shillings with a money changer and bought myself a new SIM card. I opened my phone, flicked out the old MTL Rwanda SIM and replaced it with my new MTL Uganda SIM, quietly cursing the whole concept of nationhood in the process.

The bus pressed on through the capital Kampala and towards Kenya, crossing the White Nile at the delightfully-named city of Jinja. I decided there and then that if I ever won an island on a gameshow, I would call it Jinja Island.

Stranger things have happened...

Being so close to the equator means night falls around 6pm every day and so it was dark by the time we reached the border. I went through the usual formalities, although after a whole day sitting on a bus I was in a bit of a daze. I was stamped out of Uganda, and made my way over to the Kenyan side of the complex. After getting my entry stamp I noticed a bureau de change nearby.

For some reason, changing a hundred dollars into Kenyan Shillings took the best part of half an hour, but I wasn't concerned, this was my 43rd African border crossing of the year — it had never taken less than a couple of hours on a bus.

But when I emerged from the bureau de change, the bus wasn't where it was supposed to be. I looked around. I couldn't see any familiar faces from the bus.

Bugger.

Panicked, I started to run. In the dark. Africa isn't big on street lighting so I didn't get very far before I fell afoul of one of the numerous potholes in the road. And so that's how I entered Kenya. Arse over tit. Backpack, bags, stuff; everywhere.

And of course as things turned out I could have sauntered. I could have crawled. I could have single-handedly performed *HMS Pinafore* in its entirety and I still would have made the bus in good time. It was parked around the corner and the other passengers were still at the first passport check. Gah!

Anyway, where are my manners? Helloooo **Kenya!**

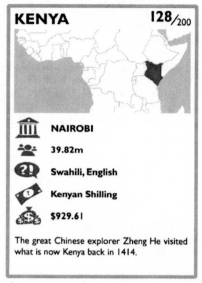

KENYA 128/200

🏛 **NAIROBI**

👪 **39.82m**

❓ **Swahili, English**

💵 **Kenyan Shilling**

💰 **$929.61**

The great Chinese explorer Zheng He visited what is now Kenya back in 1414.

Kenya is named after Mount Kenya, the second highest mountain on the continent and has been a happy hunting ground for us humans since the year dot. Ever since we quit being all *Homo heidelbergensis*, in fact. Where the name "Kenya" comes from has been the matter of dispute for years, but it was probably a corruption of "Kiinyaa" meaning "God's resting place" or else "Kĩ-Nyaa" which means "cock ostrich".

I hope it's cock ostrich.

Kenya is famed for its coffee, Maasai warriors and being home to all of the "big five" game animals (lion, leopard, buffalo, rhinoceros and elephant). Economically it's on the up and up and the international port of Mombasa is booming. Well, it would be if the dock officials would just do their bleedin' job without demanding more backhanders than a Wimbledon final.

My plan in Kenya was to grab visas for my next two countries: Ethiopia and Djibouti. That meant it was embassy time again. I was hoping it wouldn't take too long as it was now December 21st and I had just ten days to reach Egypt or else Mandy would "string me up by my giblets" (her words, not mine).

In other news, the series editor Matt would be joining me in Nairobi to film the last leg of this year's record-setting journey. I hadn't had a camera op with me since Rocco left in August, so it was about bloody time — I'm supposed to be making a TV show here!

This of course is the same Matt who had succumbed to amoebic dysentery in Senegal whilst waiting for me to finish fannying about with Mauritanian visas and the Sahara Desert.

Well this time I'm happy to report that he didn't get ill awaiting my arrival. Although his hotel did catch fire.

After an indeterminate time spent waiting for the bus to leave (and attending to my exciting new injuries) we set off into the night, Nairobi-bound!!

I arrived in "Africa's second most notorious city" early the next morning. I navigated my way through the mean streets to Matt's hotel, which was still smouldering from last night's fire. It was good to see him again, but I have to admit feeling some trepidation that he might slow me down as I entered this critical final stretch.

But as things turned out he actually made things easier, which was a massive relief. Case in point: I got to send Matt off to the Djiboutian embassy while I headed over to the Ethiopian embassy. Double the manpower, half the time, awesome!

Joining me on my run to the Ethiopian embassy would be my friend Aengus Stanley. Aengus was a fellow adventurer from the Republic of Ireland; he had driven all the way to Nairobi from Tipperary a few years earlier. He had come down the route I'm about to take up.

I had to ask, 'So is it dangerous — northern Kenya I mean?'

Aengus grinned. 'Not really. Although we did get shot at while changing a tyre.'

'Wait, what?'

Best not think about it. Or tell Matt.

Nairobi gets a bad rap (people call it "Nairobbery"), but I really gelled with the place. It didn't seem to have the same edge as Lagos or Joburg. It's a big, cosmopolitan city with everything a wide-eyed urban backpacker could desire. I guess if you go out looking for trouble you'll probably find it, but you can say that about anywhere in the world, right? Well, maybe not Halifax, Nova Scotia. Ahh — lovely, lovely Halifax.

Amazingly, Matt and I ended up getting both visas *before lunch*. Based on everything that has happened so far on this adventure you know how remarkable that is. It was like a meteor just landed in my pocket. And it was made of gold. Somebody must have activated the Infinite Improbability Drive — it's the only logical explanation.

Our itinerary did not leave much room for error, but if we could get to Ethiopia the next day, I might just make it.

After saying goodbye to Aengus, Matt and I raced over to Eastleigh, a grotty suburb of Nairobi where the buses leave to head up North. We found a minibus that was heading to the border with Ethiopia. It was a brightly-coloured Japanese school bus, all pinks and yellows and adorable cartoon bunnies; equipped to ferry kids around suburban Tokyo and clearly *not* designed to survive African highways.

'When is it leaving?', I asked.

'Very soon', they said.

Ha! It's bad enough wasting an entire afternoon sitting on a stationary minibus sweating your face off in the heat and dust of what is arguably the worst part of Nairobi, but when your eight-year relationship hinges on you getting to the church (well, pyramids) on time, frustration can quite easily turn to despair.

It was 7pm before we began the 24-hour journey to the Ethiopian frontier.

Sleeping on buses is tricky at the best of times (although I had a lot of practice that year) but this journey was an absolute nightmare — the road was utterly dreadful and the driver had a nasty habit of slamming on the brakes every time he saw a pothole. Which was every few metres.

Dear Lord — this was the *main highway* between two capital cities. It was bad enough to begin with, but after we passed Nairobi's last satellite town in the early hours of the morning, we hit the dirt track that stretches 350 miles all the way to the border. Then all bets were off. The bus had a ground clearance of about three inches.

We bumped, scraped and scratched our way along the road at a respectable fifteen miles an hour, dripping oil, water and brake fluid, busting our exhaust and losing chunks of metal as we plodded along. The suspension groaned with every bump and the engine heaved under the strain of having to deal with a bus packed with adults and heavy luggage rather than a handful of tiny Japanese schoolchildren and their Pokémon backpacks.

By 7am we had slowed down to a crawl. The minibus pulled into a small town for repairs. After losing a couple of hours while the oil leak was plugged (with bubble-gum no doubt) we were told that it would take us two hours to get to the next town. It took eight.

Eight torturous hours. We picked our way along the road so slowly it would have been quicker to walk. When we finally reached the town we were told that we would not be continuing our journey until the next morning.

This called for a good old-fashioned bus mutiny. We abandoned our shitty school bus and found an 18-wheeler truck that was heading to the border and — even better — taking passengers.

But not in the cab. Up top.

Matt and I clambered on top of the 40-foot shipping container that was attached to the truck and prepared to ride through the desert, Mad Max style. Unfortunately, Matt had left his leather bondage gear at home.

As we were setting off we noticed two little local girls standing at the side of the road. They were smiling up at us so Matt and I waved to them, all friendly like. They didn't wave back. Instead, they slowly drew their index fingers across their necks — the universal hand sign for "you're totally gonna die".

The truck gathered pace and thundered off into the night.

After a few hours of bumping and shaking, sitting atop a cargo of God knows what, we arrived in the town of Marsabit, 130 miles from the border. The border wasn't open at night and so we were told there wasn't much point in pressing on. We slept on concrete beds in what was perhaps a barn. The Marsabit Marriot is presumably still under construction.

This was all a bit of a baptism of fire for poor old Matt, but he seemed to take it in his stride. I woke him at 6am to crack on to the border. We couldn't find the truck we came in on but we found another without much delay — there is, after all, only one road around these parts.

This bit of the journey was a real pleasure. Sitting atop of a massive lorry, far above the dusty highway, health and safety be damned, the wind in my hair, Kenya stretching out to the right of me, the foothills of Ethiopia to my left, music blasting into my ears from my iPod. Travel heaven.

We arrived at the border around midday.

We may have survived the northern wastes, but thanks to that awful minibus I was a day behind schedule. Time and tide wait for no man. Barring some kind of miracle the *CMA-CGM Turquoise* would be leaving without me.

Bollocks.

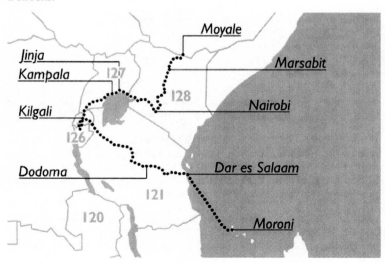

Chapter 30
Six Minutes Past Midnight

For those of us who grew up in the 1980s, **Ethiopia** (the only country in modern Africa that was never colonised) is synonymous with famine, skeletal children with bloated stomachs and flies on their faces and Bono thanking God that he wasn't born in a country with such a lack of basic tax loopholes.

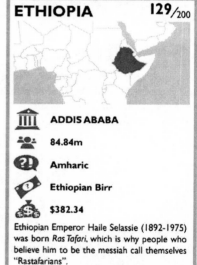

ETHIOPIA 129/200

🏛 **ADDIS ABABA**

👥 **84.84m**

💬 **Amharic**

💵 **Ethiopian Birr**

💰 **$382.34**

Ethiopian Emperor Haile Selassie (1892-1975) was born *Ras Tafari*, which is why people who believe him to be the messiah call themselves "Rastafarians".

Today's Ethiopia is a far cry from those dark days. Addis Ababa is flourishing, the roads are pretty good, people are healthier than ever and economic growth is in the double digits.

That's not to say it's all wine and roses. Ethiopia still has major problems — child labour is rife, the horror that is female genital mutilation is an everyday occurrence (which is unusual for a mostly Christian nation) and the country has a less-than-stellar record when it comes to democracy and freedom of speech.

While the scars of its war with Eritrea (a province of Ethiopia from 1950 to 1991, now an independent nation) are more readily found in Eritrea itself, the border between the two countries is permanently closed and Ethiopia is now a landlocked country with all of the inherent problems that come with not having your own seaport.

Cards on the table though, I have a huge soft spot for Ethiopia. The food is to die for, they have medieval castles (really!) and it might well be the last resting place of the Lost Ark of the Covenant. *Cue Raiders March!*

The language, Amharic, has its own alphabet that looks like little dancing men. Ethiopia still uses the Julian calendar (when I visited in 2009 it was still 2002), new year is celebrated on September 11th, and, as I was soon to learn, "three in the morning" doesn't necessarily mean what you think it does.

Crossing the border was (thankfully) a piece of cake. We then took a local bus to the town of Yabello, hoping to find an overnighter up to Addis, perhaps even recoup some time back and get to Djibouti before the *CMA-CGM Turquoise* departed for Egypt.

However, it seems that Ethiopia, like Mozambique, does not have overnight buses. Okay, yes, I understand it is for safety reasons, but it's still rather inconvenient for us adventure-y types on noble quests. We would have to wait until the following morning. Any last hope I had of making the ship to Egypt was pretty much gone. But that wasn't going to stop me trying.

We left the following day, nice and early, 6am. It was Christmas Eve. We thundered north in a minibus with a couple from Spain and Switzerland called Asier and Silvia and were making really good time until BANG we hit an eagle.

Yes. An eagle.

Now in Ethiopia (unlike Senegal where it seems *mandatory* to have a cracked windscreen), driving with a broken windshield is a big no-no. So the driver's mate had to grab the (now exceptionally dead) eagle and throw it in the minibus — for some reason it had to be at my feet, but whatever, it was a fresh kill and didn't smell half as bad as those severed cow's legs that doubled as my footrest through northern Congo.

We stopped in the next town. While the driver filled in an incident report with the local police, Matt and I went to find a Coke.

One thing that will never cease to amaze me is how Coca-Cola manage to get their product everywhere. And I mean *everywhere*. I swear that there are undiscovered tribes in Papua New Guinea that somehow have access to Coca-Cola. If only medicine and clean water had such logistical omnipresence the world would be a much better place.

We found the local store. I asked the shopkeeper for a Coke which I glugged down in next to no time. Matt then asked for a "Coke Light". The guy, who spoke no English whatsoever, looked confused. Matt reiterated, 'Diet Coke, you know — Coke Light?'

The shopkeeper furrowed his brow, grabbed a normal Coke from the fridge and put it on the counter. 'Coca-Cola?'

Matt pushed the Coke back towards him. 'Sorry mate, I want Coke Light.'

At this point I took Matt gently by the arm, dragged him outside and whispered in his ear 'we're in Ethiopia mate — who the f--- do you think is going to be on a diet?'

This is not to say people are starving, but the typical body shape in East Africa is tall and slender — needless to say, the slimming industry is yet to make inroads around these parts.

After an hour or so we were back on the road, and eventually managed to hit Addis Ababa without also hitting any more raptors.

We arrived late that night. Christmas Eve in Addis Ababa — or was it?

"Do they know it's Christmas?" sang Band-Aid in order to raise funds for Ethiopia. A noble effort, but somebody should have told Geldof, Midge Ure, Bono and co. that Christmas in Ethiopia is not celebrated until January 7th.

This was great news for me. Since they didn't know it was Christmas, public transport would be operating like any other day. With any luck we could be in Djibouti by the evening of Boxing Day[42]. There was no mathematical way I could make the *CMA-CGM Turquoise* in time, but my hope was that there would be another ship — Djibouti City is a very busy port and any ship going north towards Europe would have to pass through the Suez Canal at some point.

That night Matt and I checked into a hotel near the bus station. I was told that the bus to the town of Dire Dawa near to the border with Djibouti would leave at three in the morning, so I dragged my weary carcass out of bed at 2:30am, having managed just a couple of hours sleep. I said I'd go check it out, buy our tickets and then come back and get Matt.

Arriving at the bus station I quickly realised that it was closed. Gates shut, no buses, nobody around. A guy shouted over to me that there were no more buses that night.

'But I was told my bus was at three!', I explained.

'Three in the morning?', asked the guy.

'Yes.'

The guy burst out laughing. 'My friend, that'll be three in the morning *Ethiopian time.*'

'Ethiopian time?'

'Yes. Three hours after the sun rises.'

That meant the bus would actually be leaving around 9am.

---

[42] Editor's Note: As noted previously — December 26th.

'You're kidding.'

The guy continued to laugh. I laughed too. It was either that or cry.

When I got back Matt cheered me up by giving me my Christmas present off Lonely Planet: a brand new iPod Touch. Get in!

I loaded it with songs as I knew that Christmas 2009 would be spent mostly travelling through a country that was resolutely not celebrating Christmas.

We hadn't got far before Matt and I learnt another quirk of life in Ethiopia: people hate it when you open a window on the bus. It can be a zillion degrees Fahrenheit, sweat may be cascading off your face, the powerful stench of vomit could be hanging in the air like the corner of some student disco, but touch that window and you're in big trouble Buster.

An urban myth that diseases come from the wind has taken root in Ethiopian culture (much like the equally ludicrous belief that vaccines cause autism in the West) and so opening the window of the bus, even while driving through the stifling heat of the Great Rift Valley, is a big no-no.

I lasted about half an hour before making my move. I cunningly handed out biscuits to my bus companions to get them "on side" and, just as everything seemed hunky-dory, I opened the window a crack.

My impudence was met with howls of disbelief.

'Are you crazy?! Shut the window!'

A lady who was clutching a baby gave me a right dressing down. Happily, it was in Amharic, so I could legitimately claim to not understand what she was getting at (even though I totally did).

Lunch was a traditional Ethiopian spread — lots of different bits and bobs served on a massive "plate" of bread. The bread is spongy and best described as flatbread meets crumpet. The idea is that you break a bit off and grab the food with the bread. It's kinda cool. Although I think Matt was less impressed with this unconventional Christmas dinner.

We spent the night in Dire Dawa and the next day we were up at some ungodly hour as it was time to cross into country 130: **Djibouti**.

A tiny country located just west of the Horn of Africa, Djibouti is the former French Somalia. After de-colonisation it (sensibly) opted not to join with the former Italian and British Somalias, instead taking Fleetwood Mac's sage advice of *go[ing] your own way*. Since then it has become a significant port on the Red Sea, not just for ships travelling to and from the Suez Canal, but also for goods coming in and out of Ethiopia.

Djibouti is bordered by Eritrea to the north and Somalia to the south-east.

The process of crossing the border took several excruciating hours, made all the more excruciating by the fact that the *CMA-CGM Turquoise* was scheduled to leave that very same morning. Matt and I had both been stamped in, but we found ourselves kicking stones at the side of the road waiting for our bus to be inspected.

When I was planning *The Odyssey Expedition*, I was aware that the border between Eritrea and Ethiopia was closed (and littered with landmines!) but I thought I could cross the border into Eritrea from Djibouti without too much fuss. However, a small border skirmish shortly before my arrival put paid to that idea. The story I got told was that a few Eritrean soldiers asked if they could nip across into Djibouti to get some sand. The Djiboutian border guards said something along the lines of 'umm, sure.'

DJIBOUTI 130/200

🏛 **DJIBOUTI CITY**

👥 **821,865**

💬 **French, Arabic**

💵 **Djiboutian Franc**

💲 **$1,458.87**

Lake Assal in Djibouti is the saltiest lake outside of Antarctica, even saltier than the Dead Sea.

The Eritreans entered Djibouti, dug a big hole in the sand, jumped inside and refused to leave. As a result, the border was swiftly closed to everyone.

So Eritrea was out of the question for now, but the border with Somalia was only ten miles from the Djiboutian capital (also called Djibouti), so a day trip to the Most Dangerous Country In The World™ would be fairly feasible.

After waiting over an hour at the Ethiopia-Djibouti border for no discernible reason, Matt and I carried out yet another bus mutiny and soon we were on another coach trundling towards the Big Smoke.

We were about halfway there when the bus stopped at a checkpoint. Inspection time! Papers please!

I hadn't been hassled by checkpoint trolls since I left Angola back in October — I found Southern and East Africa refreshingly free of the bastards. And, true to form for my experience of francophone countries in Africa, there was apparently something wrong with my entry stamp. *Of course there was.* I was told I could return to the border and get it sorted or else pay a "fine".

I paid $20 and we continued on our way. Having missed the boat I was already in a fairly shitty mood, this just compounded my negative disposition. We reached the hot, dusty capital around noon. I made a beeline for the local CMA-CGM office to find out if there was an alternative boat I could take to Egypt — but I arrived to find it closed.

At that point I may have had a little bit of a breakdown.

In an effort to cheer me up (or perhaps because he was sick of slumming it) Matt had checked us into the Djibouti Radisson. Ooh! A bit of luxury!! Well, it would be, but first Matt would have to do battle with the hotel manager who would not accept that Matt had already paid for the room through an online booking service.

After an hour or so of arguments, emails and print-outs, I left them to it and headed back to the shipping agents, hoping for some sort of miracle.

And, would you believe it, I got one.

The *CMA-CGM Turquoise* had been delayed by a day.

It would not be leaving until the following morning!

While this was bad news for the ship operators (you don't want to know how much extra it costs to pass through the Suez Canal if you're a day late), it was great news for me. All being well, we'd hit Egypt on the afternoon of New Year's Eve and I'd be with Mandy well before the stroke of midnight.

WOO HOO!!

Not only that, Abdourahman and Deyan, two of the guys at the agency said they'd escort me to the border with Somalia so I could tick it off the list.

On the way we stopped by the Radisson to pick up Matt. He was still arguing with African *Basil Fawlty* over the booking. Agreeing to sort it out later, we headed to the frontier. Abdourahman, Deyan and Matt stayed on the Djiboutian side of the border while I walked across the thin strip of No-Man's-Land into **Somalia**.

If you feel I'm being a wee bit blasé about walking alone into a warzone, worry not fair friends, I wasn't entering *Somalia* Somalia, I would be popping into the infinitely safer breakaway republic of Somaliland.

Once upon a time there were three Somalias — French Somaliland, British Somaliland and Italian Somaliland. French Somaliland would eventually became Djibouti, but in 1960 Italian and British Somaliland teamed up to form the independent state of Somalia. All went (relatively) well until 1991 when everything turned to shit. Warlords overran the capital city of Mogadishu and the government was left camping out at the airport.

The old British Somaliland part of the country (sensibly) thought "sod this for a game of soldiers" and announced its independence from Somalia, declaring itself the Republic of Somaliland.

I for one, see no reason why Somaliland has failed to achieve international recognition. It was historically a separate territory and it's attached to the Most Dangerous Country In The World™. Not only that, Somaliland has its own currency, flag, national anthem and government (with remarkably free and fair elections). It looks like a country, smells like a country, tastes like a country, I don't know why it's not a country. In any case, it's not like the government in Mogadishu is in any position to argue.

SOMALIA 131/200

🏛 **MOGADISHU**

👥 **9.381m**

💬 **Somali, Arabic**

💵 **Somali Shilling**

💰 **$400 (estimate)**

Horrifically, it is estimated that 99% of Somali women have undergone female genital mutilation.

But as things stood, Somaliland was still a part of Somalia as much as Tibet was a part of China and West Papua was part of Indonesia — and while I am a believer in self-determination I also have to be pragmatic. Somaliland was the only genuinely safe place to cross the border into Country 131.

Once my GPS was confident that I had entered the country, I swapped a few US dollars for a nice fat wad of Somaliland shillings, turned on a sixpence and returned from whence I came. Done and done!

That night Matt treated me to a farewell meal — he wouldn't be joining me on the ship to Egypt — he'd be flying there and (hopefully) getting things set up with Mandy so it all looked spontaneous and dramatic for the telly.

Around 3am the phone in our room rang. I half-remember answering it. 'Graham, the boat is leaving, you must come down immediately.'

I muttered something about doing it tomorrow and fell back asleep. Ten minutes later the phone rang again. 'Graham, you must come to the reception immediately, the boat is leaving now.'

'Ah that's nice!' I said. I put the phone down, flipped my pillow to the cool side and closed my eyes.

Then, as the words slowly percolated through my half-awake brain, I had that feeling like I was falling from a tree and was jolted awake. *HOLY CRAP THE BOAT IS LEAVING EARLY.*

I jumped out of bed, got dressed, stuffed my life into my backpack, said goodbye to Matt and legged it downstairs. The port agents were at reception. 'Graham, we need to go! Now!!'

After what I can only describe as the fastest (legal) exit stamp in the history of Africa, within an hour I was aboard the ship and we were pulling out of port.

Phew!

So there I was on the *CMA-CGM Turquoise* heading towards Egypt and the promise of a spectacular reunion with the woman I loved. Nothing could stop me now! Oh, did I mention we would be popping into **Saudi Arabia** along the way?

A scorching hot desert theocracy notorious for human rights abuses and funding terrorism, Saudi Arabia is that spoilt rich kid who can get away with murder because his family has enough cash to make any given problem go away. It's like if Patrick Bateman was a country. Needless to say, I wouldn't recommend it for a family outing.

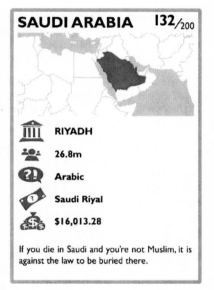

SAUDI ARABIA 132/200

🏛 **RIYADH**

👥 **26.8m**

❓ **Arabic**

💵 **Saudi Riyal**

💰 **$16,013.28**

If you die in Saudi and you're not Muslim, it is against the law to be buried there.

I was nearly arrested for carrying a video camera which I wasn't even using when we were in port in Jeddah. Thankfully, the crew came to my aid and defused the situation. I even got to keep my (briefly confiscated) video tape.

As was my experience on all the major cargo ships I had been on thus far, the crew of the *CMA-CGM Turquoise* were wonderful. Most of the officers were from Egypt and the Middle East, while most of the crewmembers came from The Philippines. Once again I had a cabin to myself, all air-conditioned and clean, I was free to stroll around the ship to my heart's content and the food was superb. Needless to say I didn't think I'd be clambering back on board a pirogue any time soon.

When I awoke on the morning of December 31st, I looked out of my porthole and there she was: Egypt.

As far as backpacking is concerned, Egypt is where it all began for me. It was the last summer of the 20th century when I took my first overland adventure as a grown-up: Cairo to Istanbul with my friends Dan and Dino (of Team Odyssey fame). It was on that journey I met a certain

Miss Amanda (aka Mandy) Newland, resolved to backpack the entire world (or die trying) and decided I absolutely loved the bones of Egypt.

I loved it so much that I returned a few months later with my friends Mary and Paul for the turn of the millennium itself. There was an epic Jean-Michel Jarre gig at the pyramids. Yeah, Jean-Michel Jarre. The French synth-pop guy. With the lasers. Don't judge.

And here I was, exactly ten years later. Doing it all again. This time sans any French synth-pop. Or lasers. Well, you can't have everything.

If all went to plan, Mandy and I would meet at the (hilariously situated) KFC by the Sphinx, climb up onto the roof and watch the last sun of the decade set behind those ancient tombs.

But by sunset the *CMA-CGM Turquoise* had only just dropped anchor outside the Egyptian city of Suez. It was a bit far to swim and lacking a rubber dingy in my backpack, I would have to wait for the Suez authorities to arrive on the pilot boat before I could disembark.

Luckily we were close enough to shore to get mobile phone coverage, so I was able to knock back my ETA at the pyramids from 5pm to 8pm. But in the event, I was a little optimistic. By 8pm I was still on the ship. By 9pm I was beginning to panic.

The pilot boat had arrived, but there was a mountain of paperwork that had to be laboriously read through and signed. I texted Mandy and told her to hang tight in Cairo until I gave the signal — I didn't want her hanging about in Giza at night on her own.

It wasn't until 10pm that the pilot boat was ready to head back to shore. After saying thanks and goodbye to the captain and crew, I clambered aboard.

Ten minutes later we pulled into dock. Terra firma, at last. Hello again **Egypt,** my old friend.

EGYPT 133/200

🏛 **CAIRO**

👥 **76.78m**

❓ **Arabic**

💵 **Egyptian Pound**

💰 **$2,461.53**

More time passed between the building of the pyramids and the reign of Cleopatra than has passed between the reign of Cleopatra and today.

Even though I was the only person there who needed to purchase a visa, the border formalities seemed to take an eternity.

Matt from Lonely Planet was waiting for me in a taxi outside the port. The driver and his mate didn't speak a word of English, which made explaining the urgency of the situation difficult, although they really should have guessed by my frantic gesticulating. By now it was 10:30pm and the Pyramids were over 100 kilometres away.

The urgency of the situation was completely lost on the *Chuckle Brothers* who were driving us — they seemed more keen on taking us on a tour of Suez, stopping to pick up some bits and bobs on the way. By the time we were on the freeway it was already approaching 11pm. I watched out of the window as the milestones (well kilometre signs) clocked down to 50km to Cairo.

At 11:35pm, I actually thought that we were going to make it — we had passed Cairo airport and there was little traffic at that time of night. I rang Mandy and told her that it was time for her to head to the pyramids.

It was at that exact moment that the driver decided that now would be a super time to take a 20-minute detour in order to get some fuel from his favourite garage, presumably saving himself a few cents and saving me the indignity of actually hitting the pyramids on time. Guys, *we're happy to pay!*

Tweeting a blow-by-blow account of the whole howling adventure, the humour of the situation (our driver didn't actually know where the pyramids were) was lost on me at the time. How can you be a Cairo taxi driver and not know where the goddamn pyramids are?!!

At 11:55pm, we were pulled up at the side of the road getting directions from a random pedestrian. I had completely forgotten that this was how most taxi-drivers found their way around Cairo — memories of similar frustrating situations came flooding back.

There are only two roads to the pyramids — one, the imaginatively titled "Pyramids Road" which runs to the north of the complex, and the other, which runs to the south-east through the Giza suburbs — near the Sphinx (and the KFC).

Mandy rang. She was already there and was waiting in the dark. She wasn't happy. Thankfully, her own taxi driver had stayed with her to make sure she was all right. I put him on to my taxi driver and he explained the situation in Arabic. With new-found fervour, our driver headed the right way (for a change). But by now it was too late. The clock had struck midnight.

The next five minutes were the longest of my life, racing through the maze of streets that is modern Giza. But we turned a corner and suddenly, there, towering over us was the Great Pyramid of Khufu.

A left and then a right and there was the KFC.

And standing outside...

Mandy.

She ran towards the taxi...

I opened my door, but Matt ordered me to WAIT! There was no time to set things up. This was a shot that he didn't want to miss.

Matt tried his door. Unfortunately, it was locked. 'LET ME OUT!', he screamed at our poor bewildered driver — *CLICK CLUNK*. Out he got.

'ACTION!'

I took a deep breath and stepped out of the taxi and WHAM into the loving arms of my Amanda, for a kiss that was 100,000 kilometres, 365 days, 133 countries and six territories in the making.

There in the shadow of those timeless, perplexing giants, the place we first met, I whispered 'I love you.'

Mandy pulled back and smirked. 'I know.'

It was six minutes past midnight. Happy New Year.

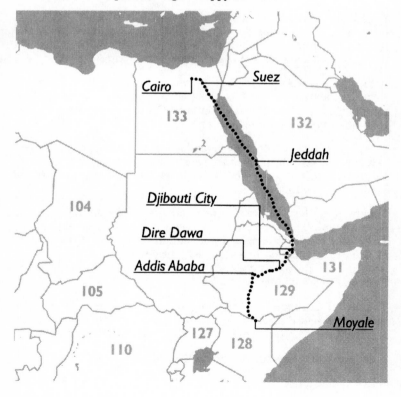

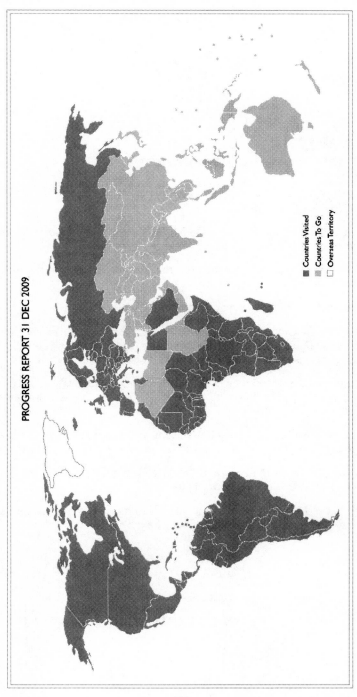

PROGRESS REPORT 31 DEC 2009

■ Countries Visited
■ Countries To Go
☐ Overseas Territory

Epilogue
Where Now But Everywhere?

Mandy and I took a night-time horse ride up to the plateau overlooking the pyramids.

And so there we were, back in each other's arms. All we had to do now was to work out what we would do next.

I had failed in my primary mission: to visit every country in the world in just one year without flying.

But I had gotten further than anybody else.

I had set the Guinness World Record for the *Most Countries Visited in One Year By Scheduled Surface Transport* (133), which, as yet, nobody has come close to breaking (Top Tip: don't bother with the islands).

I could call it a day with my head held high. I could go back to Australia with Mandy, settle down, get married, have kids, live that life more ordinary.

Or I could continue. I had gotten this far. I had overcome hell and high water. There were only 67 countries left to go.

Nobody had done this before. It didn't really matter how long it took so long as I finished before dying of old age.

But if I did go on it wouldn't be easy. Mandy had already waited an entire year for me. Would she wait any longer?

The Odyssey Expedition

continues in Book 2

"TOP OF THE WORLD"

Team Odyssey

They say it takes a village to raise a child. I discovered it takes a small army to get a ginger travelling monkey around the world.

So first up, thank you Mum and Dad for creating me and for instilling in me the spirit of adventure required to make this thing happen. For believing in me when others didn't and for giving me the kick up the arse I needed to get on with the damn thing.

Huge thanks to Leo Skelly for webmastering for me throughout 2009, ably assisted by the irrepressible Colm Broaders.

Lorna Brookes, we met at a Lyons and Tigers gig and I told you I wanted to visit every country in the world without flying. Anybody else would have thought I was bonkers, but you were there cheering me on, making phone calls, emailing shipping companies and sweet-talking PR departments from the inception to the very end.

Dino Deasha, who joined me on my first backpack adventure from Egypt to Turkey back when we were young and whose mad skillz were responsible for finding and getting me wherever I needed to go next, thank you. I owe you a lifetime supply of *Abdul's* kebabs.

Christian Olsen, the nicest man in the world, it's an honour being related to you. Thank you for all your help throughout the journey.

Mum, Dad, Leo, Dino, Lorna and Christian: you guys were the core of Team Odyssey. If it wasn't for you I'd still be stuck in Guyana. THANK YOU.

Huge thanks and kudos also to Thierry Klinklin for your assistance and language skills.

Thank you for the music, Simon Barber, as well as the web hosting.

Thanks to design supremo Scott Jones for not only *The Odyssey* logo but also helping me conceptualise *Man of the World's* cover art.

Huge thanks to Vicki Eccleston for all your incredible designs and your work on *The Odyssey* board game which graces the cover of this book.

Thanks to my two gorgeous models Raven Skobe and Stephanie Cogal

McLean who join me on the cover of this book and to Graeme Hill for taking the photos.

Big shout-out to the Heebie-Jeebies Liverpool for allowing us to do our rather impromptu photo shoot in the basement.

Thanks also to Grethe Børsum for taking my original publicity shots.

Camera ops Laura McGann, Rocco Fasano, Matt Bourke and Carlos Pauluk — thanks for putting up with me for a few days (or weeks) on the road with camera. Sorry for all the stuff that went tits-up.

Thanks to Matt Eland, Stuart Lanceley, Laura, and Jewles for helping me make the pitch video.

Thanks to the team at Lonely Planet TV: David Collins, Tony Jackson, Peter Beilby, Sally Storey, Thomas Aylesbury et al. I know we had our ups and downs but we still put together a really great show.

Special thanks to Hugh Sheridan for teaching me how to sail and generally being awesome.

Thanks to John Howell for lawyering for me where lawyering was required.

Thanks to Mel Tompkins and the team at WaterAid for spurring me on.

Thanks to Mary and Paul, Katana, Lindsey, Michelle, Matt the Mick, Steve Clarke, Stan and Helen, Lucy and Tim, Sarah Newton, Mave, Denise, Helen Raghu, Kjell, Soraya, Kaya, Laura Worthington, Brian O'Connor, Tom Dowrick and Danny Alexander for helping me along and being such bloody awesome mates.

Leo, Matt, Katana, Alex Hanyok, Marcelle, Ben and Kathryn for helping proofread this rambling nonsense: Thnak You.

Thanks also to my brothers Alex and Mike, cousins Yvonne, Kenny, and John, and my nephews Alan, Gwyn, Joe, David, Matthew, and James.

A special thanks also to Alex Zelenjak, Sari Stein and Gavin Mac for the advice and tip-top banter on the old Odyssey Expedition blog site.

Mr. Jared Bendis; publisher, agent, gamer, castle hunter, dancer and fellow border detainee I really wouldn't have got this book written if it wasn't for you. Thank you from the bottom of my heart.

A huge thanks to everyone who put me up or helped me along the way:

AMERICAS

Mia in Buenos Aires; Mario and family in Venezuela; Francisco on the bus to Brazil; Cedric and Bevaun from Gulf Shipping; the crew of the *MV Miriam*; Annette in Trinidad; Linda, John and Ted from the

September Song; Kim and Rochelle in St Vincent; Captain Ainsley Adams and the crew of the *Melinda II*; Martin and Fabio in Martinique; the staff of Whitchurch & Co. in Dominica, Captain George Solomon and the crew of the *Eastpack*; Seamus and Wayne in St Kitts; Captain Grant of the *Vagrant*; Christal, her family and Joanne in Antigua; Kerri and Andrew of the *Mariposa*; Sarah in the US Virgin Islands; Captain Claudio, the officers and crew of the *Costa Fortuna*; Mehrdad, Ken, Esperanza, TJ, Lu, Robert and Roman in the Dominican Republic; the crew of the *Linge Trader*; Jorge and Memo in El Salvador; Sofia on the bus to San Jose; Ishmael in Guatemala; John Curryman in The Bahamas; Midge, Admiral Finbar, Captain Seth and Mike Bellows in the Conch Republic; Captain Johnny of the *Bootlegger*; Monica in New York; Patricia, Seppe and James in Halifax.

EUROPE

Guðbjörg from Eimskip and the captains, officers and crews of the *Reykjafoss* and *Dettifoss*; Auntie Christine and Uncle Jens in Denmark; Lynn Robinson in Lithuania; Delia in Hungary; John and Vlad in Romania; Tom in Croatia and Ors (kinda) in Budapest.

AFRICA

Semi, Anis, Wahleed in Tunisia; Fatima in Morocco; Adam and Michel in Western Sahara; Mentor in Senegal; The Fishermen of the *Mustafa Sy*: Captain Mbeye, First Mate Modou, Saliou, Ablaye, Adama, Aleen, Aleen, Mahmoud, Doudou and Elage; Piran, Mito, Maria the Lawyer, Tomek, Gary, Callee, Yuri, Ines, Maggie, Debbie, Margarita and Nazia in Cape Verde; Milan and Sebastian of the *Fleumel*; Jared in Senegal; Isaac in Mali; Helga and Paul in Sierra Leone; Shadi in Liberia; Aya in Côte d'Ivoire; Tanko in Ghana; Fred in Burkina Faso; Tony and Roland in Nigeria; Hugo and his family in Cameroon; Vivian and Kamikaze in Gabon; Estelle, Tatayo, Dimitri (Mobengo), Justin, Alex and Steve the Fishmonger in Gabon; Marc of the *Reol*, Molo and the São Tomé boat saviours; Christophe and Max, Dominique and his wife in Congo; Parul, Holgar and the British Embassy staff in Kinshasa; Michael, Laure and Alex in DR Congo; Emilio in Angola; Tashia in Namibia; Eileen, British Andy and friends in Pretoria; Nenien and her boyfriend in Zeerust; David, Jenna-Lee and David's dad in Johannesburg; Dr Daniel and his girlfriend in Lesotho; Liliana in Swaziland; Flore and Gui in Mozambique; Jason in Malawi; Dylan in Tazania; Mickael in Réunion; Captain Jens-Uwe, Captain Klaus and the officers and crew of the *DAL Madagascar*; Commissioner Madhi, Yaya, Fanja, Keith, Stephanie, Alice and Daniel in Comoros; Sevene and Thomas on the *Simacom*; Aengus in Kenya; Silvia and Asier in Ethiopia; Abdourahman and Deyan in Djibouti; and the officers and crew of the *CMA-CGM Turquoise*.

The companies that helped along the way:

CMA-CGM, Vodafone, Eimskip, Lonely Planet, Gulf Shipping,

Deutsche Afrika-Linen, Algeos, BBC Worldwide, Nat Geo Adventure, Costa Cruises, Distant Horizons and Fantasea Tours.

The people who backed our Kickstarter:

Julia Schramek, Simon Hoare, Elaine Jones, Kevin Williams, Sarah Hardy, Hannah Atkinson, fod, Leo Skelly, Yvonne, Daniel Dryden, Madelyn Carey, Tom Wellman, Matthew Eland, Jessica, Adam Irvine, Pradeep Gopalakrishnan, Marcelle Porteous, Erik Gurkan Nilsson, Chris Pye, Matthew Lumby, Gavin Brightman, Pad Regan, Rob Skyner, Christopher Nelson, Maria Annette, Douglas Baker, Felipe Guerrero, Brad Carlsson, Mary Pasqualetto, Brendan, Greg L, Miguel Chafen, Matthew Hanna, Guilherme Ferreira Carvalho, Tom King, Cody Redshaw, Alastair, Dennis Prangle, Peter Allen, Fülöp Tamás, Vicki, Alan Roberts, Jason Smart, Claire Wright, Rafal Rudzinski, Mark Anthony B Hobbs, Ian Deasha, Kirsty Elizabeth, Amanda Newland, Matthew Gage, Toby, Michael Graziano, Adrien Behn, Alex Hanyok, Thomas Johnson, Cliff O'Neill, Thomas Pohl, Julian O'Shea, Melissa Brooks, Michael Shanahan, Mason Lorenz, Billy Hicks, Todd Marks, Dominic Fitzpatrick, Sarah Newton, Gareth Richards, KC Erb, Cricket Averett, Alfredo Luque, Hanna Dameron, Eric Kothe, Oliver Parker, Mark Cundall, Glenn, Stuart Lanceley, Andy Scott, Tracey Morgan, Marina Schultes, Herb Kim, Neil Jones, Carolyn Jones

And last, but by no means least, Mandy.

I want to hurry home to you

Put on a slow, dumb show for you

And crack you up

About the Author

As an original member of Team Odyssey, Graham asked if I would take a crack at writing his "About the Author" section, so here goes....

Graham David Hughes was born in Liverpool at the wrong end of the seventies. If you had to define in a sentence what drives him perhaps it's his desire that years from now schoolchildren across the land will be required to learn his date of birth.

From an early age Graham stood out from the crowd. With his striking auburn hair and encyclopaedic knowledge of smutty jokes he was always going to be noticed and now he has grown up into a person that once you meet him, he's kinda hard to forget.

Graham has always had a plan to make his mark and has always has a madcap scheme or three in the offing — once he finds something he wants to do he sets about it wholeheartedly. He is the one shouting the loudest, his hand is up highest, the squeaky wheel after the oil.

He is a keen reader, and has a range of knowledge that includes (but goes way beyond) current affairs and copious amounts of pop culture. If you're ever at a house party with him, be prepared to find yourself deep in conversation about anything from the Crab Nebula to the politics of modern Africa to the films of Akira Kurosawa, via Jabba the Hutt, monkey butlers and Viz Magazine.

Graham's major passions are travel and cinema, both were cultivated from childhood. He was in Eastern Europe as the map was redrawn after the end of the cold war, and partook in some eccentric summer holidays road-tripping in a Cadillac through the country lanes of Wales.

After leaving Manchester University with a degree in Politics and Modern History, Graham single-handedly travelled around the world, picking up his sassy Aussie girlfriend Mandy along the way. A trip to Serbia's Exit Festival in 2007 took in Albania, Bosnia and Kosovo (amongst others) on a meandering return leg, brought his "country tally" up to a total of 70.

Since returning to Liverpool, Graham devoted his time to a number of enterprises, specifically his company, Hydra Studios. With Hydra he wrote and directed a number of excellent short films and won the inaugural Liverpool 48 Hour Film Challenge in 2006. From 2002-2008 he was heavily involved in the Liverpool Music Scene, shooting or producing videos for the likes of The Coral, The Zutons, China Crisis, and filming for the release of Arctic Monkeys' second album, *Favourite Worst Nightmare*. He has also written numerous treatments for larger film projects and has developed scripts with the support of the UK Film Council.

Never one for the "normal" 9-to-5 lifestyle, Graham can normally be found beavering away on a project or painting the town red. Or (more typically) both at the same time. He is at his best with a deadline and a plan of how to get it done. Forever plunging headfirst into new experiences — he's the guy who always says "yes" and then worries about how he's going to do it afterwards. Anywhere he lays his head is home for the night. It is this spontaneous and unpredictable attitude that has shaped his life so far, given him some of his funniest stories and his incredibly eclectic group of friends.

The Odyssey Expedition is the culmination of his decade-long dream to travel to every country in the world, set a new world record, raise money for a worthy cause and entertain people along the way. Christ knows he's been banging on about it long enough.

– Dino Deasha, December 2008

For more of Graham's blogs, videos and daft adventures, visit

theodysseyexpedition.com

grahamdavidhughes.com

jinjaisland.com

globalscouseday.com

eurodyssey.com